D0855976

THE CURIOUS
GARDENER

The Flowering Year

The Border Book

The New Kitchen Garden

The Tulip

Plant Partners

Searching for Order
(originally published as *The Naming of Names*)

Bulb

THE CURIOUS GARDENER

ANNA PAVORD

With thirteen wood engravings by Howard Phipps

BLOOMSBURY

LONDON · BERLIN · NEW YORK · SYDNEY

First published in Great Britain 2010

Copyright © 2010 by Anna Pavord

Wood engravings copyright © by Howard Phipps 2010

Frontispiece: Kitchen garden doorway

Bloomsbury Publishing Plc
36 Soho Square
London W1D 3QY
www.bloomsbury.com

Bloomsbury Publishing, London, New York and Berlin

A CIP catalogue record for this book is available from the British Library

ISBN 9781408808887
10 9 8 7 6 5 4 3 2 1

Typeset by Hewer Text UK Ltd, Edinburgh
Printed in Great Britain by Clays Ltd, St Ives plc

MIX
Paper from
responsible sources
FSC
www.fsc.org
FSC® C018072

This book is dedicated to all my editors at the *Independent*, from Hilly Janes to Laurence Earle. They have given me plenty of rope, but have also prevented me from hanging myself. Thank you

CONTENTS

OCTOBER

NOVEMBER

DECEMBER

Introduction

I used to hate gardening. I grew up with parents who were always bottom-up in the borders. Lurking round the edges of their horti-conversations, I couldn't see the point of it all. Gardening seemed to be one long roll-call of disaster: black spot on the roses, blackfly on the beans, canker in the apples, pigeons among the peas. Why did they bother, I asked myself? The shops were full of excellent vegetables and blight-free flowers.

The garden always seemed to get in the way of things that I wanted to do. There was no end to its demands. Hedges needed cutting week after week, as did lawns. Weeds grew with hideous persistence between the big flat flagstones of the terrace by the French windows. So family expeditions became nerve-racking affairs for me. Would my father, who had promised to take me to spend my pocket money in town, finish hooking out those weeds from the terrace before the shops shut? He didn't believe in weed-killer. Could I drag my mother away from the lupins (very fifties) and towards the Coliseum cinema where there was a film she had said I could see? As I was a country child, trips to town had huge significance. Glamour hovered around the hissing coffee machine in the town's Italian café, not over the ancient stone troughs where my father cultivated alpines with exquisite care and attention: gentians were his speciality.

I tried the 'if you can't beat them, join them' approach. Both my brother and I had gardens of our own at home, though I think they were probably given, rather than asked for. He had a pear tree in his. The centrepiece of mine was a 'Beauty of Bath' apple tree, planted by my mother way before I was born because it was her mother's favourite fruit. But, as a child, I never grasped that this was an early, short-season apple. If my grandmother wasn't about in early August, then the chance to shower her with booty was gone. And nobody explained that it wasn't my fault it sometimes didn't fruit at all. 'Beauty of Bath' is early into blossom, as well as fruit. If blossom and frost come together, you kiss goodbye to your apples.

Marriage brought with it a patch of ground where once again I tried to grow things. You couldn't exactly call it a garden. It was eighty feet of river bank on the Thames at Shepperton where we were living on a Thames sailing barge. It was a fantastic boat, with a hefty wooden hull and vast fat tree trunks for its masts. We had an Aga on board and stoked it with coal we kept in the fo'c'sle. We had to row the coal up the river in our clinker-built butty boat. Once we overloaded it. The coal (it was a kind of Phurnacite) started to soak up the water oozing in between the wooden boards and by the time we arrived alongside the barge, we were practically rowing underwater.

We spent the first few months clearing the rubbish from the river bank against which we were moored: plastic bottles, fertiliser sacks, hunks of rusting iron. Then my parents brought flag iris to go at the water's edge, together with primroses, primulas, snowdrops and small Welsh daffodils for the bank and a wildish kind of rose (*R. gallica* 'Complicata') to go on the railings by the towpath. The dream was romantic – very pastoral.

But in our first winter, the flags got washed away by the torrential floods that surged down the river. The following spring, all the daffodils and primroses we'd planted were picked by people out on their Sunday promenades along the towpath. The rose finally gave in to the determined onslaught of the horses in the paddock on the other side of the railings.

'Perhaps some pots on deck?' asked my mother hopefully, but pots were dismissed as un-nautical, as was safety netting round the sides of the boat. When our first daughter began to crawl, my husband hitched her by her harness to the barge mast on a rope just long enough to encourage the spirit of adventure but short enough to stop her falling off the edge. So, with the loss of the flag iris, our first grown-up foray into gardens came to an end with yet more disasters to add to the list.

It was at our first house and on the first patch of ground that we actually owned that I really discovered the point of gardening. It wasn't a Pauline conversion. There was no sudden, blinding vision of beauty. I didn't see myself (still don't) trolling through bowers of roses, straw hat just so, gathering blooms into a basket. Nor had I any idea at first of the immense joy of growing food. But I had at least begun to understand that gardening, if it is to be satisfying, requires some sense of permanency. Roots matter. The longer you stay put, the richer the rewards.

I also realised how completely I had missed the point as a child. Gardening was not necessarily about an end result. The doing was what mattered. At this time too, I learned about gardening as therapy. Banged up with small children all day for the first time, I thought I would go under. When a confrontation seemed to be looming of a kind that had no solution (apart from giving away the children to the first person that passed by on the lane outside) I would race to the newly made vegetable patch at the bottom of the garden and furiously hoe beans. The children's legs were shorter than mine and if I was lucky, I'd have at least a minute and a half on my own before they caught up with me and wanted to hoe too. Later on, when they were five or six years old, gardening with the children became a pleasure. But at this early stage – not.

This first garden (I don't count the river bank) was a square patch in front of a brick cottage. It was a pleasant jumble of roses, honey-suckle, japonica, white iris (the iris are with us still – the only plant to provide a connecting thread between each of our three gardens), peonies and madonna lilies, planted by generations of previ-ous owners. It was tidy enough not to be daunting and provided enough unfamilar plants to keep me tethered in the evenings to the first gardening book I ever had: the *Reader's Digest Encyclopaedia of Garden Plants and Flowers*. It hadn't the sexy pictures that you take for granted in gardening books now, but I learned a lot from it and still use it more than any other in a library that must now contain over a thousand gardening books.

During the five years we stayed there – caretaker years, in terms of gardening – we planted nothing new, but learned how to cope with what we had got, mostly under the guidance of our hawk-eyed neighbour, a magnificent woman called Jo Schwabe. 'Don't touch that border!' she would shriek from a hastily opened window, as I stood poised with a fork over a narrow border under the east wall of the house. 'There's lily bulbs under there. Madonna lilies. You'll ruin them with that fork.'

And as I prowled with secateurs round a summer-flowering jasmine which, in season, scented the whole house, she would yell, 'Leave that bush alone. You'll have no flowers next year if you hack at it now. Do it in September.' At the beginning, it made trips into the garden nerve-racking affairs, but she was right. I could easily have murdered a perfectly good garden in my ignorance. She hid Easter eggs in old birds' nests for our small children to find and gave me anemones to plant in the border in front of the house.

Over the years, she taught me the value of patience. She also, in no uncertain terms, taught me that plants are not designer playthings, not merely accents, dots, drifts and drapes, but living creatures with needs and desires of their own. She introduced me to the witchy belladonna (*Amaryllis belladonna*) and explained why she'd put it in a sunny gravel patch at the foot of a brick wall. She showed me how to prune the hybrid tea roses that had been planted in a bed by our back door. When she asked us to water her bonsai while she went away for a rare break, I felt I had passed a very important test.

Once upon a time, you would have picked up all this information from your parents. But so few of us now stay where we were initially put. In this first house, I was at least four hours' drive away from my home in Wales. But my parents saw what was happening. My Christmas present that year was *Hillier's Manual of Trees and Shrubs* in the old, green paper-covered edition. I started marking it up, asking them for the names of the rhododendrons and camellias that I particularly liked in the garden where I'd grown up.

But that's when I discovered another important thing about gardening. If you move away from home, you'll probably end up in a place where the soil and growing conditions are different. *Hillier's Manual*, with its vast list of rhodos and other lime-hating shrubs, was my parents' gardening bible because they gardened on leafy, acid soil. Our first house was in Sussex, with a garden made on heavy clay. They had shade. We had sun all day. Fortunately, I cooked only one rhododendron before the penny dropped.

Herbaceous plants grew well, though, and I learned that they had a way of putting themselves in combinations rather better than any I had thought of. It would have been lunacy not to take advantage of all the self-seeding that went on, even if the end result did not fit the plan that had taken me three months and ten library books to prepare.

The children went to bed promptly at six o'clock. I longed for the clocks to go back in spring because then, in the extra evening light, I could climb over the wall to the field at the bottom of the garden where, in a fenced-off corner, we made a fruit and vegetable garden. In clay so thick you could have made pots with it, I grew the best sprouts I have ever produced. Carrots were more difficult, but I grew globe artichokes from seed, leeks, potatoes, courgettes, beetroot, asparagus peas (a waste of time), French beans, lettuce, onions, shallots, tomatoes and sweetcorn. We had several rows of raspberry canes, brought by my parents from the beds at home, strawberries, gooseberries and three different kinds of currants. That patch was my salvation.

It was also, in a roundabout way, the reason we left Sussex and came to West Dorset. England was weird in the early seventies. Things you needed – like bread – kept disappearing. Oil went on the first of its expensive sprees and I got slightly obsessed with the idea of self-sufficiency. I don't mean the full-on, weave-your-own-salvation kind. I just wanted to be somewhere where we could raise enough food to feed the children and have some spare to barter. I wanted chickens and a good supply of firewood. And Sussex, though lovely, was slightly too brushed and combed for me, raised as I had been in the wild border country between Wales and England.

So we bought a Queen Anne rectory, the kind of house nobody wanted then: too big, too cold, too demanding. Little remained of the roof, but it had an acre and a half of garden. I had another baby (odd how often that goes with moving house); the health visitor called and found me crouched over a fire in the scullery, ivy growing up the insides of the walls, the stone floor covered in plaster and rotting timber. There wasn't an entire floor or ceiling in the whole place. To her credit, she said nothing. Nor did the health visitor who, several years earlier, had visited the barge in winter and found me crawling on all fours up the gangplank to the deck with our first baby strapped to my front. It was too icy to risk any other way of getting aboard.

For thirty-five years, the rectory was the lynchpin of our lives. At the beginning, it took eighteen months just to hack our way through to our boundaries. Standing eventually on the space that became our top lawn, looking out over the valley, I saw our neighbour, a farmer, staring at me. 'Well,' he said, after a long country silence. 'I've not seen anyone up there since the last war.'

This place, which I loved with a passion, taught me everything else I learned about gardening (though actually the more you go on, the less you realise you know and the more extraordinary the whole process seems). Although, at the beginning, we couldn't see it for elders, brambles and general chaos, the rectory had a walled kitchen garden. We made monumental compost heaps, hauled in heroic quantities of manure and, a piece at a time, got this garden back into full production. I plastered the walls with fruit trees – pears, cherries, plums, apricots, peaches – and taught myself how to train them into espaliers and fans. We made an asparagus bed (a real sign of roots).

The garden became the focus of all my dreams: I would lay paths of intricately patterned pebbles, brought up from the beach; I would make a flowering meadow, build a stump garden. Reality gradually tempered the megalomania. There was never enough money. Never enough time. But I did not want to impose myself on to that ground. All I ever hoped was that a stranger, walking in, would suppose it had always looked like this: the kitchen garden divided once again like a noughts and crosses board into its nine seventeenth-century squares, the cobbles of the stable yard now cleared of the detritus that on our arrival had lain two feet deep. The messages we found pencilled on the stalls of the stables were to me as important a part of the history of the place as the house itself.

It was, apart from the big kitchen garden, rather a shady place, dominated by big yew trees, beech and evergreen oaks. In the far corner was a bit of a wood, where the tree trunks reared up like cathedral pillars, rooks clattering about in the branches overhead. Gradually we cleared ivy from the trunks and the stone walls that bounded it on two sides. We planted snowdrops and bluebells. I loved it there, especially in winter with the wind roaring in from the sea and the trees shouting back their defiance.

The first plants I ever put in the rectory garden were snowdrops, brought by my mother from a ruined cottage on the Llanwenarth Breast, where we used to walk when I was a child. Shortly after that first visit, she died. She never saw what we did with the rectory. She never knew that I would start writing about all these things. But writing (I became gardening correspondent of the *Independent* in 1986 when the paper was first set up) forced me to think much harder about what I was doing, to question whether I couldn't be doing better. The writing fed the garden. And the garden certainly fed the writing.

Two of our daughters were married at the rectory, walking up the lane, in their long white dresses to the church, awash with cow parsley and apple blossom. Almost their whole lives had been lived in that one house. The garden was woven through with their camps and secret places, where they pounded potions in jam jars, set up shops and traded dares. Then, after thirty-five years, we left. In gardening, the future is what matters. As the removal van turned into the drive of the rectory, that phrase became like a mantra. What we had done once, we could do again. And so, chanting inwardly, I glided through the first day of the move (it took three days) in a curious trance, scrubbing the beautiful big blue lias slabs we had laid in a terrace by the back door, scrubbing the wide stone steps (the best gift we ever gave to the garden) that led from the stable yard to the top lawn.

The move had been long planned and it was, without doubt, the right thing for us to do, but on the last day, I wobbled badly. The sun was streaming through the young foliage of the beech trees. The border outside the study window was at its jungly best with royal ferns not quite fully uncurled. The plants on the bank, silhouetted against the sun, had a radiance about them which suddenly made me want to scoop the entire garden up and take it with me. My mantra about the future was drowned in an urgent need to stay with the now. My husband broke open the champagne he had foreseen that we would need.

We toasted the past. We toasted the future. I thanked the garden for all that I had learned from it. I laid my cheek against the moss of the courtyard wall. I said goodbye to the pear trees I'd trained out on the kitchen garden walls. Then we walked away, leaving the garden blazing in the June sun.

Avon Meadows in winter

STAR STRUCK

How can it be that some serious newspapers — even the *Independent* — are still without horoscopes? Everybody knows what an important part they play in public life these days, and yet here we are, left often with no Mystic Meg, no Petulengro to guide us on our way. It really is too bad. Most horoscopes, though, tend to be obsessed with periph- eral matters: career opportunities, emotional relationships and such like. These are interesting enough in their way, but cannot compare with the really big issues in your life: the arrival of a new pot, the anxieties caused by a demanding aspidistra. Star-gazers — start here.

AQUARIUS (22 JANUARY—19 FEBRUARY)

Dream on, Aquarians. One day, you too could appear on *Gardeners' Question Time*. But there is a danger that in your own garden, your dreams will never be translated into reality. Design gardens for other people instead. The future will always be more interesting to you than the past. Junk Jekyll. Think instead of pergolas of spun steel, water gardens of perspex and laser-light shows among the lilies. Uranus in your birth sign makes it likely that you will want to try out things that others regard as slightly eccentric. But if they don't like your *trompe l'œil* Taj Mahal in mirror and bottle tops, more fool them.

PISCES (20 FEBRUARY—20 MARCH)

The Sun in your birth sign after the 19th means that you will be able to do whatever you set your mind to over the next few weeks. But still, choices must be made. 'Kiftsgate' rose or 'Rambling Rector'? 'Mermaid' or 'Paul's Himalayan'? Letting nature take its course is a doubtful doctrine, as you may have already found this winter. Drains and poplars do not mix. Pisceans are apt to take the line of least resistance. You are curiously drawn towards wild-flower gardens. But Pisceans are also intuitive. You will recognise that a plant is in difficulty long before it is past saving, a useful trait in a gardener.

ARIES (21 MARCH—20 APRIL)

Ariens are energetic and good at getting round obstacles. All your ebullient energy will be needed this month to circumvent a drama, not at this moment clearly delineated. It may involve a neighbour. It may involve a boundary. You like quick results, which makes you an impatient gardener. Try this year to curb the trait. In the garden centre, avoid annuals which will die this year and go for perennials which will die next year instead. After the 15th, Mars, your ruler, moves into a tricky part of your chart. Avoid this period for servicing lawnmowers.

TAURUS (21 APRIL—21 MAY)

Happiness is a more obscure salvia than your neighbour's, and in this game of horticultural one-upmanship, Taureans will score every time, for they are careful and tenacious gardeners. Venus, your ruler, enters the bossy sign of Aries on the 9th and the days there-after may be full of anxiety. Should it be petunias rather than busy lizzies in the front border this year? Choose carefully, for old ties, once severed, may never be remade. Your worst fault is stubbornness. Try and accept advice more readily. But on the positive side, you do not believe in short cuts. Taureans always read the instructions on a weedkiller pack.

GEMINI (22 MAY–21 JUNE)

Criticism never goes down well with Geminis, but is it such a good idea to plant an all-black garden? It is vogueish, certainly, but just the teensiest bit limiting. You can have too much even of ophiopogon. Finance continues to be a problem and will be until you learn that you do not *have* to throw away the potted camellias after they have finished flowering. You are good at pretending to know more than you do, love variety and are a compulsive buyer of garden gadgets. Speaking of which, there is the most amazing gizmo around now which cuts edges, shaves legs and minces parsley. Not all at the same time, of course.

CANCER (22 JUNE–22 JULY)

Your delight in the difficult comes to the fore this month when seedlings, always keener on dying than living, demand your undivided attention. Pluto, warring with Mars on the 19th, indicates difficulties in your personal life. Take heart. Your partner's predilection for mixing purple and orange in the herbaceous border has almost run its course. Known for your nurturing, you are likely to find yourself in charge of tricky alpines. You also invent complicated life-support systems for your house plants when you go away. But listen to this: you can actually get seeds which take less than a year to germinate.

LEO (23 JULY–23 AUGUST)

This is a decisive month for Leos as it marks the start of the giant onion season, the Leo's favourite plant. Make the most of it. Pluto has a challenging aspect: slugs are massing on the horizon. The lime-light that you enjoy will pass you by unless you attend assiduously to watering and pricking out. Gladioli and dahlias, chrysanthemums and begonias are more likely to be your thing than tasteful euphorbias and hellebores. Leos are generous, though, and good people to have as neighbours. 'My rose is your rose,' they will say munificently as their 'Bobby James' rambler mounts the boundary fence and takes over your lawn.

VIRGO (24 AUGUST–23 SEPTEMBER)

The Sun in something or other provides just the boost you need to lash out on a really exciting new asset. A lawn edger, perhaps. You know how you fret if the grass is a whisker out of place. Loved ones do not help this month by leaving tools unseen in the shrubbery. All the portents suggest that your black eye will have healed by the solstice. You are likely to be a good planner and organiser but you must learn not to fret if things do not always go as they should. That's gardening. You are probably best left to garden on your own, for you can be hypercritical, often unfairly, of other people's efforts.

LIBRA (24 SEPTEMBER–23 OCTOBER)

Unexpected developments are about to alter the whole course of your gardening life. Look for love among the bonsai, however unlikely this may seem. Everything this month points towards a complete break with the past. Chuck out the hostas and think Japanese. Librans are star gardeners for they are diplomatic, love harmony and are brilliant mediators. Get yourself elected chairman of your county's National Gardens Scheme committee. Occasional indecision is your only downfall, but when you *have* decided, the results in your own garden are much photographed. Librans get their gardens into all the best magazines.

SCORPIO (24 OCTOBER–22 NOVEMBER)

Your delight in a bargain has unexpected consequences when officers of the Fraud Squad turn up to repossess the *divine* little cherub you picked up for two songs in Pimlico. Never mind. Back to Haddonstone. You are likely to have a beady eye for everyone else's business as well as your own. Trust a Scorpio to give you the cheapest source of supply for anything from compost to cotoneasters. You are also likely to be argumentative. Stay off contentious issues such as peat and pesticides.

SAGITTARIUS (23 NOVEMBER–21 DECEMBER)

Assert your independence this month. No matter what the style gurus say, you can live without a crushed-glass water feature. Try it and see. There are other changes on the horizon. Goodbye chrysanthemum. Hello dendranthema, leucanthemopsis, arctanthemum, tanacetum … You do not always realise how hurtful your bluntness, a characteristic of all Sagittarians, can be. Some people really do love cacti dressed up in sunglasses and paper skirts. You rarely sulk, but it is equally rare for you to learn from your mistakes. Sagittarians murder more rhododendrons than any other group of gardeners.

CAPRICORN (22 DECEMBER–21 JANUARY)

For once, forget the pennies and lash out on a pair of secateurs. They will be so much easier to use on the philadelphus than the bayonet from the hatstand in the hall. Economical is the polite way to describe Capricorn's gardeners. They save their seeds wrapped in screws of paper in old Ovaltine tins and hover round paper-recycling bins, waiting to retrieve *Gardens Illustrated* magazines that others are throwing away. But you are likely to work hard in the garden, not shirking even the most hideous chores,

such as scrubbing down the greenhouse. If you are hiring help in
the garden, check birthdates before anything else.

MORE HASTE, LESS SEED

I have recently driven to Penrith with George Orwell, been on a
trip to East Anglia with Julian Barnes and whiled away some time in
London with E. F. Benson. Talking books, since I discovered a public
library with a vast stock of unabridged editions, have revolutionised
my life. Orwell's *Down and Out in Paris and London* was so riveting, I
missed my exit on the M6 motorway and had to make a forty-mile
detour to get back on route.

Choosing the right tapes is, of course, crucial. You are allowed
three, so there is room for one flier that you don't know much
about. One can be a safe bet, an author you know you will enjoy.
My third is usually an ought-book, one that you take because you
are so tired of people saying 'I can't *believe* you don't know Süskind/
Hesse/Ondaatje,' as though you might die of the deficiency.

Flipping through the seeds that I will start to sow this week, I see
that the same principles have guided my choices there too. There
are the bankers: stocks, violas, poppies. There are a few fliers such
as a low-growing white evening primrose, *Oenothera caespitosa*, and
one or two oughts such as the pink-flowered form of the short-lived
perennial *Verbascum blattaria*.

Oughts in the plant world are notoriously fickle. No sooner have
you congratulated yourself on tracking down the right form of herbaceous elder or sky-blue salvia, than you find the goal posts have been
moved and you are left holding yesterday's plant. There is a type of
gardener for whom scarceness is the only criterion of a plant's worth.

They will not be growing *Limonium* 'Azure', the popular everlasting sea lavender with papery flowers that you can cut and dry. These can be sown any time now and the seed will take one to two weeks to germinate. Then you need to prick the seedlings out in boxes, grow them on and finally plant them out in May where you want them to flower. They are generally in bloom by late July and then stand in excellent condition through to late September.

Some sea lavenders are sold as mixtures with lemon, pink, white and blue flowers. 'Azure' is just clear, solid blue and grows to about 24 inches (60 centimetres) with characteristic flanges or wings running up the sides of the stems. Plant about 12 inches (30 centimetres) apart, for the leaves make quite large basal rosettes. I am using it in a blue and yellow planting to replace *Salvia farinacea* 'Queen Victoria', which I can never get into flower early enough to justify the fuss of raising it.

Any statice plants left over can go with *Rudbeckia* 'Goldilocks', an exuberant double form of this orange-yellow daisy, commonly called black-eyed Susan. Because of the doubleness, the central cone is not so clear and prominent as it is in other varieties, but the shagginess is appealing, though politically incorrect. We are supposed to have only single flowers in the garden to be sure of approval from the style police.

Some rudbeckias that you can grow from seed, such as 'Goldsturm', are perennial, unlike 'Goldilocks', and if you are trying to persuade rudbeckias to flower in shade, the single 'Goldsturm' with long strappy petals will perform better than any other variety. The soil needs to be moist, though, not starved. If you sow 'Goldilocks' in March, you should have flowers by August. Then they will continue until the frosts.

One important advantage of growing from seed is that you can fill your garden with flowers that no garden centre or street market will supply. But conversely, I no longer grow flowers such as petunias or lobelias from seed. These can be bought in so easily as bedding plants in May. And if you have a street market such as London's Columbia Road to hand, you save very little money by growing your own.

But seed sowing is an essential rite of passage for a gardener. For years, as a novice, I felt it was all too complicated to get into. When my father-in-law died, my supply of custom-grown plants dried up and I was forced to raise my own seedlings. They grew successfully and my pride was even greater than when I produced my first decent soufflé. Optimism is an essential tool in the gardener's kit. Much more important than a strimmer. And quieter.

Penstemons have become very vogueish plants. There was a time when you only ever saw 'Garnet' or 'Ruby', stalwarts of the August garden, flowering like shrunken foxgloves in shades of deep red, pink and pale mauveish blue. Now there are at least a hundred named varieties, but they all need to be propagated by cuttings, taken in August, for they do not come true from seed. But you can get seed mixtures of penstemons such as 'Cambridge Mix', which grow into bushy plants no more than about 10 inches (25 centimetres) tall. They are useful for filling gaps where other things have thoughtlessly died. If you sow early enough and grow the plants without a check, you can get them to flower the same year. Or you can treat them as biennials, sow them in early August, overwinter them in a cold greenhouse and plant them out the following spring. That way they come into bloom earlier.

Stocks come from the same bit of the rainbow as penstemons, but have the huge extra advantage of smelling like a celestial Body Shop. They are a confusing family because they bob up under too many divisions: Park, Ten Week, Brompton, Night-scented, Regular, East Lothian, Mammoth. The ones I usually grow are the biennial Bromptons, which, like wallflowers, you sow in summer to flower the following year.

This year I am splashing out on a night-scented annual stock called 'Starlight Scentsation'. It looks desperately wholesome: pink and white and mauve, single but heavily scented, and about 18 inches (45 centimetres) tall. It affects me like the young Shirley Temple. Half of me goes 'Aaaah!', the other half goes 'Arrrgh!' I must hope the first reaction is stronger than the second. At least the stock won't sing.

Stocks have been cultivated for almost as long as there have been gardeners. They were written about in the eleventh-century gardens of Islam, they crop up in the illustrations that decorate some of the earliest printed books in Europe, they appear on the famous Unicorn tapestries (woven in about 1500) that now hang in the Metropolitan Museum of Art in New York.

The Italian agriculturist Agostino del Riccio had them growing in his courtyard garden in 1597. They survived through the anti-flower pogrom of the English landscape garden and emerged triumphant into the High Victorian gardens of the nineteenth century, when they were used extensively both for cutting and for bedding out. Contemporary gardening books recommended them for 'flower beds and borders, for edgings, ribbons and pot culture'.

Victorian garden writers advise frequent applications of guano water for the best stocks. This was a fertiliser made from dissolving bird droppings in water. First find your guano, but the inference is clear. Stocks do best on good, rich, well-fed ground. I am planning two patches in the certain knowledge that Joshua, the most hopeless cat that ever cadged free board and lodging, will certainly make his bed on one lot.

GARDENING CLOTHES

A change in gardening jacket is a traumatic affair. I have just lost my old one and am breaking in a replacement. It will be a long, painful process. My first gardening coat was an extraordinary cream corduroy thing, which called itself a safari jacket. It was windproof (though not very warm) and had four patch pockets on the front. I acquired it with my husband, who used to wear it with hair ever so

SOWING FOR BEGINNERS, WITHOUT A PROPAGATOR:

1. Use fresh compost. I find soilless multi-purpose compost the easiest and most convenient to use.

2. Make your initial sowing in a 5-inch (13-centimetre) plastic pot filled with compost which you have pressed down gently. The base of another similar-sized pot makes a convenient tamping-down tool.

3. Scatter the seeds as thinly as possible over the surface of the compost. Very small seeds (such as begonia) need not be covered at all. Cover others with a layer of vermiculite.

4. Water the pots, either from above with a watering can, or by letting them soak up water from the bottom.

5. Wrap them in clingfilm and keep the pots on a warmish windowsill until seedlings show through. Zinnias are fast (about four days), others much slower. Some seeds, such as primrose, need to be kept cool, so are best left outside to germinate.

6. Make sure the seedlings are well watered before you prick them out into seed trays – twenty-four seedlings to a tray. Handle them only by the seed leaves (called cotyledons), which, if you are clumsy, are expendable.

7. Water the seed tray and set it somewhere in full light. Turn the tray regularly so that the seedlings do not grow in one direction. Brush over their tops with the edge of a piece of cardboard. This encourages strong stems and stops the seedlings becoming leggy.

8. If you have sown a mixture of one type of flower, do not always choose just the strongest seedlings to prick out. The weaker plants are often those with the most unusual colours.

slightly too long. It eventually fell out of favour, had an unproductive spell in the dressing-up box and was fished out to put on a guy one bonfire night.

Absent-mindedly, I put on the coat to carry wood through the chilly garden ready for the bonfire. It was by then so far past being fashionable that it had almost acquired retro status. And what is more, it was comfortable. I kept the jacket; the guy made do with an iffy trench coat forgotten under piles of wet weather gear on the hatstand by the back door.

All my gardening coats have been my husband's cast-offs. He is sufficiently bigger than me for the coats to be roomy and snug. They all have the same faint smell of wet dog which I find strangely comforting and they are all well endowed with pockets. Why do tailors think that men need more pockets than women? Surely it should be the other way around.

Though the strange metal buttons that fastened it gradually rusted their way out of the corduroy, that hideous cream jacket saw me through some serious spade work in our garden. I replanted the lane hedge in it, I cleared much of the bank in it. I pruned hateful 'Mermaid', the most spiteful rose known to man, in it. I cleared out gutters and hauled compost in it. Because it had button-down pockets, my secateurs didn't fall out every time I bent over. That was a huge point in its favour. I've never graduated to a holster for my secateurs. Too Clint Eastwood. My nerves couldn't take the strain of trying to beat him to an imaginary draw every time I wanted to snip a twig.

Coat number two was warmer, but less well pocketed, in the sense that the pockets didn't button shut. It was a blue bum-freezer jacket with knitted stuff round the bottom of its too short hem. It came to me quite quickly, my husband having bought it in a great rush of optimism on a day trip to London. In the mincing streets of the metropolis, it looked fine, but it never took to the country. Its punishment for being sniffy was to accompany me on some of the filthiest jobs I've ever attempted at our place: cleaning out drains, carting stone for walls, wrestling with railway sleepers. Stuffing (kapok-like fake lambswool) started to ooze out of the cuts and snags that it acquired with each strenuous new task. The fabric caught very easily on thorns, tore, and then these messy entrails spilt out of the holes.

That jacket was silently confiscated by one of the children, mortified that I had been wearing it when she brought a friend home for the weekend. It was a fair move. I'd confiscated an army combat jacket of hers, to which she was deeply attached and which had almost as many slashes in it as my bum-freezer. At least hers didn't have a stuffing to lose.

So now I am faced with the newcomer. Not new at all, of course. Very old, because deeply favoured by my husband. I saw some time ago that it had possibilities, but have been biding my time. The difficult thing at the beginning is that a new (to me) gardening jacket has none of the built-in associations that a well-worn one has. When the sun suddenly shines in the afternoon and I decide to abandon work, I walk fast to the back door, hooking up the gardening coat on the way. The coat speaks of escape, and this patina takes time to build up. The scars it bears are a record of the things we've achieved together. But as an object, this new old coat is way beyond its forebears. It is canvas. It is faded blue in colour and it has pockets fitted with Velcro closers. What more could a gardener want?

BY HEAVENS, WHEN DO YOU PLANT?

I tidied the duster box recently. Don't ask me why. I can only think that it was a way of putting off the more gruesome tasks that took me to the duster box in the first place: blackleading the grates, cleaning the brass, polishing the poor, abandoned hatstand in the passage. But as a symbol of the transitoriness of things, nothing could be more potent.

Take Shaky. There was a time when one of the children's bedrooms was a shrine to the pop star Shakin' Stevens. In the duster box was embarrassing proof of her obsession: half of a red sweatshirt, with Shaky emblazoned on the front. She must have been very young at the time (at least that will be her excuse) because it is a very small sweatshirt. But there he is, shoulders hunched, legs splayed out, balanced precariously on the inside edges of his startlingly white shoes, with the notes of some forgotten song swirling round his overloaded hair.

The remnant of a hideously shaming dress was my own. Well, the seventies were weird, but were they really this weird? And yet this dress, with its brilliant psychedelic swirls of shocking pink, magenta and orange was once the star of my wardrobe. Now it was one of the few rags in the box that actually looked better encrusted with Brasso than it did in its original state.

There is nothing more transitory than style. That is the point of it, that it moves on all the time. Clothes and pop stars are more at its mercy than gardens, though there have been some high-spirited attempts to subjugate gardening to the cause. The difficulty is that gardens (ones with plants in, anyway) won't stay where they are put. This is a nightmare for stylists because their whole world depends on domination. The only way out is to get rid of anything that grows, and spread crushed car windscreen where the grass should be. Crushed car windscreen is the gravel of the nineties.

Transitoriness provides excitement and freshness in a garden. Sometimes it is a style thing, a craze for a certain colour, like the brilliant blue that is vogueish in gardens at the moment. There are styles in plants too. Hostas used to be stylish, but aren't any more. Hellebores are certainly stylish. So are certain sorts of primroses. Daffodils have never yet made the leap.

There is an inbuilt transitoriness in gardens too, created by the ebb and flow of seasonal plants. Jasmine and viburnum have taken over from the summer's roses. New views open up as leaves fall from the trees. And each year gardeners introduce different plants into the garden picture, some of them perhaps never intended as permanent fixtures. Marigolds, for instance, flowered spectacularly among the beetroot in our vegetable garden this year. I enjoyed that show, but it is more fun to plan a different performance there next year than to repeat the old one.

But underpinning these fleeting effects in a garden is a foundation of enormous strength and stability. The resilience and timelessness of gardens, the slow growth of trees, the immutable change of autumn into winter and winter into spring, the consequence those changes have on plants – no one can garden and remain unaware of these things. Indeed, they may provide reasons why we took to gardening in the first place.

Tapping into this underlying strength is one of the things that makes gardening important to me. This, of course, is not a conscious feeling. When I wander out of the back door to do some casual weeding I do not say, 'Fancy that. I am part of the great diurnal round.' I just get on with the job in hand. But while you are there, idly looking at the silhouette of the mahonia in the dusk and the sun sets round you, bleeding across the sky with the savage intensity that only happens on winter afternoons, you feel a whole lot better than you do inside. Colder, but better.

I don't feel I have to burrow around in my subconscious for reasons to garden. Fortunately, nobody else seems to feel the need either. Psychologists and psychiatrists leave us alone with our happy mania. My own theory about this (you have to have a theory in the psych-business) is that the act of gardening itself is what keeps you out of the hands of the shrinks in the first place.

There is no more boring subject to think about than oneself. One knows oneself too well. There are no surprises. But it is impossible to be self-obsessed if one is a gardener. You become subsumed in an immense and absorbing process that has nothing to do with the way you look or your own importance (always over-estimated) in the greater scheme of things. From that detached viewpoint you can (fortunately) afford to find gardens made from crushed car windscreen a joke. For surely only their style-blinded begetters can take them seriously?

For some gardeners, the greater scheme itself becomes all-important. Instead of underpinning the calming chores of pruning and sowing and harvesting, it becomes the driving force of everything they do in the garden. Over Christmas, I spent some time puzzling over *Gwydion's Planting Guide* by J. R. Gower, which describes itself as 'the definitive moon-planting manual'.

The guiding principle is not difficult to grasp. Root vegetables should be sown, planted or transplanted in a period that starts two days before a full moon and ends three days before the following new moon. All other fruits and vegetables (and presumably flowers?) should be sown, planted or transplanted in a slot that starts two days before a new moon and ends three days before the following full moon.

Now, you don't necessarily have to go along with these rules (which have long been a part of gardening lore), but at least you can understand them. J. R. Gower adds a further complication: signs of the zodiac. The beneficial signs for sowing and planting are Taurus, Cancer, Virgo, Scorpio, Capricorn and Pisces, all either earth or water signs. The trick, says Gower, is to get the phases of the moon working properly with the movements of the zodiac.

That means, according to the example he gives, that tomatoes should be sown between 14 January (22.04 hours) and 17 January (8.42 hours), or 19 January (21.22 hours) and 22 January (9.35 hours). I enjoy the thought of JR standing with seed packet in hand, waiting, when most of us are thinking about bed, for the hand of his watch to creep round to the 22.04 position.

Nick Kollerstrom's *Planting by the Moon* is a much fuller and better-designed guide to the same subject, though still wonderfully arcane. There is a generous day-to-day diary in this book with full instructions on the state of play up there in the heavens. On 5 January, 'The Moon has reached its north node, which is usually a stressful time, but is quickly followed by the trine aspect, which is more harmonious. Work only in the afternoon.' Oh! If only I could. Afternoons are so wonderfully short in January. But dear Mr Kollerstrom, afternoon-only hours just aren't an option. Will a thunderbolt strike me if I dig compost before noon?

I do hope not, because I am intrigued (though not persuaded) by this book. It tells about cycles of the sky, how the moon may affect fertility and crop yield. It explains the rhythms of the sun and sets out sensible principles of organic gardening. It includes a modern-day plan of work for a productive kitchen garden, which appears alongside its eighteenth-century equivalent, garden notes taken from Martha Bradley's *The British Housewife*, which was first published in 1756. 'December is a dead season of the year for gardening,' says the sensible Mrs Bradley. That's all the excuse I need to stay by the fire.

ACE OF SPUDS

What honours are there left in life since I scooped the big one – a first prize for my potatoes at the Melplash Agricultural Show? I fear I may have peaked too early, for since that seminal summer, I've never again grown potatoes perfect enough to set before the critical gaze of the Melplash judges. The winning spud was 'Catriona', a long, oval second early variety with purple eyes marked on a smooth white skin.

It is an old potato, known since 1920, and a useful one in our neck of the woods because the haulm dies down early and so does not get blighted as readily as other varieties. The ironic thing about those prize-winning 'Catriona' potatoes is that they were what my mother called 'moochers', potatoes that got left behind in the ground when I was digging the main crop. They started themselves into growth in the spring, but were never earthed up. Instead, they got covered rather thickly with grass cuttings.

This kept the ground underneath moist during hot weather. It also made lifting incredibly easy. I scarcely had to dig, merely scraped away the 6-inch (15-centimetre) layer of grass. There were the potatoes, sitting like a nest of goose eggs, clean and gleaming. Having by accident discovered this labour-saving way of growing, I've tried it several times since. It works well on a plot in our kitchen garden that is mulched thickly with leaves every winter, and never dug.

Why bother, some gardeners ask? Potatoes are so cheap to buy. True, but the selection in supermarkets is pathetic, compared with the 118 varieties of seed potatoes offered, for instance, by the Scottish firm of Webster's. And if you like cooking, you need different kinds of potato to do different things. For baking, you might turn to 'Epicure', 'Osprey' or 'Romano'. For roasting you'd perhaps choose 'Accent', 'Edzell Blue' or 'Dunbar Standard'. For boiling, you need 'Marfona', 'Argos' or 'Maris Piper'. For mashing, I like 'Winston', 'Desiree' and 'Sante'. For salads you have to have waxy potatoes such as 'Pomfine', 'Belle de Fontenay' and 'Pink Fir Apple'. For chips, you might reach for 'Swift', 'Cara' or 'Pentland Dell'.

Once you are committed to the idea of growing your own, you face another series of choices to find the clutch of potatoes most likely to succeed on your kind of ground. If it's a windy or exposed plot, try the first early 'Colmo', with low, spreading foliage. The new second early 'Bydand' will also survive howling gales. Where slugs are particularly ghastly, choose 'Vanessa', the old variety 'British Queen' (1894), 'Kestrel' or 'Pentland Squire'. On dry soils,

'Arran Pilot', 'Rocket', 'Estima' and 'Pentland Dell' all survive and crop in drought-ridden summers.

If you suffer from retrostalgia, an overwhelming conviction that nothing now is as good as it used to be, send to Edwin Tucker for a selection of potato plants, micropropagated from varieties now more than a hundred years old. These exist in such small quantities that you can't buy them as tubers. Instead Tucker's send out ready-grown plants in late May and early June. They have twenty-two of these rare varieties on offer, including 'Shetland Black', known since 1900, 'Skerry Blue' from 1846 and 'Champion', reputed to be the best-flavoured potato ever raised. It's been known in Arbroath since 1862.

As well as tasting better than you had ever imagined a potato could taste, many old varieties have blessedly strong constitutions. In the slap-happy, spray-happy post-war years, this was not valued as much as it perhaps is now, when the effects of eating poisons for lunch are beginning to be more clearly understood. 'Edzell Blue' is immune to wart disease. 'Dunbar Rover' is resistant to blight.

Even their best friends would not call potatoes a decorative addition to the kitchen garden, though 'Red Duke of York' took my fancy this last summer, with its dark purplish foliage and purple flowers. It's a first early, producing red potatoes that bake well and can also double up as salad potatoes.

Early potatoes mature in about fourteen to sixteen weeks, so from a March planting, you might be eating the first new potatoes by the end of June. Before you plant, you have to 'chit' the tubers by laying them out in trays to sprout. Planting time depends on the weather. If you plant too early, sudden frost may cut down the nesh, green foliage. Commercial growers use spun polypropylene covers over their crops to protect them against this. In Lincolnshire and Bedfordshire, the flat fields look like lakes, covered entirely with a shimmering web. The system works for gardeners too.

You can grow early potatoes in containers with reasonable success, but the bigger the container, the greater the success.

Crops from early potatoes are, anyway, lighter than the load you might expect from a maincrop potato, so it is best to use the fast-maturing, lighter-cropping earlies if you want to grow in a pot (or a dustbin – they work very well). Extra early types such as 'Dunluce' or 'Rocket' are best for this.

In the unusually quiet days that lay between Christmas and the New Year, I read happily through lists of old potatoes and sorted out an order. I love mail order, because by the time a parcel arrives, I've usually forgotten what I've sent for. Amongst others I put in for 'Red Duke of York', bred around 1940, 'Dunbar Rover' (sounds like a football team), which is a few years older and 'Edzell Blue', grown in Edzell, Angus a year after the First World War broke out. What supermarket can produce such delights as these? And what restaurant can provide a treat as good as a fluffy pile of 'Edzell Blue' mash, whipped up with good farm butter, a twist of pepper and a dusting of freshly grated nutmeg? Even dear Jamie would be pushed to match that.

Having completed the order, I announced the fact brightly to daughter no. 2. 'And?' she replied after a pause just long enough to wither entirely any hope on my part that potatoes might be a subject fit for family conversation. But in the solitude of the hell hole that is my potting corner, I continue to be quietly excited.

GRACE AND FAVOUR

'Suppose Endsleigh had never been built,' wrote William Adam, land agent to the Duke of Bedford in 1826, 'your Grace would in 1824 have received £3,090 more from Devonshire than you did ... I have always thought that your Grace never did a wiser thing than to build a residence in Devonshire, tho' of course the expenditure there was necessarily increased by it. The only question is whether that Expenditure is greater than it need or ought to be … All this expenditure however carries no advantage except the amusement it affords your Grace. Which I admit is a sufficient exception. Only it is fit that you should know the price it costs you.'

Worth every penny, I'd say, as Endsleigh is now a hotel (the latest venture by Olga Polizzi of the Hotel Tresanton at St Mawes) and the 'amusement' once only enjoyed by the Duke and his family is now available to us all. The garden is open every day and it gave me the best day out I've had for years.

Don't go there expecting a garden in the modern sense. There's a sensational pergola of roses (ten each of nine different varieties), an enormous herbaceous border, said to be the longest in England, and water features round every corner, but the real point of the place is the clever exploitation of its situation, the rambling house – the Duchess's idea of a cottage – set by the architect Sir Jeffry Wyatville above a bend in the River Tamar, with thick woods rising behind.

The Duchess chose the spot herself and the great eighteenth-century landscape architect Humphry Repton was brought in to advise on the layout of the grounds. His speciality was the pictur-esque, views composed like the ones you might see in paintings by the French artist Claude Lorrain: rushing water, awesome cliff faces, huge trees, a dramatically romantic style that looked as though it might be natural, but in fact was tweaked to the last grotto. Repton was the antidote to Capability Brown, whose shaven grass style came to seem too tame, lacking in excitement. Intricacy and variety were keynotes of the picturesque style and Repton built both into the Endsleigh landscape, which included the enchanting buildings designed by Wyatville: an ornamental dairy, a Swiss cottage, a shell house. A couple of them now belong to the Landmark Trust, who rent them out as holiday cottages.

The drive to Endsleigh twists down through vast mounds of rhododendron and camellia past a lodge house with a verandah supported on great barked tree trunks. Go to the hotel reception, pay your fee and get hold of a map. If you are in funds, book lunch, which will fit in nicely between the eastern side of the grounds and the Dell on the west. You can't miss either of them.

Lunch (or tea ...) will also give you access to the area immediately around the house and the view from the principal rooms that was the whole reason for Endsleigh being built in the first place. From the verandah here (incredible knucklebone floors) you can stroll along the broad grass walk that runs underneath the sloping herbaceous border on the left. Or you can climb higher and take the same line through the rose pergola. The hoops (Regency style) over which the roses grow are set up in pairs, which cross over at the top. That was a way of doing things I've not seen before but it gives the structure strength, as well as more space for the gardeners to tie in the roses.

Higher again is a yew walk, a third parallel line leading between tall Irish yews to The Georgys, the wooded area beyond the formal grass walks and borders. It's wild and wonderful in there – steep paths, the occasional precipitous sight of water charging down the hill to join the river below and fabulous trees. A few, such as the Douglas firs, now more than 160 feet high, are probably survivors from the original plantings. Others, such as maples and a huge *Aesculus indica,* were probably added later in the nineteenth century.

The marker between the tamed and the wild is Wyatville's gorgeous shell house, with small, high triangular windows casting bright orange prisms on the intricately cobbled floor inside. It's a fantastic creation, one of the best I've ever seen, with whorls of oyster shells and abalone making exotic flowers on the vaulted ceiling, while the walls are set with the feldspars and minerals that were responsible for much of the wealth pouring from his Devonshire estate into the Duke's purse.

Seen from the house, the shell house sits romantically at the end
of the long, mown grass walk. Approaching from the woods the
other side, it's far spookier, as the path leads into a dark tunnel,
the floor superbly patterned with pebbles, and brings you round the
side of a cliff face – the old quarry – back into the light.

Wyatville designed the Duchess's 'cottage' in a curve, to take
advantage of the views up and down the river. The central part was
where the Duke and Duchess lived. Bending to the east were the
servants' quarters. On the west, linked by a verandah, was the children's domain – Georgiana had ten of them.

Set in front of this verandah is an enchanting small garden,
designed with the children in mind and now beautifully restored.
Lions' masks mounted on the buildings either side pour water into a
channel set into the top of a retaining wall, a feature I've never seen
before. Repton's watercolours show the Duchess's children sailing
toy boats in the water. Repton was famous for his before-and-after
views, bound into red leather-covered books. The one for Endsleigh
still exists and there's a copy of it in the hotel.

The curved verandah seals off the children's garden on the north
side, with a pool and fountain in the centre of geometric beds,
fanning out like the spokes of a spider's web. This is the last bit of
formal gardening you'll see on the western side of the house, but
the bit beyond is almost the best of all. A winding path leads up
the steep slope to the thatched dairy, beautifully restored (it's lined
with marble and fancy tiles with an ingenious hydraulic system to
draw water up to the middle of the central marble worktop and
keep it cool for the dairymaid's cream and butter).

You'll pass the intriguing remains of an engine house and a greenhouse. You'll stumble into an extraordinary rockery, as big as most
people's entire gardens, and if you push on up the valley towards
the catchment pond, you catch the essence of Repton's genius.
Water charges under paths, tips down rock faces, meanders obedi-
ently along the leats that were dug to supply water to the house. 'Of

all picturesque subjects there is none so interesting as Water in rapid motion', he wrote. The natural advantages of the site at Endsleigh gave him a brilliant opportunity to display his gifts.

The present head gardener at Endsleigh, Simon Wood, arrived as part of a chainsaw team brought in to clear the debris created by the devastating storm that swept through the West Country in January 1990. It was far worse, in these parts, than the storm of 1987. Wood, who had spent the previous eleven years brewing beer in his father's Devon pub, clearly loves Endsleigh and is doing a fantastic job, clearing the place just enough to enhance the picturesque effect of areas such as the Dell, without robbing it of its romantic wildness. Endsleigh is lucky to have him, for this is not easy work. Strimming in this garden of 100 or more acres has to be done by hand, as the slopes are too steep for machinery. Fallen trees have to be cut up and carried out a piece at a time.

And the superb trees that remain – a pair of weeping beech, a vast kalopanax, a nordmannia (one of the biggest in Britain), a giant sequoia 167 feet tall – have to be nursed along very carefully, the trunks limbed up just enough to reveal views, but not so much that they lose their natural grandeur. Endsleigh has a quality that is increasingly difficult to find in a garden: a strong spirit of place. Now I'm saving up to stay a night there. The thought of wandering in the Dell at dawn is irresistible.

Tasks for the Month

General

- Prepare for the new season by washing pots and seed trays ready for reuse.
- Continue to dig over soil outside when the weather allows.
- Cut back overgrown deciduous hedges. Aim for a shape that is wider at the bottom than the top. This allows light to reach the lower branches more easily. Pull out any perennial weeds from the bottom of the hedge.
- Check staked trees and adjust the ties if necessary. The aim is to support the trunk, not throttle it.
- Prune overgrown laurel, cutting it back hard with a saw or secateurs.
- Overhaul mowers by cleaning the air filter and the spark plug. Mechanics manqués will also drain and replace the engine oil. Or you can pass the buck and take the mower to the service engineers.
- Brush off snow from shrubs and trees before it settles and freezes. The weight may cause branches to crack.
- Prune and train ornamental vines such as *Vitis coignetiae* and 'Brandt' which are growing on walls or pergolas.
- Protect fish and garden pools by ensuring there is always an ice-free area on the surface of the water.

Flowers

- If you are planning to grow dahlias, dig plenty of muck into the patch where you want to plant them. Dahlias are hungry feeders and will only thrive in rich ground.
- Remove any dying leaves from pelargonium cuttings.
- Order flower seed: catalogues make heady reading in the drab, damp days of January. Ageratums are useful half-hardy annuals, usually not more than 12 inches (30 centimetres) high, with neat powder-puff clumps of flowers in shades of lavender-blue and pink. They flower well even in a murky summer and the blue varieties make an excellent edging mixed with creamy helianthemums. Late blooms also look good under the purple berries of *Callicarpa bodinieri*. Sow seed in March and set out plants in late May to have flowers by July.
- Biennials take longer to come into flower. They spend the first year building themselves up, then flower from spring in the year after they

were sown. Try a foxglove such as Suttons 'Apricot', which has tall spires of a glorious soft apricot colour. They prefer cool, damp growing conditions, and look good mixed with honesty, another biennial, especially the variegated form *Lunaria variegata*.

Vegetables

- Sow greenhouse tomatoes towards the end of the month.
- Order seed ready for planting later in the year.

Fruit

- Check regularly apples in store and remove any that are rotting.
- Mulch gooseberry bushes with plenty of well-rotted manure or compost.
- Continue to prune established fruit trees where necessary.
- Plant rhubarb. Plants should be positioned at least 36 inches (1 metre) apart. Set the crowns about 1 inch (2 centimetres) below the surface of the soil and then spread strawy manure round each crown.

Loscombe

LOVE IN BLOOM

Fifty million stems of red roses will be saying 'I love you' on Valentine's Day. If only the poet had said 'My love is like a yellow, yellow tulip', life would be much easier for the flower growers and sellers who have to fly roses thousands of miles from the more equable climates of South America and Kenya to satisfy demand at this unseasonable time of the year.

I've gone off red roses in a big way since a trip to Ecuador this time last year. Vast tracts of the country were covered in polythene tunnels filled with bushes of red roses and further vast tracts of native wild flowers were being bulldozed to prepare for yet more of this rapacious monoculture.

Production was just coming to a peak for St Valentine's Day. The compounds were guarded by blockhouses and sub-machine guns. From the barbed wire of the perimeter fence, you could see girls picking the flowers, the air in the tunnels (and outside) thick with the acrid smell of sulphur. It's burned to destroy pests and disease. It does a good job on lungs too.

So I hope nobody sends me red roses next week, even though the ones from Ecuador are reckoned to be the best in the business. 'Fat as cabbages,' said a wholesaler approvingly. They are different beasts entirely from the plastic-wrapped sheaves of roses sold in quick deals to motorists with guilty consciences held up at traffic lights on the way home from work. These are cheap, but having been kept in suspended animation for weeks in sub-zero storehouses, the poor things have forgotten how to live. The buds droop. The flower never opens up. Worst of all, they have no smell.

But roses, even at £5 or £6 a stem, still dominate the St Valentine's Day market. Florists describe the suddenly inflated price of these flowers as 'a market reaction to a supply and demand situation'. I'd call it a rip-off. Interflora, which handled about half a million St Valentine's Day orders last year, says that 90 per cent of the bouquets they send will contain roses. Seven million of them are sold in the UK on Valentine's Day. The trade is mostly one way, though they have noticed an increasing trend for women to send flowers to men. Even so, that accounts for only 10 per cent of the business.

Lovers, though, do not equal mothers when it comes to receiving flowers. Mother's Day is still best bonanza day for florists, though the Valentine trade has been steadily catching up over the last ten years. It's now worth at least £22 million a year.

What, besides roses, are the other most popular flowers to send on St Valentine's Day? Carnations, chrysanthemums, daffodils, lilies and tulips appear in the top ten of most people's favourites. Does the kind of flower you send say anything about you as a lover? I think it does:

ROSE: From a lover who feels safest as one of the herd and for whom imagination will never be a strong point. Life with this person will be safe but predictable. Acceptable but unexceptional. Extra marks, though, for a Valentine who buys yellow roses rather than red. Yellow is the colour of the Monet moment and choosing it shows at least the kernel of a desire to break away from the pack. Roses, though, are best kept for a summer surprise, when a bunch fresh-picked from the garden and drenched in swoony scent does have the authentic touch of romance. Even when they are crawling with greenfly.

CARNATIONS: Acceptable only if they overpower you with their smell. If they don't, then your lover too must be under suspicion of being unable to deliver what the outside appearance promises. Much, too, depends on the colour and style of the carnations. Some are of a pink vicious enough to sear the irises out of your eyeballs. No future in that relationship. The picotees, dark colours edged in light, or vice versa, indicate greater subtlety. Good for those in long-term relationships. Few flowers match the carnation's grim determination to hang on in there, long after lesser flowers have thrown in the trowel.

CHRYSANTHEMUMS: Definitely a no-no on St Valentine's Day. Mums – as they are affectionately known in the trade – smell of harvest festivals and funerals, neither of them appropriate reminders at this particular juncture. Anyone who hands over chrysanthemums on 14 February must be suspected of a huge gap in understanding what is an appropriate response to life's little circumstances. This is a lover who later on, on your birthday perhaps, will give you new insoles for your wellington boots, when you dream of Johnny Choo's strappy, showstopping, designer-chic sandals. This is a lover who will say, more times than you want to hear, 'I do like a nice pizza takeaway on a Thursday.' Steer clear.

DAFFODILS: I'd trust a man who gave me daffodils. Hackneyed, say some, but I don't think so. Daffodils fit the bill, seasonally, and in love as in life, you like to feel you are getting the right things at the right time. Look for the bright two-tone 'Soleil d'Or' jonquils grown in the Isles of Scilly, rather than the blunt-faced, knock-you-down-at-twenty-yards yellow trumpet types. The smell will lead you to jonquils in a flower shop, even if you go in blindfolded. There's hope in daffodils. That's a dangerously fragile commodity at the best of times, but now is the season to indulge it.

LILIES: Fine if you feel you can live up to the theatrical aura they throw around them. Lilies will come from people who care very much about their appearance – perhaps more about theirs than yours, which is scarcely in the spirit of Valentine's Day giving. Let the stamens be the deciding factor. If your Valentine insists on cutting them off, on the grounds that the pollen will stain the Armani suit, then get free of the relationship as soon as you can. Just think how such a suitor would hog the bathroom. Impossible. In a crisis remember that white lilies such as 'Casablanca' are better than pink. 'Stargazer' lilies are worse than nothing.

TULIPS: As far as I am concerned, these are the best, indeed, the only flowers to send or receive on Valentine's Day. Wild, irrepressible, wayward, unpredictable, strange, subtle, generous, elegant, tulips are everything you would wish for in a lover. Best of all are the crazy parrot tulips such as 'Rococo' with red and pink petals feathered and flamed in crinkly lime-green. 'When a young man presents a tulip to his mistress,' wrote Sir John Chardin (*Travels in Persia*, 1686), 'he gives her to understand by the general red colour of the flower, that he is on fire with her beauty, and by the black base, that his heart is burned to coal.' That's the way to do it.

FOWL PLAY

Business being slow in the antiques trade at the moment, my cousin has turned to chickens instead. Hers must be the only chickens in England living in eighteenth-century hen houses. She made them herself from some Georgian doors and odd bits of dining table that she had about the place and has got so enmeshed with the business of the fowls that she now does little else.

When I called, she was transferring some hens, recently liberated from a battery, into a new palace. The water trough was a rather pretty blue and white Victorian bowl, the sort you used to see on bedroom dressing tables. The perch was a mahogany towel rail, the nesting boxes cobbled together from the fittings of an old chemist's shop. In the gloom you could just make out flashes of gold from the truncated Latin script.

The hens are ugly, nondescript things, but they lay with a fury, almost an egg a day each. My cousin, who used to think nothing of bidding perhaps eighteen or twenty thousand pounds for stock at auction, is now enraptured by the sale of a dozen eggs. 'Far more satisfying,' she says.

The problem with modern hybrid hens is that they do not go broody. Broodiness is an uneconomic activity on a commercial egg production line and the trait has been bred out of hens that are used in batteries. Consequently, in the kitchen an incubator gently bubbles away, hatching a clutch of eggs brought in by a neighbour.

So far the hens outnumber the ducks, which are Muscovies and Aylesburys. The Aylesburys are the white kind of duck that you see in children's picture books. They do all the waddling, quacking and up-tails-alling that you expect of ducks.

The Muscovies are less appealing, especially the drake, which has an unfortunate tendency to latch on to the back of your leg when you are not looking. It has a strong grip. I was standing on one leg – the one with the drake attached – swinging at it with my other leg, but the drake did not let go until my cousin shook a feed bag in front of its red, piggy eyes and it dropped off to gorge on layer pellets instead.

I don't feel lasting malice towards the bird. There is no long-term future in being a drake. Or a cockerel. There are few instances in which it is a disadvantage to be male, but the domesticated bird world is one. Drakes are for the pot. Nature arranges, as in all the animal kingdom, that there should be more males born than females. But you only need one cockerel or drake to keep a host of fowl in business. Which is why there is a large parcel in my cousin's freezer labelled 'Toots: 8lb 11oz'.

When we had our bantams – which we did until recently when fox raids became insupportable – I always funked eating our surplus birds. Instead our neighbour took them away in a sack and poussined them himself.

The original bantam cockerel was a battered campaigner called Wellington. For years he was king of the strictly hierarchical pack. One day there was a fight to the death between him and a shiny upstart called Robinson (because he crew so – there was a time when the children thought that the most hysterically funny joke in the world). Finally I had to put the boot in. Robinson ran off, cackling, and quickly rounded up all the hens with the wing-dropped, side-stepping, bossy shuffle that is the dominant cockerel's sign of authority.

I washed the worst of the blood off Wellington and put him in a haybox with food and water. He did not die, but it was a long time before the flock allowed him to live. There is no loyalty amongst hens. They did not let him eat with them, or roost with them. He mooched about alone, never going far from the stables where he roosted alone each night.

Robinson got his come-uppance. He was taken by a fox, and in the interregnum, Wellington neatly established a place for himself again in the crowd.

EARTHLINGS

Mr Major's Back to Basics programme was wasted on the rabble at the House of Commons. He should have launched it on a more discriminating audience such as the Huntingdon Gardening Club. It would have struck a sympathetic chord there. Basics are what gardening is all about, though there has been a dangerous tendency over the last couple of years for basics to be delicately, superciliously stifled by aesthetics. First you need to know what makes plants grow. After that you can enjoy the agony of deciding which plants they are to be. If you do it the other way around, you find the garden littered with corpses. This is expensive for the gardener. Pretty sad for the plants too.

Gardens are shaped essentially by soil and climate. The gardener contributes a signature scratched on the surface of the contours. The only signatures likely to last are those made by gardeners who work with rather than against the prevailing conditions.

Climate we can do little about. We have to learn to accept what we are given and to take the long, rather than the short view. A couple of sunny summers does not turn the British Isles into the Mediterranean. Who wants that anyway? We have better, more elastic growing conditions here than almost anywhere else in the world. This enables us to experiment endlessly with plants that nature never intended us to have, plants designed for deserts and alps and tropical rainforests. But like wild animals that you may think you have tamed, these exotics can turn on you at any time. You need to know something about their ways before you introduce them into your home. Knowing where they come from is the first step in understanding them.

Soil is less inflexible than climate, though it is cruelly insensitive to tell that to a new gardener labouring over a plot of virgin clay.

Even so, in the broadest sense, you need to go with the flow. If your soil is alkaline, avoid rhododendrons. If it is fast-draining, stay away from bog-dwellers such as rodgersia and gunnera. Growing calcifuge shrubs such as azaleas or rhododendrons in soil that does not suit them is not an experiment. It is murder.

The alkalinity or otherwise of your soil is a fixed constant that in the broadest sense you need to accept. Megalomaniacs find this difficult. They dig pits in their gardens and fill them with a different kind of soil, hoping to hoodwink plants into believing that everything is as it should be. For a while this works. But gradually, the soil's true constituents leach into the pretend patch and take it over. Or the roots of the shrub in question wander outside the cordon sanitaire and choke on the unfamiliar food.

You do not expect a building to last unless it has decent foundations. The same goes for plants. If the roots are happy, the rest will mostly take care of itself. Roots anchor a plant in the ground and draw in the food and drink that it needs to pump up through the stems into the leaves.

Roots have a growing point at the tip, the meristem, protected by a helmet of disposable cells. The meristem tirelessly produces new cells which stretch themselves out behind it, pushing the growing tip further into new territory.

Once put, a root has to stay. Only the tip can move and choose where it wants to go. It wants to go, of course, where it can find what it needs to keep the plant's head on its feet and it wants to get there with the least possible hassle to itself.

On both counts, gardeners can help. The essence of success lies in the structure of the soil, which should have exactly the right ratio of earth crumbs to air pockets. On heavy clay soils, there is not enough air. The roots keep bumping their noses on the underground equivalent of brick walls. On light sandy soils, there is too much air and the fine, hairy rootlets that absorb essential nutrients find themselves hanging in space, unable to clutch at what they need.

Somewhere between the two there is a perfect soil, the gardener's nirvana. This is loam, and you can begin the long journey towards it by adding humus to your soil at every possible opportunity. The easy way to do this is by surface mulching, leaving the earthworms the harder task of dragging it underground. Humus opens up heavy soils, adds bulk to light ones. There are not many remedies that work on diametrically opposed problems. This is one of them.

Fortunately, there are few places in England where the soil contains more than 50 per cent clay. The two worst patches are in London and Oxford. Clay is hard work. It is a slow soil: slow to warm up in spring, slow to release its nutrients. Despite this, I would not swap my clay for sand. Clay, treated with respect, is a sustaining medium. In hot summers, you do not feel that everything in the garden is gasping for a drink. In wet winters, you learn to stay off it.

On light soils, humus acts like blotting paper, hanging on to moisture more efficiently than the sand particles around it. Roots can only absorb nutrients in liquid form, so if they are not drinking, they are not eating.

Mulches break down into humus at different rates, depending on what they are made of. Leaves of ash and apple disappear very quickly. Leaves that contain resins, such as pine needles, or have waxy finishes, such as holly, break down very slowly, presumably because earthworms and millipedes do not like the taste of them.

Humus itself reacts in different ways. Some offers itself up very quickly as a food source, the instant takeaway. Some needs longer cooking but in the end is more sustaining. Some is in long-term store, like the cans of soup and tins of anchovies that you keep on the back shelf of the larder.

The rate at which plant debris breaks down in the soil depends on the ratio of carbon to nitrogen in the living plant. Grass has a low carbon to nitrogen ratio, about 5 to 1, and breaks down fast in the soil. In straw the ratio is twelve times higher, in pine needles higher still, about 100 to 1. By varying the mulches you use, you provide long- and short-term supplies of humus.

Mulches, compost and farmyard manure all compensate for our tidiness in gardens. We rake up leaves, cut down herbaceous perennials, remove annual weeds. Somehow we have to give all this back to the earth. In a deciduous woodland, trees provide at least five pounds of leaf litter for each square yard of ground. Now you know what you have to match.

VILLA LANTE

The garden at Villa Lante, which crowns the small hill town of Bagnaia in Lazio in Italy, is said by connoisseurs to be the least changed and best preserved of any of the great gardens of the Italian Renaissance. On my first trip to Italy, I approached it in the spirit of a pilgrim. For anyone who loves gardens, this place seemed to be a touchstone, the beginning (almost) of the story of the pleasure garden in Europe, the font of many of the ideas that still have an abiding influence on the way we plan our patches.

Bagnaia, with houses that grow seamlessly out of the vertical rock faces rising from the valley, is one of those small places that minds its own business, has plenty of business to mind and therefore provides endless delight for day-trippers. You can sit for hours in the square over coffee or grappa, drawn willy-nilly into the soap opera going on round you. In no other country does it seem to matter less that you cannot speak the language. Here, body language says as much as words.

From the square, the narrow Via Giambologna leads directly to the gate that was designed as the main entrance to the garden. This is the endstop of the dramatic long vista that stretches up and back over fountains and pools, terraces and stairways, to the grotto at the far end of the garden where the water that provides the central backbone of the design starts its long journey.

This is the entrance that Cardinal Gambara, who started making the garden in 1568, would have used. Visitors were brought in by another entrance to the right, past the fountain of Pegasus shown in an early seventeenth-century plan of the garden. The *Lex Hortorum*, law of the garden current at the time, guaranteed access for all. Free.

This same side entrance, still in use today, brings you out on a broad walk between the great parterre at the end of the garden on the left and a bank, sternly bisected by box hedges, which rises between the two square villas that make a matched pair either side of the central vista.

The big parterre on the left with its dramatic centrepiece of fountain and stone boats was all roped off. Since the garden was empty of people, I tried hopping over the rope in order to get to the fountain, but a roar and a great deal of body language from the ticket collector put paid to this little bid for freedom. The parterre was off the menu. As it turned out, so was much else.

The garden climbs up the hill by way of a series of dramatic set pieces: the Fountain of the Lights, the Water Table, the Fountain of the River Gods, the Water Chain, the Fountain of the Dolphins and finally the Grotto. The whole sequence tells the story of man's journey from the wilderness (the Grotto) to the state of high civilisation that married nature and art in the intricacies of the final parterre.

Having marked me down as a troublemaker, the ticket man shooed me off the broad walk and up the stairs at a brisk trot, which meant that it was only at the Fountain of the Lights on the next terrace that I could turn again to look at the bottom parterre.

The initial view from Gambara's entrance gate had shown that it was thick with weeds. That didn't matter. But there were puzzling

ragged holes in the middle of the big clipped squares of yew that
punctuate the twelve box-edged beds.

A photograph in Mark Laird's fine book *The Formal Garden* solved
that problem. Every photograph you have ever seen of that famous
parterre shows big terracotta pots containing orange trees filling
these holes and flanking the steps between the terraces. But there
was not a single pot in the entire garden.

And the fountain was not playing. Now that all the flowers that
Gambara planted in the parterre have gone, along with the fruit
trees that once surrounded it, you need moving water to bring life
to the layout. But the water surrounding the stone boats whose
boatmen once blew jets from their stone muskets (I think they were
muskets – difficult to tell at the distance I had been put by the ticket
collector) was as still as glass.

'Up, up' was the unmistakable message from the ticket collector's arm. He was still hovering, perhaps to see whether I was
going to jump the barricades that shut off the grottoes to Neptune
and Venus. The rose garden on the left-hand side was also out of
bounds. So were the loggias of the muses. Up, up was the only
option, especially as the Fountain of the Lights at this level had
evidently jammed. The concentric semicircles of stone, lined with
miniature jets, were scarcely dribbling. A broom handle thrust up
a pipe between one level of the fountain and the next suggested
that somebody, somewhere, might be doing something about the
problem. But not today.

An immense stone table lies between the Fountain of the Lights
and the Fountain of the River Gods, with a deep water-filled channel about a foot wide carved down its centre. This makes a serene
link between two grotesque masks either end which spew water
into a shallow, narrow moat around the base of the table. It's always
described as a table, but in fact when you look along it, you see that
the top is laid not flat but in a smooth gentle convex curve: very
beautiful, but expensive on plates.

Behind the massive, benign figures of the sea gods, stairs lead up either side to meet on the next level. A descending series of pillars, each topped by an empty urn, makes a stone banister up the edge of the steps. Spouts in the top of the urns show that they too had once been miniature fountains.

But there was a wonderful surprise in the stairway. As you turn to go up it, you find that the entire balustrade, which seems to be just stone, is in fact a water chute. The water passes under each urn in turn and rolls down a scroll of stone into an oval basin hollowed out at each level step. At the top is another balustrade, which I had seen in a picture spewing water patterns as intricate as lace, but now dry and lifeless.

It was at this stage that I stopped making excuses for the Villa Lante. Perhaps there was a water shortage, I had thought at first, having just arrived from drought-stricken England. But the previous day, Italian neighbours had been saying that this had been a staggeringly wet summer for them.

Then I wondered if there was a problem with gardeners, but there were three men sweeping gravel together on one of the paths. Why was so much of the garden roped off? Why were so many of the waterworks not working? Why were the box hedges quite so full of holes? Why, in a garden full of fabulous stonework, were the paths covered in gravel of such a deadly colour?

Meantime, I had worked my way to the Grotto at the top of the garden and back down again, past the brilliant Water Chain. This is made by a series of stone scrolls, almost meeting and dividing in a sinuous double string down the hillside, the water rushing down through the middle. I had only been in the garden for three hours and since there was still an hour and a half till closing time, I thought I would do the circuit a second time. Something might have happened with the broomstick. The rose garden might suddenly be open.

But the man on the gate had other ideas. Advancing sternly down the broad walk, he started tapping his watch fiercely and pointing to the door. In what I hoped was a meaningful way, I pointed in turn to the board that quite clearly stated that the garden was open until half past five. But it was an unequal contest. As the door was locked behind me, I heard the soft musical sound of water. The fountain was beginning to play in the parterre.

THE KINDEST CUTS

Plants present many of the same characteristics as children. The intense period of bringing them on, worrying about the right food and so on, is followed by an equally intense period of trying to rein them in. There's no equivalent to pruning in childcare, but gardeners have this one enormous advantage over parents.

It is a mistake, though, to look at secateurs primarily as offensive weapons. Good pruning is a matter of working with rather than against a plant. The most important thing, before you make any cuts, is to have clearly in your mind the essential qualities of the plant you are about to attack.

From this time of the year onwards, gardeners get infected by a kind of fever. We want to get outside and start flailing around, trying to regain possession of the battleground. There's a tendency to snip away at everything in sight, turning all shrubs, whatever their habit, into barbered buns. Resist the temptation. The garden may be tidy, but, by reducing all the shrubs to the same common denominator, you will have missed the point of growing them at all.

In the most general terms, shrubs that flower in the first half of the year do so on growth made the previous year. These can be pruned after flowering. Shrubs that flower in the second half of the year bear the flowers on the new wood they have made in the first half. These are best not pruned straight after flowering, but left until about now. These are the ones I'm going to concentrate on.

Pruning kicks a shrub into top growing gear. 'Crumbs,' it says to itself. 'Someone's trying to do me in,' and it pumps energy into dormant growth buds lying along its stems to replace what it feels it has lost.

If you pruned a late summer-flowering buddleia or caryopteris when it had just finished flowering, the resultant tender new growths would coincide fatally with the first frosts. So you leave them until February before pruning. Buddleia thrives perfectly well without any pruning, as you can see on any railway embankment. But, left unpruned, the bushes get very big. And the trusses of flower coming from old wood are smaller than the ones that are produced on new wood. So, to get the shrub to produce the showiest flowers, you need to persuade it to produce new wood each season.

First, cut out all weak and straggly growths altogether. Then cut back the rest of the growths drastically, leaving just one or two pairs of buds on each branch. Old specimens may become congested after years of this treatment. If a likely-looking new shoot springs from below the main framework, take the opportunity to saw away one of the old branches completely.

Rambling roses should have been dealt with when they finished flowering last year. The climbing roses that need attention now are sports of hybrid teas, such as 'Étoile de Hollande', 'Guinée' and 'Meg'.

Roses in this group flower on new wood but (unlike ramblers) rarely produce new growths from the base of the plant. You are much more likely to find new shoots growing from old wood higher up the plant. Cut old stems back to the junction with the new growth and tie the new growth in. Cut back the lateral growths (the side branches springing from the main ones) to about 6 inches (15 centimetres).

Now and again, it pays to take out a stem completely at ground level, especially when the main framework of a climbing rose has crept higher and higher up its support. This drastic reduction sometimes forces the rose to send out a new shoot from the base. A hefty mulch helps, too.

All dogwoods, such as *Cornus alba* 'Elegantissima', grown for their decorative winter bark, should be cut hard back now. The bark colour is much brighter on new growth than old, so you want as much of it as you can get. I cheat here and cut just half back each season. That is because I do not want to lose entirely the bulk of the shrub in spring.

For the all-or-nothing effect, cut back all growths to within 3 inches (5 centimetres) of the ground. Ambivalent gardeners can cut out the dullest-coloured wood and leave the rest. 'Elegantissima' has pretty variegated foliage, so there is some merit in having this sooner rather than later.

Wisteria needs severe pruning so that it is jolted into making flower buds rather than more growth buds. Pruning is usually done in two stages, half in summer, when you shorten the shoots you do not want, and half now, when you cut them back to within two buds of the previous year's growth. You need to be up the ladder while you are reading this. Then it becomes much more obvious how to tackle the job.

The task is easier if you have trained the main growths of the wisteria on wires. Then you can clearly see what you need to extend the framework and what you can lop off. When you are training, bear in mind that the Japanese wisteria winds clockwise, the Chinese anticlockwise. If in doubt, just follow the direction that the tendrils seem to be taking for themselves.

Jasmine needs more thought in pruning than any of the previous shrubs, though it all too seldom gets it. A brutal redesign is often its fate, transforming it from a languid, weeping, waterfalling sort of shrub into a bristling hedgehog.

Prune it by keeping as many as possible of the long bright green shoots that will flower next season, and cutting out bristly growths covered with short stems. If there are one or two good strong green stems arising from the base of the plant, cut out the same number of old stems entirely at the base to encourage more of this kind of regeneration. Pin the old buff growths as high up the wall or support as you can and allow the green growths that spring from them to fall in a kind of bead curtain in front of them. Do not clip the bush all over as if you were an army barber.

Tackle mahonia too, if you want the tassels of flowers to remain within sniffing distance. A young bush will not need any attention. It is only when you realise that you are looking at stems rather than leaves that you need to step in. Each year, shorten the longest stem by at least half, cutting above a side shoot or the old leaf scars from which a bud might shoot, if pushed hard enough.

Most hydrangeas need thinning, rather than drastic pruning. The old flower heads that have been left over winter to provide cover against frost can be whipped off now. Cut back to the point where a strong pair of leaves or buds are ready to take over. Cut the spindliest stems out entirely to encourage the bush to make good new growth from the base.

You need to be tougher with *Hydrangea paniculata*, where size of flower is all that matters. The blooms of 'Grandiflora' can be up to 18 inches (45 centimetres) long, appearing in August and September. When they first come out they are white, but flush gently to pink as they age.

Prune this hydrangea like the buddleia, taking all the previous season's growth back to within two buds of the old wood. The purpose is the same in both cases: to force the shrub to produce the vigorous growth that will carry the best flowers.

A lot of pruning is fuelled by fear. We feel a shrub is getting out of hand, that it is going to block a path or a gutter or a gate. Reducing its size is the only criterion. But if we take the trouble to understand the consequences of our pruning, the results will be a hundred times better.

PRUNING CLEMATIS

Some clematis need to be hard pruned now. Others don't. How do you tell the difference? The key is flowering time. The earlier a clematis comes into bloom, the less pruning it will need. Think of them falling into three categories: no pruning, light pruning and hard pruning. Early varieties – *C. alpina, C. macropetala, C. armandii* – need no pruning. Light pruning is enough for June-flowering kinds such as 'Beauty of Worcester', 'Nelly Moser' and 'The President', which often bear a second, lighter crop of flowers in late summer. Light pruning means cutting back tangly growth on the top part of the clematis just as far as a plump bud or growing shoot.

Later flowering clematis, such as 'Comtesse de Bouchaud', 'Gipsy Queen' and all the *C. viticella* types, need hard pruning. These clematis all flower on new growth (unlike the others) and this will be more vigorous on a pruned plant than an unpruned one. Make the cuts about 18 inches (45 centimetres) above the ground, slicing, if you can, just above a likely pair of buds.

If, as will be the case with a well-established clematis, you have five or six stems to deal with, splay them out and tie them in over as wide a space as possible, so that when they begin to grow, they will not tangle with each other. To encourage new growth, mulch liberally with compost or manure. This will also keep the soil moist and the roots cool. Clematis heaven.

A BRUSH WITH BASIL

The last of my basil plants, grown last summer, has finally turned up its toes on the kitchen windowsill. Its companions, a stalwart half-dozen, have been giving up at intervals since mid December. I shall be bereft without them.

Even the most hastily constructed salad or dish of pasta is transformed by a whiff of basil, and gardeners have at last discovered how easy it is to grow. Even five years ago, it was unknown in any seed company's list of top ten varieties. Now it's a regular. I packed the last pathetic leaves of our windowsill plants into a jar, and poured olive oil on top of them. If you leave the mixture to steep for two weeks, you have a pleasantly scented olive oil to use in salad dressings. You can enjoy the ghost of the plant, if not its substance.

I've tried growing basil in three different ways: in the open ground, in the cold frame and on the kitchen windowsill. The last has been the best, but I've also seen excellent crops in small green-houses and polytunnels. If you choose the windowsill, you can sow seed in late March or early April. Use ordinary multi-purpose compost, but make sure it is fresh. If you want to sow direct into the ground outside, wait until early June. Basil is a native of countries warmer than ours. It hates growing in temperatures that wobble too much between highs and lows and a cold night will kill it off altogether.

Suffolk Herbs offer twenty-two different kinds of basil in their new catalogue — a sure sign that this herb is now as much about cult as cultivation. I love the stuff, but a windowsill can't offer room for more than three different kinds in a summer. You need 'Neapolitana' for the authentic Italian swish it gives to food; it has large lettuce-like leaves too, which makes it a particularly productive variety. You need one kind with purple leaves – 'Purple Ruffles' – because they look sumptuous on a tomato salad.

Your third choice might be a variety with a very particular tang: 'Horaphu Rau Que' is a favourite from Thailand and tastes of aniseed; 'Cinnamon' is a spicy, tallish basil brought in from Mexico; 'Lemon' comes from Indonesia, where it's widely used to make herbal tea; 'Sacred Kha Prao' is another Thai basil, planted round Buddhist temples and excellent in stir fries.

Sprinkle a tiny pinch of seed on top of a 3-inch (8-centimetre) pot filled with compost. The typical Mediterranean sweet basil (*Ocimum basilicum*) has bigger seeds than the sacred or Thai basil (*Ocimum tenuiflorum*), which generally makes a shorter plant. Cover the seeds with a fine layer of vermiculite. Water the pot carefully, then cover it with a piece of glass or clingfilm until the seedlings emerge. This shouldn't take more than one to two weeks at about 68°F (20°C), a typical temperature on a kitchen windowsill.

Let them grow on in the original pot, giving them plenty of light and watering in the morning rather than the evening. Basil plants hate being wet at night. When the seedlings seem sturdy and reasonably well established, tip the whole lot out on newspaper and tease the plants apart, replanting them two at a time in pots 3–4 inches (8–10 centimetres) in diameter.

Once pricked out like this, our plants stay in their pots and spend their whole lives on the kitchen windowsill, along with the usual collection of stray buttons, screws, corks and safety pins that experience has taught should never be thrown away.

From time to time the whole lot spend an hour soaking in the sink, the water beefed up with a touch of Baby Bio. The plants try to flower but you must not let them. Pinch out the flower heads to keep a good supply of leaves coming on.

If you want plants to grow outside, you can sow direct in short drills, setting contrasting types side by side to make a corduroy patch of perhaps half a dozen different kinds. Or you could trace out a circle, divide it into eight segments and broadcast different seed over each of the eight portions. Alternatively, you can raise plants in separate pots, as if you were growing them inside and then transplant them outside when they are already well grown. Water them in well, remembering still that morning is better than evening. Choose a warm, sheltered sunny place if you want to grow basil outside. Lay some fleece over the seedbed to prevent cats (or birds) scratching it up. If nights seem unseasonably chilly, leave the fleece in place as the seedlings grow, or cover with cloches.

Outside, basil plants must be gradually acclimatised. If you get it wrong, the leaves turn a dramatic black overnight. Because our weather is so unpredictable (frosts in June are not unknown) you may need to fiddle with covers and cloches, providing protection at night, but plenty of light and air during the day. If you sow direct into the soil, you will also need to thin the seedlings as they develop so that they are eventually at least 6 inches (15 centimetres) apart. Left to themselves, most types leap straight up in a single stem. If you pinch out the growing top, you can persuade them to make bushier, leafier plants. Greek basil (try 'Greek Fine Leaved Miniature') is by nature more bushy. Whereas the Genovese type makes a plant at least 18 inches (45 centimetres) tall, the Greek is half that height, with tiny leaves. It is excellent in pots, as it looks like a small topiary tree, ball-shaped and prolific. 'Green Globe' is an Italian refinement of the Greek miniature, very neat, uniform and excellent in pots.

Tasks for the Month

Flowers

❧ Prune late-flowering clematis, those that bear their flowers on new growth made this season. Cut down all stems to about 24 inches (60 centimetres) above the ground. You will probably have to sacrifice precocious fat buds, but the clematis quickly makes up for lost time. Clematis in this group include 'Ascotiensis', 'Comtesse de Bouchaud', *durandii*, 'Ernest Markham', 'Gipsy Queen', 'Hagley Hybrid', all the *heracleifolia* types, 'Huldine', 'Jackmanii Superba', 'Lady Betty Balfour', all the orientalis types, 'Prins Hendrik', *rehderiana*, 'Rouge Cardinal', 'Star of India', *tangutica*, all the *texensis* varieties ('Gravetye Beauty', etc.), 'Victoria', 'Ville de Lyon' and all the small-flowered *viticella* types ('Abundance', 'Royal Velours', etc.).

❧ Winter-prune wisteria, finishing off the job you started (or should have) last summer. Continue to train in all the growths you want to keep. Cut back the rest of the lateral growths (those springing from the main stem) to two buds. Hard pruning encourages flowering in wisteria, which otherwise produces a mass of leaf. Hot summers also have a marked effect on the following season's performance.

❧ Hard-prune late summer-flowering shrubs such as buddleia. In the north or where late frosts are the rule, this job should be left until March.

❧ Hard-prune dogwoods and other shrubs grown for their winter bark. Hard pruning encourages the fresh growth that is more brightly coloured than old stems.

❧ Feed herbaceous borders, spreading well-rotted manure or compost between the plants. If plants need splitting and resetting, do this before you mulch.

❧ Mulch lily of the valley and Solomon's seal with well-rotted compost. Mushroom compost, the waste product of the mushroom-growing industry, is excellent for jobs such as this as it is friable and weed-free.

❧ Prune winter-flowering jasmine as soon as the flowers have finished. Take out some of the old brown wood entirely, making the cut at the base of the plant. This will mean sacrificing some of the new green wood that shoots from the brown, but it is the best way to renew the plant. Do not give it an all-over haircut, which reduces most of the wood that you want to keep.

๛ Start to sow annuals. Use good, fresh compost. Compact it firmly before sowing and water it. Spread the seeds as thinly as possible over the surface of the compost. Cover them with vermiculite, much easier to use than compost as covering. Some very small seeds do not need covering at all. Sprinkle the surface lightly with water and cover with a sheet of paper and a sheet of glass to conserve moisture. Do not let the compost dry out. Prick out seedlings when the first true leaves have developed. Handle them only by the seed leaves, not by the stem. Set the seedlings so that the leaves rest on the surface of the compost. Water lightly and protect from direct sunlight until the seedlings are established.

Vegetables

๛ Plant shallots 6 inches (15 centimetres) apart in rows 9 inches (23 centimetres) apart.

๛ Feed asparagus beds with a general fertiliser.

๛ Lay seed potatoes in shallow trays to sprout before planting.

Fruit

๛ Cut off the tips of raspberry canes so that they do not wave around above the topmost supporting wire.

๛ Spray peach trees against peach leaf curl, where this is a problem. Providing some sort of overhead cover for trees cuts down the likelihood of infection.

Propagating

๛ Take cuttings of fuchsia and pelargonium.

A primrose bank

SPRING IS IN THE AIR

Perhaps you've turned to a gardening column to get away from recession fever and banker phobia. Bad luck. But gardeners are surely in a fortunate position. The value of the patches we look out on every day – the real value I mean, not some notional price per square foot dreamed up by a wonky estate agent – doesn't zoom up and down because of events out of our control. Its pleasures don't diminish because the stock market is dropping like lead. The plant for which you paid £2.50 yesterday is still worth that today (in fact it is surely worth three times that – the cheapness of plants is one of life's great mysteries).

Only fools view their gardens in monetary terms, supposing that any amount spent on hard landscaping must automatically be grappled back in the asking price of their houses. The real point of a garden is to increase the value of our lives. It gives us the best chance we have of fitting ourselves back into a world that cities make us forget. A garden locks you into the slow inevitable rolling out of the seasons, cycles of growth and decay, the lengthening of days and shortening of shadows.

A garden gives pleasure, instils calm, grafts patience into your soul. Gardening slows you down, masks worries, puts them in proportion. A garden teaches you to be observant and how to look at things. You become less inclined to leap to quick conclusions. Or to jump on the latest bandwagon. A garden hones your senses. You can hear the sound of dampness creaking through the soil and smell it hovering in different guises over the compost heap. In a garden, you never feel lonely.

Nor can you ever feel bored. Though constant in the sense that it is rooted in one particular place (and roots you with it – that is an important part of its power), it is deliciously inconstant in its particulars. The light falls on it and reflects from it in a different way every day. Breezes move through it from different directions. Trees provide different silhouettes at different times of the year. And from now on, the arrival and disappearance of seasonal plants happen almost faster than you can keep up with. And this is all free. You don't need wads of money to garden.

The best trick it plays, at this time of the year, is that you never quite remember how it's going to be, that first day you go outside and can stay outside all day, fiddling about with jobs that aren't pressing enough to weigh heavily, but will nevertheless pay dividends. A garden is made up of thousands of small interventions; each one represents a choice, though you aren't thinking like that when you finally fetch the fork to heave out a bramble. It's just that the bramble has got to the point where it's more in your sight than not. And experience has taught you that if you don't hoik it out, a stem will drop and root and before you know it there will be a patch rather than a plant.

I had a great Saturday, the first warm day of the year, doing jobs like that – nothing too daunting. It was a day of reacquaintance, ambling about the place, fitting myself back into the plot. I could have spent the entire day carting mushroom compost up the bank to the bed where the cyclamen and eucomis grow. But though, in its way, this is a rewarding job, like feeding a family, it's also physically quite demanding. The bank is too steep to push barrowloads of mulch up to the border and I have to cart it up in buckets, which takes much longer.

So I larded that job with other quieter ones: ten buckets followed by a session in the gravelled yard on the west side of the house, which is always a pleasing place to work, because it is so small. *Iris lazica* and *Iris unguicularis* grow there in rubble against the west wall; cleaning up a clump of *Iris lazica* (darker blue flowers and brighter green leaves than *I. unguicularis*) absorbed more time than, at busier times of the gardening year, is available to give, but on this morning, it was a perfect limbering-up exercise. Dead leaves pull off quite easily, half-dead leaves have to be cut. General debris and snails need to be cleaned from the centre of the clump and more gravel needs to be added where I prised out some dandelions and unwanted evening primrose.

Your mind goes into delicious limbo when you are doing jobs such as this. They are undemanding, but in terms of improving the general look of things, very rewarding. Some of the time you may be thinking about the plant you are dealing with. For instance, why does *Iris lazica*, which is a native of scrub and woodland along the eastern end of the Black Sea coast, grow so well in this sunny, gravelled yard? Would it grow even better if I dug up a chunk and tucked it under the hazels on the bank? Why is *I. lazica* not scented when *I. unguicularis* is? In the wild, the two iris are separated only by 250 miles of bare, brown hill. If the point of the scent is to lure in insects, then the two iris must be pollinated in different ways. Why don't I know more about insects?

Then, after another ten buckets of mulch, I go back to the courtyard because a *Helleborus foetidus*, now gone, has left behind a patch of sturdy seedlings. There's a big plant sale locally in May, in aid of the lifeboats. If I pot up the plants now, they would look quite saleable in three months' time. So I do, and as I'm setting them out by the cold frames, I remember the foxglove seedlings I potted up last autumn. There's a rough patch by the hammock house where they fitted comfortably against the holly and hawthorn hedge.

And so that happy day passed: more buckets of mushroom compost carted to the cyclamen bed, viticella clematis and wisteria pruned and tied in, holly cut back where it was dropping too low over snowdrops, the last of the Paperwhite hyacinths carried out of the house, *Rhododendron fragrantissimum* carried in. A quiet day at Lake Wobegon. But each small act a defence (defiance even) against a world without anchors or safe harbours. Gardening – recession-proof, I'd say.

THE FREEDOM LAWN

Somebody somewhere is probably already writing a thesis on our relationship with lawns. 'Man v. Nature: rediscovering harmony', 'Songs of the Sod: an Assessment of Mowing', 'Striped State: Man, Machine and Mindset'. I use the word 'Man' optimistically, for I depend on having nothing to do with our lawn. My husband, who is gloriously unreconstructed, thinks that mowing is Man's Work. That is fine by me. I do not have great expectations of a lawn. I like it greenish and flattish. Daisies and blue-flowered speedwell seem a positive benefit. Sometimes we have had sprinklings of violets in the lawns, too.

An American thesis on the subject has already been published in this country: *Redesigning the American Lawn*, by F. Herbert Bormann, Diana Balmori and Gordon T. Geballe. Lawns there are even more of a fetish than they are here. Fences are frowned on so lawns are rather public places. Whoever lets the side down by not mowing the sward in front of his house gets cross letters from the county authority reminding him of his duty as a citizen to keep the wilderness at bay.

Murray and Ann Blum of Athens, Georgia, refused to toe the line. To save face, the town council designated their unkempt one-acre garden a bird sanctuary and put up a large notice on one of their trees explaining this to the world at large. A picture from the *Atlanta Journal* shows Murray Blum laughing in his garden under the headline 'The Yard From Hell'.

The authors argue for a less fascist approach to the garden lawn. 'Properly' maintained, that is, maintained according to the instructions issued by manufacturers of fertilisers, weedkillers, moss killers, lawn sand, lawn aerators and the like, a lawn is a monoculture. The best-kept lawns are those with the least diversity of plants; several million blades of fescue living in a botanical ghetto, untroubled by interlopers such as daisy or celandine.

Bormann and co. are proponents of what they call The Freedom Lawn (as distinct from The Industrial Lawn, the one with no weeds). It sounds good to me. The Freedom Lawn, they say, 'results from an interaction of naturally recurring processes'. I think that means you mow, but not too close. You leave the clippings to feed the lawn. You tolerate interlopers, as long as they do not get too bossy. I wage occasional war on lawn weeds with wide skirts, such as dandelion, plantain and thistle, but it is quicker and far more satisfying to whip these out with a penknife than to spend hours like a donkey on a treadmill, walking up and down behind a spreader, scattering weedkiller.

Lawns cover 20 million acres of the USA, making lawn grass the biggest single 'crop' produced in the country. But the Americans, like us, moan about what farmers are doing to the environment, while, like us, spending millions on various chemicals to tip on to their own patches of ground. The National Academy of Science in the States discovered that homeowners use up to ten times more chemical pesticides an acre than do farmers.

The arguments against The Industrial Lawn are ones we know already, but don't always care to take on board. There is the argument about the fossil fuels needed to power the ever-increasing range of machines we are told we need to maintain our lawns: mowers, aerators, leaf blowers, strimmers. More fossil fuel is burned up transporting herbicides and chemical fertilisers from mines to factories and garden centres.

We shrug and say, 'Well, our lawn machines don't use *much* petrol.' That's true, but the two-stroke engine is a dirty, wasteful converter of fuel to energy. There is, as yet, no legal requirement to fit catalytic converters to lawnmower engines, although the engine's relative inefficiency means that, for each horsepower produced, it creates fifty times more pollution than a long-distance lorry. Or, to put it another way, if it takes you one hour to mow your lawn with a petrol-driven lawnmower, you will have produced as much air pollution as if you had driven 350 miles in your car.

Another argument for The Freedom Lawn has to do with a different kind of pollution, as excess fertilisers and pesticides wash off our lawns into springs and streams. Then there is the problem of water shortage. Our obession with the greenness of a lawn tempts us to water it in a dry summer, when they come. Hose-pipe bans are difficult to police. But if you leave it alone, with the first rain a lawn will green up of its own accord.

Part of the problem is that our expectations of our lawns (and much else in the garden) are unrealistically high. We expect them to be perfect and unblemished, whatever the prevailing conditions. That can become a fetish.

The creed of The Freedom Lawn will be anathema to the fanatical acolytes for whom a single daisy can be cause for hara-kiri. These are more likely to be men than women. Perhaps it is the ritual that attracts: the weekly cut, the edge clipping, the stripes. The need for stripes is particularly intriguing, but deeply ingrained enough for Flymo to have introduced a Hoverstripe mower, that stripes as it cuts as it hovers. Before, only cylinder mowers and some types of rotary mower gave the desired effect.

In the UK the timing of the first cut varies from season to season. After a cold winter it may not be until early April, as grass only starts growing when temperatures lift above freezing. This weekend, our lawn will get its first cut. By osmosis, almost, the feeling grows that the mower must emerge from hibernation and once again 16 million British lawns will be fussed and fretted over, fed, spiked, raked and rolled. If you do everything that you are told to do to a lawn in a year, it can become the most demanding area of the garden. The most expensive, too.

However much you do on top to a lawn, its appearance, ultimately, is most affected by what is going on underneath: fertility and drainage. If the underpinning is not ideal, as is often the case, then fertilisers, herbicides and moss treatments can only ever be props. Not cures.

Low nutrient levels and poor drainage are the usual causes of moss build-up. Mowing too close also has a bad effect. The cut shouldn't be closer than about three-quarters of an inch (15 millimetres). Compaction, where the lawn is heavily used for games, bike riding, football, will also promote moss at the expense of grass.

Whatever the benefits to the environment, I don't expect great support for The Freedom Lawn. Here, badly kept grass is a moral slur. So, for those who are already fuming at the state of their turf, here is a calendar of jobs to keep a reasonable family lawn in good fettle. We are not talking bowling greens here.

- As soon as possible in April, rake out as much as you can of the moss and thatch in the lawn. If you have a large area to cover, you can hire a scarifier to do the job for you (noise, fumes ...).

- Then treat the lawn with a mosskiller combined with a fertiliser (the Japanese think moss gardens the height of refinement).

&❧ Between now and the end of September give the lawn one or possibly two treatments of a fertiliser combined with a weed-killer (goodbye to bio-diversity).

&❧ In October, spike and aerate the lawn to ease compaction. On a smallish lawn you can do this with a garden fork, wiggling it about after you have stuck it in the ground to open up the holes (The Freedom Lawn needs this too).

&❧ Follow on with a sieved top dressing of sharp sand – not builder's sand – mixed half and half with garden soil. If your ground is heavy and sticky, increase the proportion of sand. If it is very light and dries out quickly, add more soil, garden compost or fine leaf mould to the mix. Spread about a spadeful of this stuff over each square yard of the lawn (top dressing is exhausting, but it is one of the best things you can do to lawns, Freedom or otherwise).

COSTA RICA RAILWAY

Browsing in the travel section of Waterstone's, Piccadilly, recently, I picked up one of the many handbooks on Costa Rica. I was there twenty years ago and thought it rather a tame place, memorable only for the train journey we made from the capital, San José, down to Limon on the Caribbean coast. Idly, I flicked to the index to check out trains. Nothing. Nor in the next book, nor the next. Finally, Christopher P. Baker, author of Moon Travel's guide to the country, revealed why. The line closed down in November 1990, the very year we rode its rickety coaches through gorges and across bridges spun from hope rather than substance.

The journey took at least eight hours, because the train made fifty-five stops on its journey to the coast. The ticket, listing all the stops in order, was as long as a lavatory roll. The railway, built by Minor Keith, a twenty-three-year-old stockboy from a Broadway clothing store, was finally completed in 1890, by which time four thousand labourers had died in its construction. Coffee was the catalyst. Taking the crop direct to the coast, rather than via Puntarenas, Chile and Cape Horn, shortened the journey to Europe by months.

So this line, paid for in so many lives, lasted little more than a hundred years. But the wonder was, in this unstable area, that it was ever built at all. It ran for 99 miles, inching its way first through the mountains and gorges below the Cordillera Central, then rattling through the flat plain beyond Siquirres, past banana plantations and small wooden houses perched on stilts above the swamp. For a third of its length, between Turrialba and Siquirres, it followed the course of the Reventazón river, and I remember this as by far the most spectacular section of the journey.

The train pushed in front of it a dolly with a JCB earthmover perched on top. The carriages were like long wooden huts perched on wheels, with roughly planked floors and windows carved out of the wooden sides. At each end of the carriages were iron platforms with steps to the ground where you could ride in the open air.

The weather was fairly wild at the time and the river below us was in full spate, scouring out the bank on which the track was laid. The journey gave a whole new meaning to the word 'bridge'. There were no parapets where the line crossed over chasms. If you happened to be riding outside on the platform at the time, you looked straight down between the sleepers laid across the track into nothingness underneath.

Five landslides had been cleared on the line as the train had made its journey up to San José earlier that day, so on the return, the kilometre posts passed slowly, not more than one every five minutes.

Somewhere between Peralta and Tunel, two carriages jumped off the uneven rails and the train jammed to a halt, the derailed section fortunately leaning in towards the steep hillside, rather than out over the river. Several times the driver tried to jump the carriages back on to the line but failed. So all the people from the derailed section at the back – schoolchildren, farmers, market traders – piled into the two carriages remaining at the front and we continued on our way.

The railway engineer, who had been travelling in our carriage, increased his consumption of rum and started to write a report of the incident with a borrowed pen. He had the outrageous laugh, the explosive manner and the hundred-decibel delivery of the bandit villain in John Sturges's film of *The Magnificent Seven*. He wore gold-rimmed glasses with mirror lenses and had a closely clipped moustache and beard. He threw his head back when he laughed (which was frequently) and slapped his knee in a way that I thought only happened in bad novels.

The last hour of the journey was in darkness – the train had no lights – and we rattled along on an even track laid by the local banana company on stout concrete sleepers. Families sat out on the verandahs of the small wooden shacks that we passed. The air was heavy and damp and white malachite sheaths of arum lilies glowed in the dusk. Commerce must still drive this flat, uninteresting part of the railway. But the rest? History.

THE JOYS OF PARENTING

Propagating plants is a benign kind of disease. It can be kept reasonably under control by a surfeit of children, but advances unchecked when the number of mouths round the kitchen table starts to dwindle. The disease is made more dangerous by the fact that most plants, being infinitely more subtle than people, offer more than one way of perpetuating themselves. The exceptions are the annuals, which germinate, grow to their full potential, seed and die within the space of a single season. The only way of propagating them is by sowing seed.

But with other plants, you can choose whether you sow seed, divide plants up, take cuttings or make layers – which is a lazy kind of cutting. The method you choose depends on the end result you are looking for.

The point about cuttings is that each one will grow into a perfect replica of its parent – if that is what you want. Nurserymen depend on this sameness. But each seed in a seed pod may turn out to be a subtle variation of the parent, the progeny sometimes skipping back, as children do, to pick up a trait that has been suppressed for several generations.

The variation is a safety device. A flower that has a slightly different shape or colour from its parent may be more successful at attracting pollinating insects. A leaf that grows narrow or develops a woolly texture may survive drought more easily. Plants subscribe to the harsh doctrine of survival of the fittest. But gardeners intervene, selecting sickly seedlings to grow on, for the sake of a rare mutation in the flower or a variegation on a leaf that have nothing to do with survival.

The seed-sowing season gets into its stride about now, though you should never be in too much of a hurry to sow seed of annuals or tender bedding plants. Many trials have shown that seed sown in April catches up very fast with seed sown in March.

Use small pots for initial sowings, two-thirds filled with compost, topped up with vermiculite. Water the pots from above with a fine rose before sowing. Soaking pots in water can mean that the compost gets waterlogged. Scatter seed over the surface of the vermiculite.

Very fine seed will not need covering. Larger seeds can be gently stirred into the surface of the vermiculite.

Cover the pots with glass or clingfilm and then with newspaper to exclude light. Some seeds, including ageratum, antirrhinum, begonia, cineraria, impatiens, lobelia, mimulus, nicotiana, petunia and salvia, germinate best in light and should not be covered. As soon as the seedlings emerge, remove the covers and keep the pots well watered.

Prick off the seedlings into large seed trays as soon as the first real leaves develop. Very small seedlings such as alyssum and lobelia can be pricked out in small clumps. Harden off the plants gradually before planting out in permanent positions. In balmy coastal areas, this may be in mid April. In central Scotland, it is unlikely to be before June.

Cuttings of plants can be taken at three different stages. Softwood cuttings are those taken from young shoots between March and June. In some ways, they are the most difficult to look after as they often need mist and warmth before they will root, and they need to root fast before they exhaust their own food supplies. The exceptions are geranium and fuchsia, both of which root very easily from softwood cuttings. The system also works with cotinus, lilac, lavender and potentilla.

Fuchsia cuttings taken now will themselves be flowering plants by late summer. Take shoots with three pairs of leaves, cutting just below the last pair of leaves. Set them in a pot filled with fast-draining compost. Cover with a polythene bag and keep at a temperature between 50°F and 60°F (10°C and 16°C). Move the cuttings into separate pots when their own growth shows they have rooted.

Cut old overwintered geranium plants hard back in early spring. Water and feed them to encourage new shoots, which will provide softwood cuttings. Any healthy shoot, about 3–4 inches (8–10 centimetres) long, will make a cutting. Snap it off just below a leaf joint. Take off all the leaves except the very young ones at the tip of the cutting. Set the cuttings round the edge of a 5-inch (13-centimetre) pot of compost. Do not cover them. Pot them on when they are rooted.

Semi-ripe cuttings are the ones you take when the current season's shoots are just beginning to harden, but are still pliable (generally between mid June and August). The shoots must be healthy and vigorous. Simple stem cuttings can be snipped in 4–6-inch (10–15-centimetre) lengths from any likely-looking section of stem. Internodal cuttings are made by cutting halfway between leaf joints on a stem. Nodal cuttings are made through the bump immediately below a leaf joint. You then whip off the bottom leaves attached to the lump before putting the cutting in its pot.

Hibiscus roots well from stem cuttings, taken at the end of July or August. Take 6-inch (15-centimetre) sections of stem and line them out in sandy soil in a cold frame where they have some winter protection. Try the technique with hydrangeas too, by taking 4-inch (10-centimetre) sections of semi-ripe wood and sticking them round the side of a pot of compost. Cover the pot with a plastic bag until the cuttings have found their feet.

A heel cutting is what you get when you take hold of a side shoot (not one that is flowering) and give it a sharp tug downwards. It comes away with a bit of the old stem attached. That is the heel. Both buddleia and chaenomeles root from heel cuttings, taken in late July or August. Choose plump lateral shoots 4–5 inches (10–13 centimetres) long and pull them off with a heel. Trim off the growing top and the bottom leaves and put the cuttings in a cold frame, pushing them in the ground to about half their length.

A basal cutting is one made with a clean cut through the slight swelling that usually occurs where side shoots join the main stem. This is all that distinguishes it from a heel cutting. Basal cuttings of choisya taken in late July or August will root in pots covered with a plastic bag or (in mild districts) lined out direct in the ground. A propagating frame set at about 60°F (15°C) will hurry up the rooting process of shrubs such as choisya and ceanothus, but is not essential.

The older the wood you take for cuttings, the longer the cutting itself is and the longer it takes to root, so hardwood cuttings, taken from the ripened wood of a shrub or tree in autumn and early winter, sometimes take a year to root. Many common shrubs such as berberis, dogwood, cotoneaster, escallonia, privet and ribes root from hardwood cuttings.

A layer is a kind of hardwood cutting, with the added advantage that if it doesn't take, the evidence isn't so obvious. Shrubs with naturally low-growing branches are the easiest targets. Rhododendrons and azaleas propagate particularly well by this method and I have also had 100 per cent success with *Hydrangea villosa*.

When you notice a likely branch for layering, snick the underside of it about 12 inches (30 centimetres) back from the growing tip. Scrape out a hollow in the ground underneath this point and peg the stem down into it. Cover it with earth and put a flat stone on top of it to stop it springing free. A year later, the stem should have rooted. To free it, simply cut the stem behind the layer.

HASELEY COURT

Shabby chic is where we are all supposed to be now, style-wise. A friend, surrounded by her crew of superbly high-spirited children, moaned piteously as she looked at the latest crop of pictures in *Interiors*. 'No problem with the shabby bit,' she said. 'But how do you ever get on to the chic?' Her hound, lounging elegantly but muddily in an armchair, looked at her with an expression that said 'Don't bother' several times over.

This balancing act between the grand and the domestic, the tattered and the modish, was the essence of the American Nancy Lancaster's style. She died in 1994, aged ninety-seven, after a lifetime of decorating (she was an early partner in the firm of Colefax and Fowler), entertaining, rescuing crumbling houses and garden-making.

Her last home was Haseley Court in Oxfordshire, which she saved from ruin in the early fifties. It had been used as a POW camp and a Canadian field hospital, and the early eighteenth-century house was on its last legs. So was the garden, although the topiary chess set, laid out in a sunken garden on the east side of the house, had miraculously survived, thanks to an old man who bicycled over from the neighbouring village each year to clip what he called 'his kings and queens'.

Over the next thirty years, Mrs Lancaster remade the lines of what became a superb ten-acre garden. She planted long tunnels of hornbeam, which stretch your eye right to the boundaries of the garden. She brought in new clipped spirals and cones of box to make what she called a 'topiary parlour' of a shady courtyard on the north side of the house, brightening up the sombre evergreen shapes with bright skirts of variegated ivy.

She made a nut walk leading down a gentle bank towards the remnants of a moat, which she reinvented as a long canal garden. The nut trees are underplanted with carpets of hellebores and bluebells. She took in a hay meadow and, dividing it into four, created elaborate parterres and potagers, rose walks and herbaceous borders, the centrepiece an elegant trellis summerhouse with a scooped-up roof. Despite its scale, it has the airy, diaphanous quality of a giant spider's web.

For almost the last twenty years of her life, Nancy Lancaster lived in the converted stables at Haseley, keeping the formal, quartered garden that she had conjured from the hayfield for herself while the rest was sold with the main house. Under the sympathetic hands of Desmond and Fiona Heyward, who moved into Haseley Court in 1982, the whole property was eventually reunited.

As Mrs Heyward had for some time been such a close neighbour of Mrs Lancaster's, she absorbed many of her most strongly held principles. The Confederate flag no longer flies above the pediment on the south front (Mrs Lancaster was born in Virginia) but the garden paintwork is still Confederate grey, a soft bluish grey which is a sympathetic colour in a garden.

She had such style, said Nancy Lancaster's contemporaries, that she could even wear her tiara on the tilt. Balancing seemingly opposing forces was second nature to her, and restoring the right kind of equilibrium to the garden has been Mrs Heyward's chief concern.

The long yew alley leading down one side of the garden had become very overgrown and wobbly. Mrs Heyward saw that this was one of the lines that needed to be kept very clean and straight, with tall dark evergreen walls that pull you down their narrow confines, and an urn at the end to reward you for the journey. There was plenty of money for urns. Mrs Lancaster was already a rich widow at the age of twenty-one.

But the stone grotto at one end of a hornbeam tunnel, home to a slightly wistful cherub with water splashing round his feet, needs no straightening up. Mrs Heyward feels that the balance there is about right, wild polypody ferns seeded into the roof of the grotto, wisteria tendrils escaping from a nearby wall to coil over the symmetrically placed corner urns.

Plants are still allowed to seed themselves about in the Lancaster way. The hornbeam tunnels have rivers of scillas running along their feet, which wander now and then in an exploratory way towards the centre of the path. There are lightly built narcissus there too, quite unlike the more recent inventions with frilly snubbed noses that look as though they have been head-butting a brick wall.

A cross tunnel is made of laburnum, which used to be lined with tawny-orange, red and yellow wallflowers. 'She was not afraid of colour,' says Mrs Heyward. Provided there was plenty of green to act as a buffer, she delighted in hot colours. Yellow was a great favourite, in dress, and decoration, as well as the garden. The garden designer and writer Mary Keen remembers Mrs Lancaster wearing a brilliant yellow hat in the depths of winter. Yellow paint covered the walls of the big Mayfair drawing room where Colefax and Fowler had their office.

Her design messages were not always so clear. 'Paint it the colour of elephant's breath,' she once instructed a bemused decorator. Perhaps she meant the colours of santolina and lavender, rue and rosemary, the soft restrained tones that she used in one of the four quarters of her own walled garden, the one she made from the hayfield.

The Heywards have had some difficult decisions to make. Storms wrecked a good deal of the great chestnut avenue that led away from the south forecourt over the field to the distant horizon. After taking advice, they decided to fell the few remaining chestnuts and replant a double avenue of lime, a generous gift to the future.

Honey fungus claimed the umbrella-shaped Portugal laurels which, with flat-topped clipped Irish yew, guard the boundaries of the topiary garden. The Heywards replanted new Portugal laurels which have been growing steadily as round mop-headed unclipped trees. Now their long-term future must be decided. Umbrellas as before, or balls?

There is more exuberance, style and good design in this one garden than you might gather in a whole season of garden visiting. See it while the trees are still bare and you can pick out the lines of the garden in hornbeam and yew, box and *Rosa mundi*, hazel and laburnum. See it again in summer when roses sprawl over the octagon and tobacco plants scent the parterre.

A few years after Haseley Court, south-east of Oxford, was built, with its handsome grey front and classical pediment, the estate at Buckland, near Faringdon, south-west of Oxford, was also being developed. Richard Woods, the landscape designer, was brought in by the owners to rearrange the surroundings. His chief task was to make it look as though the river Thames was flowing through the shallow valley below the house.

Since he had only a minuscule stream to work with, this was a tall order, but he brought it off. He created a string of lakes which sit in the hollows of the land as though geography had never intended anything different. Where the little stream rises, Woods built a classically pedimented grotto, arranged so that the spring water splashes over stones as it falls.

From this modest start, the lake swells gently and then narrows again at a waterfall which connects it to the next stretch of water. Here there is a pretty boathouse in the rustic style and a summerhouse, both thatched. At some stage in the 1950s, the garden designer Lanning Roper was brought in to develop a garden around the lakes for the Wellesleys, who owned the estate. His flowerbeds have disappeared now and the shrubs he planted have grown big and wild. It does not seem a loss. The lakeside walk, along through yews and box trees, with moorhens skittering across the water, does not need prettiness of that sort.

Halfway down the path that leads to the lake you pass a thatched ice house, the interior bricked into a perfect egg-shape. Double wooden doors provide insulation at the entrance and you can read about the last time the ice house was filled: 6 April 1913. Six men barrowed ice hacked from the lake to fill the domed structure, and Mr Gough the head gardener provided hot beer, bread and cheese for the workers. It seems as long ago as a dream.

RED ALERT ON THE TOMATO FRONT

I have been defrosting the freezer. It's an antediluvian model – the kind with black flip top lids that village newsagents used to keep their ice cream in. You could fall into its icy, cavernous bottom and never be seen again. I hate the job but freezers are like filing cabinets. The system only holds up if the person who puts stuff in is the same person who pulls it out.

Buried at the bottom of the freezer among stray gooseberries and escaped broad beans were five bags of tomatoes, the remnants of last year's harvest. I froze sixty pounds of tomatoes last year, and they freeze brilliantly if you bag them up whole and unskinned. Then they don't stick together and you can fish out whatever quantity you want. If you run a frozen tomato under the cold tap, the skin peels away like silk.

We grow all ours outside. Sometimes, you can risk setting out plants at the beginning of May, but if the month is treacherously cold and windy, as it often is, you need to wait until the end of the month. If you've got a greenhouse, you can get much earlier crops. In the West Country, where I garden, blight is an ever-present threat on outdoor tomatoes, so early maturing types are generally the safest. That means growing small fruited tomatoes such as 'Tumbling Tom' and 'Red Alert' rather than tall cordon beef tomatoes, which you train up on a single stem.

The plants need watering in well when they are first set out, whether you plant them in pots, Gro-bags or the open ground. But once they have settled and are growing away, you shouldn't water too much. Research from the National Vegetable Research Station at Wellesbourne, Warwickshire suggests that overwatered tomatoes (and sweetcorn, French beans and runner beans) produce leaf at the expense of fruit. Hold off until the plants begin to flower, then start watering again.

In terms of taste, 'Gardener's Delight' and yellow 'Sungold' remain among the best of the small cherry tomatoes. Both are cordon types, which you need to train up on a single stem, pinching out the side shoots as they grow. 'Red Alert' (one of the earliest of all tomatoes to mature) and 'Tornado' also produce cherry tomatoes, but on bushes that don't need any pinching out. You just plant them and leave them alone.

If you have a greenhouse, you might start sowing tomato seed as early as February. But for outside crops you shouldn't be sowing more than six to eight weeks before the plants can be set outside. If you take that as the end of May, then late March is plenty soon enough to be tearing the top off a seed packet. Until I had a greenhouse, all my plants were raised on the kitchen windowsill. If you sow seed in a 5-inch (13-centimetre) pot, you can prick out the seedlings into individual 3-inch (8-centimetre) pots where the plants will happily stay until they get into their final quarters outside.

Bush tomatoes on their own might be enough for your needs, but they crop over a relatively short period. And for cooking you sometimes need something a bit larger, perhaps 'Brandywine', an old Amish variety with huge pinkish red fruit, or the Italian variety 'Costoluto Fiorentino', with medium-sized fruit of superb flavour. Both are available as plantlets from Simpsons Seeds (www.simpsons-seeds.co.uk), who offer nearly seventy different kinds of tomatoes as plants, even more as seeds. Orders for plants need to be in by the end of March.

The first tomatoes seen in Europe were yellow-skinned kinds, which gave the fruit their popular name of *pomodoro*. Like potatoes, they were treated with great suspicion. Gerard said the whole plant had 'a ranke and stinking savour'. Early food writers advised cooking them for at least three hours to drive off the poison that was supposed to lurk in the fruit.

Purple-skinned tomatoes such as the superb 'Black Russian' were once common, but even in 1905, the gardener William Robinson noted in *The Vegetable Garden* that 'consumers continue to favour the red varieties'. I thought 'consumer' was a modern term. Evidently not. Robinson listed a 'Mikado Purple', 'Purple Champion', 'Purple Ponderosa' and 'Apple-Shaped Purple'. Many of these must have been raised by nineteenth-century gardeners from seed saved from the best of their crops. The seedlings would not always have had the same characteristics as their parents. Tomato seed stays viable for at least four years.

In their homelands – Ecuador, Peru and Bolivia – tomatoes grow in dry, poor ground. Overfeeding, like overwatering, produces leafy growth at the expense of fruit. We noticed in Ecuador that tomatoes were often used as ground cover among stands of sweetcorn. Once planted, they were left to their own devices. The same combination would work here too, if you used bush tomatoes such as the extra early 'Red Alert' or 'Tumbling Tom'.

Over the last few years, there has been a great boom in new varieties of outdoor tomato. Grown outdoors, tomatoes are less susceptible to pests but in a wet summer they can be completely destroyed by blight. Fortunately, breeders are beginning to address this, introducing blight-tolerant varieties such as 'Ferline'. One of the great delights of growing your own tomatoes is that you can choose different varieties each year, but you need to check whether they are meant for outdoor growing.

Flavour develops more fully in tomatoes grown outside than it does in greenhouse fruit, but the first outdoor types were unpopular because they started fruiting so late that half the crop was fit only for chutney. But using small cherry tomatoes such as 'Gardener's Delight' and 'Sub Arctic' as parents, breeders have produced a race of fast-maturing, wonderfully flavoured bush tomatoes.

Because they don't need staking, bush tomatoes are easier to manage in Gro-bags than the upright, single-stem varieties. If you live in the north of the country, choose the earliest cropping bush varieties such as 'Red Alert'. Where space is limited, upright-growing, staked tomatoes may be the only option. These are often called cordon, or more muddlingly, 'indeterminate' varieties. They don't have to be confined to stakes in the vegetable garden. Olivier de Serres, agricultural advisor to the French king Henri IV, said that tall-growing tomatoes were often used in France to cover outhouses and arbours. The cordon 'Merveilles des Marches' described in the Simpsons catalogue sounds like the right kind of tomato for the job. All we need is a good, ripening summer.

Tasks for the Month

General

- Treat drives, paths and paved areas with a residual weedkiller. Used carefully, these are great allies.
- Spring-clean house plants, taking off dead leaves and dusting over the foliage with either a damp sponge or a leaf wipe. All house plants will now need more food and water. Those that seem to be bursting out of their containers may need repotting. Do not suppose that by giving it a pot twice as big, a plant will be twice as happy. One size larger will be plenty.
- Moss often has a field day in lawns through the winter. If you cannot learn to love it, hire a scarifier and sweat away a weekend tearing the stuff out of your lawn. A chemical mosskiller is a lazier option.

Flowers

- Prune hybrid tea roses and climbers that flower on the current season's growth. (In mild areas, this is a job that can be done in January and February.)
- Cut fuchsia and mallow stems back to live wood.
- Pull any dead leaves away from the rhizomes of bearded iris and give them a feed of bonemeal. If you are lucky enough to have flowers of *Iris unguicularis*, keep picking them. They will fare much better indoors than out.
- Plant acidantheras and anemones.
- Set begonia tubers in boxes of compost. As soon as they have sprouted, plant them out in separate pots.
- Start overhauling herbaceous borders, lifting and dividing congested clumps of plants and replanting them in soil enriched with compost and bonemeal. Michaelmas daisy, rudbeckia and phlox especially benefit from this treatment. As they age, growth tends to die out in the centre of the clumps. The most vigorous growth is usually round the edges: these are the pieces you should choose for replanting.
- Late summer shrubs that bear their flowers on this season's growth (buddleia, caryopteris, etc.) should be cut back hard now,. If you have inherited a really overgrown buddleia, bring it to heel gradually by cutting out half the stems this season, half next. Flowers are larger on hard-pruned specimens than on those left to their own devices.

March

- ❧ Choose some hardy annuals for sowing directly into the ground where they are to flower.
- ❧ Plant gladioli, setting the corms 4–6 inches (10–15 centimetres) deep in well-drained soil in full sun.
- ❧ Lift and split clumps of snowdrops and aconites if you want to hasten their spread through the garden. Replant them with a generous portion of bonemeal mixed into the earth. Snowdrops settle more successfully 'in the green' than as dry bulbs.

Vegetables

- ❧ Sow parsnips in drills about half an inch (12 millimetres) deep in rows 12 inches (30 centimetres) apart.
- ❧ Sow summer spinach in drills half an inch (12 millimetres) deep, the rows 12 inches (30 centimetres) apart. It will do best in a half-shaded spot where there is rich, moist soil. In drought conditions it runs quickly to seed. Some varieties such as 'Campania' are slower to bolt.
- ❧ Sow broad beans if the ground is not too wet. Take out a shallow drill about 12 inches (30 centimetres) wide and sow the beans in a broad band so that when they are grown they give each other some support.
- ❧ Sow celery and celeriac indoors, scattering the seed thinly over the compost. Celery is a hefty feeder, so if the ground is workable start to prepare the patch outside with a layer of manure in the bottom of a 12-inch- (30-centimetre) deep trench.
- ❧ Sow carrots.
- ❧ Sow leeks in a seedbed for transplanting later on.
- ❧ Sow Brussels sprouts if you need masses. If you do not, it is simpler to buy a bundle of plants later in the season.

Fruit

- ❧ Mulch currants and gooseberries thickly to keep down weeds and conserve moisture.
- ❧ Perfectionists may need to spray apple and pear trees against scab. Fortunately there are usually more pressing tasks at hand. Scab is a blemish rather than a threat. Trees will not die from it.

Propagating

- Divide aconitum, aster, astilbe, chrysanthemum, dicentra, echinops, geum, helenium, hosta, inula, lamium, libertia, ligularia, liriope, lysichiton, lysimachia, mint, osmunda, phlox, rodgersia, sisyrinchium, solidago and thalictrum.
- Take hardwood cuttings of eucryphia and willow.
- Set rooted cuttings of tender perennials such as penstemon and semitender shrubs such as argyranthemum and artemisia into individual small pots.
- Start feeding rooted cuttings of heather.

The jobbing gardener

SPRING IN NEW YORK

Spring in New York is a designer event – a concept. From the colour-coded tulips in fancy Park Avenue to the great steely magnolias in the courtyard outside the Frick Collection, style is all. The Frick was sealed off behind hoardings while I was there, while a mammoth restoration took place, but two small windows had been cut in the hoarding to give a view into the courtyard. Consequently, the magnolias stood, framed, as though they themselves were Renoir portraits.

The city can scarcely look more beautiful than it does in late spring, with big old cherry trees spreading horizontal branches of blossom over the mounded contours of Central Park, and the street trees just beginning to breathe green over endless stretches of tarmac and concrete.

But if you want your own personal spring in New York, it comes expensive. Wandering into Takashimaya, the most elegant shop on earth, perched where 54th Street joins Fifth Avenue, I enquired the price of the branches of pale pink quince blossom stacked in green glazed French earthenware urns in the shop window. Forty dollars a branch, said the assistant, giving, both in the cold tone she used and in the way her practised eye took in my clothes, the clear message: 'These things are not for you.'

No, they are not, because I've plenty of quince in the garden. But I was rather staggered, given that the blossom was fracturing and falling with each customer that jiggled against it, that there were people who would actually shell out such fortunes for this stuff. You'd need at least eight branches to make a decent show. But there were customers there, lapping it up. If Takashimaya says quince is spring, then quince it is.

The flower shop, run by a French florist, occupies the front half of the ground floor. Above are another six floors, exquisitely arranged, with clothes (mostly black, white and beige – Filippo Chiesa of Italy, Yeohlee of New York), luggage, jewellery, bedlinen and smellies. Takashimaya has even rethought the concept of the carrier bag. The big ones are like flower pots, narrower at the bottom than the top. The small ones are origami puzzles, flat packs that with a flick of a shop assistant's wrist are transformed into triangular conjuring tricks. It's impressive. And the lavatories are breathtaking.

I hovered longest in the flower shop, eavesdropping shamelessly on the conversations going on round me. 'Edgy. Very edgy,' said a young man in black, pointing to the huge bunch of snakeshead fritillaries for sale in the shop. Was that good or bad, I wondered? Good, evidently, because his client bought vast quantities of them. 'It's got to be purple,' said another, a personal stylist or interior designer by the sound of what he was saying. He swooped on some witchy arums, the colour of Biba's aubergine velvet, and expertly conjured up an instant arrangement: arums with a flicker of pale blueberry blossom, some magnolia, spotted hellebores, a few 'Queen of Night' tulips. Exquisite. And yours for 300 dollars.

The flowers were displayed with the casual flair that always means bankruptcy. On one table, among simple crystal bowls and urns of tufa, were the yellows – pale hyacinths, egg-yolk ranunculus, old-fashioned double daffodils with green round the gills, fabulous double roses of a lazy, peachy disposition. In the far corner was pink: 'Sarah Bernhardt' peonies, with lilies, white lilac stripped of its leaves, and ornithogalums. They all seemed like garden flowers, just gathered, not like florists' merchandise at all. I think that is what made them so bewitching, here in the middle of urban Fifth Avenue.

Behind the flower shop, taking up the rest of the ground floor of Takashimaya, is a display space, showing off a collection of whatever seems to be The Thing of the moment. For the time being it's coconut matting, either plain or dyed delicious shades of yellow and Tyrian purple. 'The uneven working and irregular knots are combined with meticulous study of proportions to become the somatic features of unique creations,' said the blurb. 'The rug is no longer an interior design accessory, but an independent and simple object designed to be used.' Well, fancy that.

A NEW LEAF

Holinshed, whose famous sixteenth-century *Chronicles* provided Shakespeare with some of his best plots, wrote that when Catherine of Aragon wanted a decent salad, she had to send over to Flanders to get it. Francophiles might still feel the same. But olive oil has now escaped the chemist's shop, lettuce has been reinvented, chicory and endive are listed in every seed catalogue. And we have discovered that rocket is as easy to grow as mustard and cress. Only a smudge of garlic round the inside of a salad bowl stands between us and a *mélange* as good as anything you'd find on the other side of the Channel.

Successional sowing is supposed to be the key to full salad bowls, an endless conveyor belt of salad vegetables, seamlessly presenting themselves in perfect condition, each crop neatly dovetailing with the next. A little rocket here, a soupçon of mixed saladini there, a two-week timetable of sowings; it sounds so easy, so achievable. But does it work?

If the weather is very hot, seed germination may be delayed. Conversely, the growth of rocket, radish and spinach and other crops above ground will accelerate. If it is cool, lettuces will remain in good condition for a long period, so your second and third sowings may come on tap while you are still content with your first. So it's not quite as neat as it seems, but at least you can spend this month dreaming that this year might be different and buying the seeds you'll need to provide an almost year-round supply of salad leaves. They'll taste far better than the supermarkets' bagged equivalent, washed in a chlorine solution at least ten times stronger than anything allowed in a public swimming pool.

There is at least one principle you can hang on to: the shorter time it takes a crop to come to maturity, the more successional sowings you have to make. Salad rocket, for instance, grows quite fast (wild rocket is slower) and there is a noticeable difference in taste and texture between its young leaves and its old ones, which are unpleasantly strong.

The terminal leaf of a rocket plant is much bigger than the others, and once this has been nipped off for consumption, the crop goes slowly downhill. But if you sow your first lot in spring, you can expect to pick it five or six weeks later. As with spinach, you get the best crops in spring and autumn, when the plants resprout quite vigorously. In the heat of summer, rocket runs to seed fast. Although you can use its flowers in a salad (they taste just as peppery as the leaves) they are not worth the loss of the green stuff. You can slow down the tendency to bolt by sowing summer crops in semi-shade and also by keeping the patches well watered. Watering moderates the flavour of older plants too.

For this crop, you don't even need a garden. Rocket will grow perfectly well in a pot or seed tray on a windowsill. You can sow it in a windowbox or a Gro-bag, a little at a time. There are several different kinds: salad rocket, wild rocket and Turkish rocket, which is said to be slightly more resistant to attacks by flea beetle.

Flea beetles (there are 130 species in Britain alone) feed on plants of the brassica family, which includes wallflowers, radish and turnip as well as rocket. You know they have been visiting when you find young leaves peppered with tiny holes. April and May is when they are busiest, feasting on the nesh young foliage of plants that may be so discouraged by their attentions that they keel over and die. Once plants are past the juicy stage, they become less attractive to flea beetles. But the same goes for us, too.

Flea beetles have increased hugely in numbers since oil-seed rape became a widespread agricultural crop. They can be black and yellow or bluish black all over, and are about a quarter of an inch (6 millimetres) long. You'll know them by the way they jump. But how do you deal with them? You can concentrate on keeping seedling crops growing fast, hoping to outpace them. You can also protect seedlings with fleece covers. If you are really cunning you can catch flea beetles on a sticky trap, by tickling the foliage of your seedlings while the beetles jump on to the trap you are holding over the top. But this method is very hit and miss. Mostly miss.

In a small space, one of the most productive ways of growing fresh salads is to use the cut-and-come-again technique. You can make your own seed mix of salad crops: salad rocket, oriental greens such as mizuna, mibuna and the mustardy komatsuna, a spinach such as 'Emelia' or 'Dominant' and loose-leaf lettuce such as oakleaf or 'Merveille de Quatre Saisons'. If you don't want to splash out on that much seed buy ready-made mixtures such as Misticanza (Italian), Mesclun (French) or Oriental Saladini. Sow the seed in a container or a compact patch of ground and scissor off the young leaves when the plants are about 3 inches (8 centimetres) high. Make the cut just above the first seed leaves (that's usually about half an inch (15 millimetres) above ground).

This technique, which you can use with different kinds of lettuce, young spinach, endive, chicory, purslane, Chinese mustard, mizuna and land cress, gives you the juiciest, most tender leaves. You can cut over the same patch four or five times before the seedlings either run out of steam, or shoot up to seed. Much depends on the weather and whether you remember to water.

Rocket, leaf lettuces and corn salad or mache can be sown any time from early spring on. Mache grows flat like a rosette of lawn-daisy leaves, so is best grown separately and cut as a whole rosette. Most chicories and endives are best sown from June onwards. You sow them just like lettuce, then thin out the plants so that they stand at least 12 inches (30 centimetres) foot apart. They make flat-faced mops of growth, tight-hearted, curled, crisp, stronger tasting than lettuce. If you sowed an Italian variety such as 'Grumolo Verde', you could use the summer leaves young and small for salads, then leave the rosettes to develop and overwinter so that they provide another early crop for cutting next spring.

'Babyleaf' salads may include amaranth, chop suey and choy sum, spinach, the black cabbage called 'Nero de Toscana', bull's blood beet, rhubarb chard, land cress and Greek cress, red perilla, purslane and texsel greens. Italian mixtures often use rocket with various lettuces, chicory and black kale. Provence salads may have a slower-growing blend of sorrel, corn salad, lettuce and chervil. With baby leaves, you can eat your way round the whole world.

THE MAGNOLIA MOMENT

There are moments in the gardening year when, like Cecil B. de Mille, you want to shout 'Hold it' and freeze the scene, just as it is in every detail, for a little longer. 'Get a camera, dumbo,' said one of the children, reading this introduction uninvited over my shoulder on the way back from yet another interminable conversation on the phone. It beats me the way they stand there, playing songs down the wire to their friends, jigging in a solitary fashion. 'Oh, I *love* this one, don't you?'

'But ...' I started. But the whirlwind had moved on, to sigh over a spot in the bathroom mirror. What I would have said is that a camera is not the answer. A photograph can signpost a garden, but it cannot give you the depth, the texture, the immediacy of the real thing.

Anyone with a magnolia in their front garden must think the same thing this month, when the vast, waxy blooms finally open after the yearly will-there-won't-there-be-a-frost anguish. For years, when I did not have a decent one of my own, there were two magnolia detours that I always tried to take in April. One led through Shepherds Bush in west London, the other past the Chepstow racecourse in Gwent, where beside a petrol station grew one of the most magnificent magnolias (now gone) you could ever hope to see.

If I could not get to Chepstow, I'd drive through any 1930s suburb. Semi-detached gardens never look lovelier than they do in April, where original plantings of cherry and magnolia have grown to maturity. They were the number one shrubs and trees in the thirties, popularised by Collingwood 'Cherry' Ingram, traveller, botanist, gardener and collector of Japanese plants.

I did not have an easy start with magnolias in my own garden. Although planted against the most comfortable west-facing wall I could find, two big-leaved evergreen bull bays (*Magnolia grandiflora*) were killed in youth by frost. Two *Magnolia stellata* died in quick succession on the bank. Pining for Surbiton, they did not even wait to take in the view. 'Hang on,' I told them. 'I'm sure you could get to like the place,' but they didn't.

After that I went for *Magnolia* x *soulangiana*, the most commonly planted of all magnolias. My Hilliers handbook assured me that it was the best type to use on 'indifferent clay soils'. It managed in its first spring to squeeze out a few leaves of a colour which suggested that it was finding the surrounding soil rather worse than indifferent. Then, with a scarcely audible bleat, that one gave up the ghost too.

I should have stopped when I killed the *M.* x *soulangiana*. Of course I should. It is what I would have told anyone else to do. But it is shaming to admit failure with a plant that half England seems to be able to flaunt successfully. So I tried one last throw, 'Leonard Messel', a chance hybrid that arose in the Messels' garden at Nymans in Sussex.

By this time I had swotted up more on magnolias than I did for any exam in my finals. A reasonable depth of good soil. Yes, can do. Rich living, good drainage, plenty of moisture. Yes, although the last two requirements seem contradictory. Shelter from spring frost and cold winds. More difficult. Though generally sheltered, there are few places in a garden that are protected from all four quarters of the wind.

For magnolias, shelter from the north and east is the most important. That may have been my problem, since the only place where a magnolia could spread its wings was on the bank, which caught a certain amount of wind from the north.

As a race, magnolias are very tolerant of atmospheric pollution. That explains why they are such successful urban survivors. Frost touches them less in town gardens than it does in the country, too, though they would suffer from drought more severely.

Anyway, my 'Leonard Messel' went in the only place on the bank not already tried by the three other suicidal magnolias. I planted it with as much tender loving care as happened to be left over on that day, but it was not enough. Messel struggled on in the awful accusatory way that makes you wish the wretched thing would die and stop making you feel like some horticultural Herod.

Since then, things have got better and in my new garden, seven species magnolias (including the superb *Magnolia tripetala* with leaves as big as a banana's) are growing lustily. Conversely, the great white cherry 'Tai Haku', which grew splendidly in the old garden, is struggling in the new one.

I planted it again because I didn't want to do without that moment when 'Tai Haku' is the epitome of spring, the clusters of big white flowers still not sufficiently full blown to make you feel the end is near. The foliage is just beginning to unfurl, the leaves a highly polished bronze at this stage, magnificent with the blossom and good too with other things such as golden-leaved philadelphus or choisya, just coming into bud in April.

You don't want to be away at that point when there is just exactly the right amount of bronze leaf to white flower on 'Tai Haku'. It never lasts long enough, but that is the point about cherries. They are fleeting. The less you have of them, the more you look forward to them.

Could you ever long for heather to bloom in quite the same way as you do a cherry? Heather just turns its volume up a few notches, and then sits there telling you the same story over and over again for months. Then it slides drearily back into background noise. Only on a mountain does it really begin to sing. And on a headland at St Martin's Haven in Pembrokeshire where you see it as the foreground to the gurgling whirlpools of Jack Sound beyond.

At this time of the year, garden scenarios flash by faster than you can keep up with them. Aconites, for instance. In early February the flower stems push up like small croquet hoops through the litter of winter. This month, the aconites show only ruffs of green leaves with the seed pods balanced on top like carefully made little pies on a plate. Where does the time in between go?

Between the big set pieces of the garden – the cherry, the pear blossom, the wisteria, the rambling roses – that mark its progress through the seasons, there are endless smaller tableaux that you tend to forget about until they put themselves on stage. De Caen anemones are always a surprise. One year they came up through and around the species tulips that I had forgotten were already planted in the same area, so that small red and bronze tulips were flowering rather surprisingly on top of the other's ferny, frothy foliage.

The tulips were *T. hageri*, grown in pots plunged in the bank, then lifted and ripened in the same pots in the cold frame for the summer. It is the only way that they can survive in heavy clay soil. If you've light, fast-draining ground, you can forget about the pots. The flowers make perfect goblets, wide and rounded at the bottom with the petals all meeting to make a pointed top. The colour is variable, sometimes rich red, the red sometimes overlaid with green and bronze on the outsides of the petals.

The anemones are exactly like the ones you buy as cut flowers, growing on fat juicy stems, the flowers held up by a frill of greenery under their necks. The corms are the most unprepossessing things you are ever likely to plant in the garden, small misshapen pellets of what looks like dried sheep's dung. As a transformation scene, the anemone's beats fairy tales any day.

From each of these wizened bits of nothing, you can expect up to twenty flowers, coming up over a long succession during April and May. How do they do it? What is going on underground? What wonder protein is packed inside that corm? After four years or so, they begin to dwindle. After their superhuman efforts, I am not surprised. The double St Brigid anemones are not quite as prolific as the de Caen, but the double blue 'Lord Lieutenant' is very showy, excellent later with the sulphurous flowers of a dwarf spurge. Oh, why doesn't April last longer?

SAVING YOUR OWN BACON

Martin Luther King had it right, I think. Even if he knew the world was going to end tomorrow, he said, it would not stop him planting an apple tree. In the torrents of apocalyptic prose and images of gas masks and underground bunkers that have filled our papers over the last few weeks, nobody has talked much about planting. Instead, strange websites are being raided for advice on Survival with a big S.

Quoted on the homepage of the Rocky Mountain Survival Group (www.artrans.com) is a quote from science fiction writer, Robert A. Heinlein. Redefining Renaissance man for the twenty-first century, he says, 'a human being should be able to change a diaper, plan an invasion, butcher a hog, handle a boat, design a building, write a sonnet, balance accounts, build a wall, set a bone, comfort the dying, take orders, give orders, co-operate, act alone, solve equations, analyse a new problem, pitch manure, program a computer, cook a tasty meal, fight efficiently, die gallantly'.

We'll forgive him for the desperate New Man-ness of the diaper. There's very little skill attached to that task, now that disposables have ousted the kind that need folding. But as a mantra for survival, Heinlein's recipe has got some big gaps in it. Take the pig. A pig is a precious commodity, given the time and effort it takes to raise one to the age when it can best be slaughtered. What's the point of knowing how to kill the beast unless you also know how to cure the flitches, make brawn and prepare the intestines for sausage skins, and are privy to all the other rare delights that a single pig, carefully husbanded, can provide?

A pig killing was a big event on my uncles' farms in Wales. You never wanted to miss out on one. The arrival of the pig man had a grand drama and he was always greeted with the formality appropriate to the occasion. No beast then was trucked miles to an abattoir. A pig was killed at home, in his own farmyard, with plenty of buckets standing by to catch the blood that poured from the expertly slit throat. The farm dogs used to lap it up in vast quantities, while it was still warm.

In one clean operation, the entire pig was cut up and dispatched in separate dishes to the kitchen. Some parts, like the sweetbreads, had to be dealt with immediately (though you never killed a pig in hot weather). Others, the huge flanks, were laid out on the slate slabs of the dairy to be salted into bacon. Uncle Charles, my mother's favourite brother, had a gift for curing bacon, using a secret recipe that he never even told her about. It produced flitches as stiff as boards, which, when the brine had done its work, hung from huge hooks set in the dairy ceiling. The bacon smelled sweet and dry.

So unless old Heinlein knows something about preserving his pig, killing it is not going to get him far along the road to survival. He includes cooking 'a tasty meal' as a desirable talent, but includes nothing about fire-lighting or growing food. Both are vital skills. An Armageddon, with gas and electricity still available at the flick of a switch, is an unlikely scenario. Building a fire that lights first time with a single match needs forethought. Having lived so long without central heating, our children share our obsession with dry kindling in various sizes and well-seasoned wood, preferably ash or beech, to give a fire heart. Can Heinlein handle an axe?

And most importantly, does he know how to raise a patch of potatoes, or grow an acre of corn, or in any other way provide the basic carbohydrates that survival depends on? He'll find writing his sonnet so much easier if he's got something to line his stomach with first.

SPRING FEVER

I do not see why we should not enjoy a mild winter and a early spring from time to time without supposing that the end of the world is nigh. It may yet all end in tears with a hideous summer, but it's wonderful when bulbs flower with reckless abandon: deep magenta *Tulipa pulchella*, almost smothered by spotty lungwort, bright yellow *T. grengiolensis*, the backs of their petals washed over with a complicated bronzy green. There are hyacinths everywhere.

Each year, when the bowls of forced hyacinths have finished in the house, I plant them out, more because it seems murderous to throw living things away than because I expect much from them. In the garden, they grow even better than they do in bowls, with well-balanced heads, shorter stems and leaves. Inside, I grow the bulbs in compost rather than fibre and fancy, though I have no proof that the sustenance they get from the compost makes it easier for them to pick up their socks in subsequent seasons. They have to expend a lot of their own capital if they are grown in fibre.

One group of blue and white hyacinths is clustered round a variegated brunnera (creamy leaves, forget-me-not flowers), the whole ensemble looking ridiculously like a piece of willow-pattern china. Dark blue hyacinths grow amongst the low, pale ferny foliage of sweet cicely (*Myrrhis odorata*) with clumps of a white Barnhaven primula, one of the few varieties that I got round to splitting last year. In another group, the colours are reversed, with white hyacinths, a stray bit of *Euphorbia robbiae* which absent-mindedly wandered off from the place in which it was put, and dark, almost navy blue cowichan primulas, also grown from Barnhaven seed.

I could get very interested in primroses, but I'm trying not to. As I'm already besotted with tulips and have more than a passing interest in aquilegias, our garden is in danger of screeching to a sudden, awful halt at the end of June. If I'm to fall in love, it must be with something that peaks in August or September. Sunflowers? Fun, but not complicated enough. Salvias? Too complicated by half. Penstemons? Yawn, yawn. Well, there are always pears. Pears are riveting.

Over the years, the primroses cross with each other, and drift into muddy mauves, but originally I had a mixture called 'Butterscotch', copper, bronze, apricot and yellow; another of 'Valentine Victorians', rich crimson pinks; and one called 'Rustic Reds', the colours of tawny wallflowers. Now is the time to be sowing more to flower next spring. They like cool conditions, so the seed is best sown thinly on the surface of compost in a 5-inch (13-centimetre) pot, covered with a pane of glass and then left outside in a north-facing position. Primula seed dawdles towards germination, so it may be six weeks before you know whether you are to be a proud parent.

When happy, the primulas seed round with abandon. Out on what we unimaginatively call The Bank, a semicircular sweep of sloping ground round the south and west of the house, Barnhaven 'Muted Victorians' and 'Striped Victorians' are flowering fit to bust, in weird shades of dirty pink and blue. The paths up the bank are dressed each year with crushed bark. This is evidently an ideal medium for self-seeding as there are far more seedlings there, where there is no competition, than ever appear on the bank itself. It slightly defeats the purpose of the path, of course, to have it covered with plants, but it seems churlish not to acknowledge the bounty. I dig up seedlings in trowelfuls, poly-anthus, double daisies, verbascums, foxgloves, verbena, lychnis, polemonium, and press them on anyone who calls. The milkman scarcely dares come any more, but it keeps the path more or less open to traffic.

'Cantate' tulips on the bank were originally planted out close to a young plant of *Euphorbia characias* subsp. *wulfenii*. The euphorbia has now reached its zenith, but unfortunately the tulips dwindled. I like the brilliant red of tulips with the acid green of the spurge. It's a combination to try again, perhaps using the equally bright *T. eichleri*, which has more staying power and good foliage of a very pale, glaucous grey.

The big spurges, such as *Euphorbia characias*, usually peak in late spring but in a mild season bring forward their act and flower at the same time as the purple-pink magnolia 'Leonard Messel' and blue brunnera. The spurges self-seed too, and there is an extraordinary amount of variation in the seedlings' foliage and flowers. The ones I like most have bluish leaves and very bright lime flowers, without the dark eye.

Unfortunately, they hate being moved and sulk for ages if you try. I find it best to cut down most of the tall stems and wait for new growth to sprout from the bottom. But generally, this is a good time to shift herbaceous perennials, before there is too much top growth to get damaged in the move. The difficulty lies in remembering what you said last summer you were going to do this spring. I was going to shift some daylilies, but have forgotten where I thought they ought to go. Resolution: take better notes.

For years, the most evil sight in the garden was the narcissus 'Texas' with yellow petals and harsh orange trumpets underneath the last pink blossoms of the viburnum 'Dawn'. When the children wanted flowers to take to school in spring, 'Texas' was the sacrificial victim, which I hoped would solve two problems at once. Unfortunately, the flowers survived these onslaughts, and leered horribly every time I looked out of the bedroom window. In the end I had to dig them up. It was the only answer.

GETTING TO THE CHURCH ON TIME

We have three daughters, all of whom have married, the weddings in the church a hundred yards up the lane, the parties afterwards held in a tent at home. Consequently, at various times, wedding flowers have been much on my mind.

Commercial growers, with their computer-controlled warm rooms, cold rooms, light rooms and dark rooms, can bring pretty well anything into bloom at any time of the year. Amateurs have a chancier time of it. Daughter number two chose to get married in late April, which was kind of her since it is a great time for flowers. In the previous October, I thought I had a plan, but Nature, as is her right, had different ones and laid on an incredibly mild winter and six months of almost incessant rain. Consequently, only a week before the wedding, I was still not sure what I would have to hand on the day.

In October, the autumn before the wedding, I was thinking bulbs: late, sweet-smelling narcissus, anemones, and tulips, tulips, tulips. The anemones captured the colours we wanted to work with – rich blue, red, purple, magenta, pink. So I bought fifty corms each of scarlet 'Hollandia', violet blue 'Mr Fokker', violet rose 'Sylphide', the fine blue double (my favourite) 'Lord Lieutenant' and another double with violet flowers called 'The Admiral'.

Planted in the garden, anemones have always been extraordinarily free-flowering. I thought I'd plant them in 5-inch (13-centimetre) clay pots and use them as table centres. It didn't work. The twenty-five pots were packed together in the cold frame all winter, but when flower buds started to appear in March I shifted them all to a cooler spot under a north-facing wall. Because they had been growing close together in the cold frame, the foliage in each pot supported its neighbour. Separated, the stems flopped.

That was lesson number one. Each pot should have had more space. And even planted ten corms to a pot, well fed since the first growth appeared, there were not enough flowers full out all at the same time to make any one of the twenty-five pots showy enough to work as a table centre. On average, there were just six or seven flowers to a pot. Measly. That was lesson number two.

What was the solution? The problem lay more with the containers than the flowers. Old clay pots were an important part of the picture this daughter had in mind, but I'd used all I had for the anemones. So the day before the wedding, I picked all the anemones that we could use and planted the rest in the garden.

The dishwasher delivered the pots in a fit state to pack with blocks of Oasis wrapped in plastic and I prayed that there would be enough tulips around to fill them. Because their stems are so fleshy, you have to poke holes in the Oasis with a pencil before you put the flowers in. Dressed with moss, the underpinnings are hidden from view.

Our garden is thick with moss, which likes the damp and the shade. Nevertheless, I bought in supplies from our local florist. I used our own moss at our last party. A mesmerising cavalcade of insects climbed down from it during dinner and marched across the white damask cloths of the various tables: beetles, woodlice, centipedes, ants. We ended up racing woodlice between fork finishing posts but they hadn't drunk as much as we had and kept veering off course into the butter dishes.

So I bought in moss this time, but we had our own tulips. I planted two and a half thousand of them in the November before the wedding and hoped I had covered all eventualities by choosing varieties that flowered from mid April through to mid May. It turned out to be an exceptionally early year.

The main display was to come from 200 'Purple Prince', a sturdy single early of rich purple, 200 'Sjakamaro', an equally good mid-season tulip, of roughly the same colour (though with a much more interesting centre of pale bluish green) and 200 'Purple Star', which is slightly more magenta than the other two, the flowers beautifully set off against greyish foliage.

The first of these is supposed to flower by mid April, the second by late April and the third in early May. So, theoretically (as I thought when I was planting the bulbs last year), I should have been able to count on masses of purple tulips whether the season was early or late.

Instead, by the end of the March, all were in full colour, though not fully open. I hauled all the pots into the shade and on Good Friday, when the weathermen were predicting a hot Easter, tied up 600 blooms with thick soft wool. Would it work? It's a trick that was used by florists in the eighteenth and nineteenth centuries which I'd read about, but never tried for myself. In the event, the hot weather didn't come but at least the little corsets stopped the rain beating into the centres of the flowers and splaying them open.

The moment of truth came on the Monday before the wedding when I whipped off the wool bindings. I didn't know if the tulips would then gracefully pretend that the unexpected hiccup never happened. Or would they suddenly slump, as I do when I'm kept up too late at night and required to keep going long past my natural span? Not all the tulips were for picking. Some of the biggest pots were planted to decorate the tent: pale cream 'Magier' with a purple rim round its petals, fabulous 'Couleur Cardinal', scarlet with overlays of plum, and stubby little double earlies such as 'Electra' and 'Schoonord', which I planted in wicker baskets.

'Electra' is a harsh pink, not a tulip I would use in the garden, but it is showy and can be calmed down by masses of white 'Schoonord' and the presence of stately 'High Noon'. This turned out to be one of the few things that performed to order, a mid April tulip that came into bloom in mid April with soft pink and cream flowers, the cream in a broad flame up the backs of the petals.

We made trellis panels to hang round the walls of the tent and they presented no problems. We washed them over with Cuprinol wood stain, a bluish-green colour called Sage, watered down to give a beaten-up, unaggressive finish. Oh, how dangerous this all is. I'm already beginning to talk like someone out of *Private Eye*'s Pseuds Corner. But I must plough on: the trellis was decorated with ivy and bunches of grapes.

Then there was the church. Well, you have to work hard to spoil a small Norman church with Saxon underpinnings and a sixteenth-century wall painting above the chancel arch. A gang of friends who understand flower arranging volunteered to fill it with wildness and scent. All I had to find were boughs of apple blossom to go over the chancel arch. 'Back! Back!' I kept shouting to the big old Bramley apple on the top lawn. But, like everything else in the garden, it wasn't listening. Nevertheless, it was a great day, an astoundingly great day.

Tasks for the Month

General

- If you have a new lawn in mind, do not skimp on the preparation. Choose a seed mixture to suit the site. Shady lawns will need a higher percentage of coarse rye grass. Sheep's fescue will grow well in dry places.
- This is an ideal month to plant bamboos. They make good screens but will not thrive in very exposed situations. They like good, moist soil. *Arundinaria nitida* is the most shade-tolerant, with purple-flushed canes and narrow bright green leaves.
- Mulch trees and shrubs while the ground is still damp.
- Freshly planted evergreens may need a temporary screen around them to prevent the foliage drying out.

Flowers

- Thin out flowering shoots of mophead and lacecap hydrangeas, cutting a few of the old stems to ground level.
- Sow petunias in a temperature of around 15°C (60°F).
- Start thinking about stakes before your plants need them.
- Prune hardy fuchsias, such as *F. magellanica*, down to ground level.
- Cut back perovskia and romneya near the base of the stems.
- If you have time to spare, deadhead daffodils to stop them wasting energy on seed production.
- Lift and split hardy chrysanthemums that have overwintered outside.
- Plant out sweet pea seedlings, providing support for the plants in the form of either bamboo canes or pea sticks.
- Prune forsythia, cutting out some of the old wood each year. Aim for a three-year cycle, so that within that time you have worked over the whole bush.
- Towards the end of the month, start to harden off annuals ready for planting out in May.
- Continue to sow hardy annuals outside where you want them to flower.
- Protect the new spears of hosta foliage against slugs.
- As hellebore flowers fade, new foliage starts pushing through from the base. Feed with a fertiliser high in potash at fortnightly intervals until mid June (not later, or growth will be too soft).

April

- Camellias may need picking over as they are reluctant to shed their flowers.
- Various forms of primroses and polyanthus can be split and replanted now in ground refreshed with bonemeal and compost.
- If necessary, prune grey-leaved shrubs such as artemisia, phlomis, senecio, sage, santolina and rue, cutting out any growth damaged by wind or frost.
- Summer-flowering heathers – types of calluna, daboecia and erica – can also be sheared over now, as new shoots are beginning to grow.
- Christmas amaryllis die down messily about this time of year. When the foliage has withered naturally, lay the pot and its bulb on its side to rest in an airy, dry place. In late autumn, repot the bulb and start it into growth again.
- Begonias can be planted in pots and hanging baskets inside before being set out in May.

Vegetables

- Plant well-sprouted early potatoes, setting them about 6 inches (15 centimetres) deep and twice that distance apart.
- Try an early sowing of lettuce and endive.
- Plant onion sets about 4 inches (10 centimetres) apart in rows 12 inches (30 centimetres) apart.
- Sow radish, mustard and cress, and more lettuce.
- Sow kohlrabi in shallow drills, thinning the seedlings later to give room for each plant to develop. They should be ready by July.
- For an early crop of French beans, sow seed indoors.
- Watch emerging pea crops carefully: they will be prone to attack from pigeons, rabbits, slugs and weasels.

Fruit

- Hoe carefully around raspberry canes to shift annual weeds. Do not delve too deep: raspberries are shallow-rooted.
- Remove and burn the grease bands put around fruit trees last autumn.
- Spread clean straw round strawberries and remove runners so that the plants concentrate on producing fruit.

Propagating

- ❧ Divide achillea, agapanthus, artemisia, arundinaria, carex, diascia, festuca, geranium, gunnera, heuchera, kniphofia, matteuccia, miscanthus, origanum, polygonum, sedum, sempervivum, stachys, tellima and tiarella.
- ❧ Take tip cuttings of abelia, acer, caryopteris, fuchsia, helichrysum and lavender.
- ❧ Set heather cuttings into individual small pots, using an ericaceous compost.
- ❧ Start to harden off cuttings of semi-tender shrubs in a cold frame if possible.
- ❧ Prick out seedlings of annuals as they develop their first true leaves, but keep them under cover.

Sgwyd yr Eira (Fall of Snow)

THE JOINED-UP GARDEN

I got married in the year of the casserole. We had eleven as wedding presents: French orange and black Swedish cast iron, Spanish terra-cotta, English stoneware, decorated Portuguese. I learned every stew recipe I could lay my hands on. We wallowed through osso bucco, drowned chickens of various kinds and anything with *boeuf* in its name. Even so, I was hard pressed to keep all the casseroles in full play.

Unfortunately, nobody gave us knives or forks, though we had half a dozen silver teaspoons. All our wedding money went on fitting out the Thames sailing barge *Falconet*, which was our first home; for the first eighteen months of our marriage, visitors brought their own eating irons with them.

After leaving the barge, it took a long time to put together anything resembling a domestic survival kit; even longer to accu-mulate any flotsam, the bits that join up the spaces between the bed, the table and the cooker and which make your house feel like home.

This is the way in gardens too. The basics in the garden are the major furnishings, the trees and shrubs that give bulk and perma-nence to the plot. A few shrubs are grand enough to stand in isolation, as a Queen Anne chest might. Most look better with a swirl of other plants around them.

Suppose one of your basics was a shrub rose. Most gardens have a rose, so this is a fairly safe bet. You may have sensibly chosen one of the Rugosa roses, which are trouble-free, as they never get black spot or mildew. They have masses of bright green foliage and good autumn hips. Let's say it is the white-flowered R. *rugosa* 'Alba', which comes out in June, large single papery flowers, each with a golden boss of stamens.

A useful piece of flotsam here would be catmint. There is a natural symbiosis between catmint and old roses. It is partly to do with colour. Catmint is a soft grey-green-blue that fits in well with the white and purplish pinks of these old roses.

Partly it is a matter of form and texture. Roses are usually fairly stiff and upright in growth. Catmint in comparison makes soft mounds of growth and the texture is matt. The foliage is good from spring, when it first appears, right up to the time of flowering and beyond. I like 'Six Hills Giant', which is a richly generous plant, but it requires room to grow at least 3 feet (1 metre) up as well as out. Best to plant it slightly to the side of, rather than directly under, a rose.

When the first addition is in place, there is an irresistible urge to go on adding. Perhaps you will have been to Sissinghurst and come back swooning about the white garden. You buy a handsome white phlox, carefully choosing one of the *Phlox maculata* types (perhaps 'Miss Lingard') rather than the more common *Phlox paniculata*. Why? Because it does not get nibbled by eelworm.

You plant the phlox in front of the rose and it does all that you hoped, flowering in luxuriant columns, rather than terminal pyramids. Usefully, it starts its act while the rose is resting. Even so, you begin to wonder whether white followed by white isn't a bit, well … limiting.

And you have been reading a book about foliage in the garden. You have been told you need some important leaves somewhere in what you are now thinking of as your composition. For leaves, read hostas. You fancy warming the scheme up a bit and decide on a goldish sort of hosta rather than a white variegated one. Because you are feeling impatient, you splash out on three hostas ('Fragrant Gold' or 'Lemon Lime') and plant them by the phlox.

The whole group swings instantly into a different mode. The warming happens. The balance shifts. Then you begin to worry about the first half of the year. The three bits of flotsam you have introduced will take you through summer, passing the baton from one to the other, but there is nothing there for spring.

Anemones are the answer, either the fat-stemmed, chubby 'de Caen' type or the earlier *Anemone nemorosa*. If you don't fancy anemones, think scilla, or chionodoxa. Planted in autumn, these will give you three months of spring flowers – white, pale blue, purple, pink, magenta, whatever you fancy.

All this is padding, but it is what converts a series of lonely shrub outposts into a setting that feels comfortable. The catmint and the phlox, the hostas and the anemones make a web which will reach out to touch other webs that you may weave round other pieces of basic shrub furniture. Before you know it, you will have a joined-up garden.

THE TONGARIRO CROSSING

The Tongariro Crossing is billed (in the *Lonely Planet* guide and elsewhere) as the greatest one-day walk in New Zealand. Set in the Tongariro National Park, south of Lake Taupo in the North Island, the walk takes you high up among the extinct volcano cones of Mt Tongariro (6,458 feet), Mt Ngauruhoe (7,515 feet) and Mt Ruapehu (9,175 feet). The peak of Ruapehu used to be permanently covered in snow until four years ago when it erupted in a spectacular fashion and put an abrupt end to skiing that year.

By chance, we had a free weekend when we were within gallop-
ing distance of the Tongariro Park. And the weather was settled.
That was important. The shuttle buses that deliver you to one end
of the walk and pick you up from the other, eleven miles on, won't
take passengers unless they think there's a reasonable chance of
them surviving the experience.

So at seven o'clock in the morning, loaded with water, chocolate
and three layers of clothes, we flagged down a shuttle bus. You pass
the end of the walk on your way to the beginning and the driver
pointed out what we needed to do. Aim for the shelter hut. Keep
away from the hot sulphur springs (a Maori sacred site) steaming
weirdly out of the bare slopes, and above all, avoid keeping him
waiting.

True, it is an extraordinary walk, through a moon-like landscape
where the ground is turquoise and yellow and bright mineral green.
You start gently, on low heather slopes with the saddle between two
peaks as your goal. The climb up the saddle, the Devil's Staircase,
is said to be the toughest part of the walk, but that depends on
whether you go better on the ups than the downs. I much prefer
climbing to sliding.

When you are high, you cover two extraordinary flat sections
across the centre of old volcanoes, swept bare by wind, colonised
only by pale, ghostly lichens clutching the ground. From the top,
the views are world-class: across to the milky blue of Lake Taupo,
and a spiky range of mountains on the opposite horizon. Wherever
you look in New Zealand there are mountains. That's why I liked it
so much.

The worst bit, I thought, was getting down a scree run, very
narrow with vertical drops either side into things you'd rather not
think about. It was like inching down the edge of a flapjack, the
ground crumbling and giving way in a shower of small avalanches
with each footstep. But gradually the bareness gave way to the first
spidery, tough clumps of grass, then alpine flowers – white gentians

balanced on shiny black rosettes of leaf. Lower down grew a scrub
layer of leptospermums carpeted underneath with celmisias. The
final descent (and the first bit of shade you see all day) was through
ancient, still podocarp forest, thick with sub-tropical ferns.

So a fine walk, but not the best we did. That was on Great Barrier
Island, where, unlike the Tongariro Crossing, which is now a motor-
way of a trail, full of young on their year off ticking off their Things
To Do, we saw not a soul all day.

Great Barrier sits to the east of Auckland, a couple of hours' ferry
ride away. You can fly there, but who would want to when there's
a boat tied up at Subritzky's quay in Auckland, loading up with
supplies? 'Hippy heaven!' explained an Auckland friend. 'Surfer's
paradise. Marijuana plots in the bush. A robust attitude to central
government.' He sounded quite nostalgic.

But it was too late in the season for surfers and we never stum-
bled across the marijuana, though we spent all our time in the bush.
Difficult not to, when 70 per cent of the island is covered in it. It's
administered by the Department of Conservation, who keep open
a series of superb trails, especially through the wild mountainous
country in the north of the island.

We started our best walk at a place called Windy Canyon on the
east coast, vast outcrops of rock and gulleys, a Cinemascope dream.
There's a slow climb along an open spine of land which leads the
way to the top of Mt Hobson, the tallest point on the island. As the
summit steepens you move into the shade of vast kauri trees, native
evergreens that first brought loggers here in the 1920s. They are
like cathedral pillars, all trunk and few branches, but the trunks
can be nine to twelve feet across. They are awesome trees. The long
descent brought us down seven hours later to the tiny harbour of
Port Fitzroy. As it happened our transport home was waiting somewhere else entirely. But on Great Barrier hiccups of that kind just
don't seem to matter. We still got back for a red snapper supper.
And PLENTY of wine.

FERN BRITAIN

The way people go on, you'd think that only one fern had ever been invented – the New Zealand tree fern. Yes, it's a handsome thing and just right for West Country coastal gardens where it can rear out of jungly rhododendrons and vast magnolias and give a fair impression of elsewhereness. Sometimes it works in town gardens too. Much depends on the skill of the planter. It's one of the top three plants likely to be chosen for the kind of in-your-face exotic urban space that goes with lots of glass and metal. The other two of course are the banana and the phormium or New Zealand flax.

The problem is that the kind of tree fern urban trendies want is likely to have been very expensive. They are priced by the amount of bare trunk under the fronds – the taller the trunk (which isn't actually a proper trunk at all) the more expensive the fern. There are practical advantages in having a tall one. You can plant underneath it, or place it at the edge of a deck so the fronds sway over your breakfast table. A tall tree fern provides shade and makes use of air-space that is perhaps less cluttered than space on the ground.

But the temptation, if you've paid a couple of hundred pounds for a plant, is to put it in a very prominent position, so you get the most out of what you've paid for. Ferns actually work best when they are not in the limelight. They are stars, of course, but subtle ones. They draw you in quietly, work on you modestly. A tree fern is fantastic when you come upon it unexpectedly, not so good on its own in glaring light where it looks as though it has been accidentally dropped by a passing auk.

They are expensive because the trunks, or not-trunks, take a long time to develop. They are built up gradually from the stems of the fronds. Each spring, gardeners cut off the old, battered leaves, but the base of each stem remains and gradually these fuse together

into a hairy column from which the new fronds draw their sustenance. These ferns don't have roots like other ferns, which is why
it has been so easy for importers to fly them in from the other side
of the world.

Ecologically, of course, it's better to buy home-grown ferns, but
some nurserymen with expensive goods to sell will tell you that
British-grown tree ferns never develop trunks. That's not true. It
just takes time. The first tree fern I ever had came from a garden in
Cornwall, where they self-seeded all over the place. The gardener
whipped a seedling out of a dry-stone wall, I potted it up at home
and now it has a trunk nearly 24 inches (60 centimetres) tall (and is
still in a pot, though not the same one as it started in).

The way the trunk is built up dictates the way it needs to be
looked after. The fern doesn't pull moisture up from the ground as
efficiently as a plant with roots does. You need to keep the central
column moist and I do this by emptying a can of water over the
fern's head from time to time. The ribs of the fronds collect water
and channel it down to the centre, where the dark brown hairs on
the old dead stems absorb it like moss. But if you've got a very tall
tree fern and can't reach its head easily, then hosing the trunk down
from time to time will allow it to absorb the moisture it needs to
develop its vast and beautiful leaves.

Last autumn I acquired two more tree ferns, British-grown,
at a very modest price (£4.50). They are planted in ivy behind a
holly hedge, under the canopy of an oak, both of which I hope will
protect them from frost. But I put them there too because the path
that passes that way is at a much higher level. Looking down into the
crown of a big fern is one of May's great pleasures and this month
the ferns have been fantastic, flipping themselves open in a series of
acrobatic moves more beautiful than any Olympic gymnast could
devise.

For a gardener, ferns are not demanding creatures. You need
to think a bit about suiting plant to place (frothy adiantums will

cope with dry berths, osmundas won't) but after that there's only one thing you need to do and even that is for your benefit rather than the plant's. You must cut off the old fern fronds before the new ones start to uncurl. It's almost too late to do it in May (how maddening it is to be told that – sorry) but you can always do it next year. The particular way ferns unfold themselves, slowly building a fountain of foliage, is far more beautiful to watch if your eye is not distracted by the weather-beaten fronds of the previous year. This is particularly true of dryopteris, the male fern, a British native that occasionally goes mad and produces fronds with crazy bunches at the end, or with double the amount of leaflets.

I'm not quite sure how it happened, but I seem to have nine different kinds of dryopteris in the garden, none more dramatic than *Dryopteris wallichiana*, a native of Hawaii, Mexico, Jamaica and other places that might make you wonder whether it would survive a British winter. But miraculously, it does.

I'm so mad about it there are now three big groups of it in the garden, one in a wild bit, where it grows with leucojum and ivy, another lot planted under the big arching branches of *Rubus tridel* 'Benenden', which has been flowering since the middle of May, and a third group strutting its stuff with thalictrum and the tall, sword-leaved *Iris orientalis*, an iris that actually prefers damp soil. The midribs are as hairy as a monkey's arm and at this early stage, the fronds are an almost luminous yellow-green. Full grown, they can be 4 feet (120 centimetres) long. Some groups are more shaded than others and each catches the light in a different way. This is important with ferns. Some will do in bright light, but the mystery of dappled shade gives them much greater allure. And if you have the chance to plant some of your ferns (particularly the vase-shaped ones such as *Matteuccia struthiopteris*) so you see them against the light, the drama increases considerably.

They are good mixers: Solomon's seal, primroses, snowdrops, irises such as *I. orientalis* or 'Gerald Derby', arums of all kinds, arisaemas, cyclamen, *Euphorbia robbiae*, hostas (but not too beefy), lily-of-the-valley and smyrnium all look good with ferns. Having done a quick count, I find I've planted twenty-five different sorts and that's not counting all the native ferns that were here before we arrived. Somehow I feel it's not going to stop there. They've drawn me into their net.

SAVING FOR A RAINY DAY

When water was a public utility, as it still is on our Monopoly board, you felt you ought to do something to help in a drought: put a brick in your loo, cut down the amount of showers you took, rig up some system to save rainwater, even siphon off the bath water to reuse on the flower borders. Privatisation has changed that. While those who run the water companies pay themselves so handsomely for wasting a billion gallons of water a year in leakages, you feel less inclined to help them with their problems.

Nor am I especially impressed by the fact that Brighton and Hove council (and other authorities in the south-east) say they will not be providing their usual displays of flowers in summer. Saving water is the spin, as it is with hotels that tell you they're not going to change your sheets or towels. But would either be doing it, if it weren't also saving them money to waste elsewhere?

In the UK, we've been through the drought scenario several times: in the summer of 1976, when environmentalists were predicting the end of the world as we know it, and in the spring of 1997, which was preceded, as the spring of 2006 was, by an unusually dry winter. In some parts of Britain the fifteen months since the beginning of 2005 have been the driest since 1933. In our garden, as it happens, winter rain stopped play with its usual muddy frequency.

But if gardening teaches you anything, it is the importance of the long rather than the short view. The long view on drought is that, compared with Somalia, we don't know what it means. That said, there are plenty of things gardeners can do to help their plants through hose-pipe bans and prolonged spells of dry weather. The crux of the matter is the soil. If you get the soil right, the plants will look after themselves.

On thin, fast-draining ground, the more bulky stuff you can get into the ground, the better it will be able to hang on to what moisture there is. Think of compost, muck, leaf mould as blotting paper. Soil needs organic matter like this. Nature keeps trying to provide it, but we, as gardeners, keep clearing it away. The easy way to get blotting-paper bulk back into the soil is to lay on thick blankets of mulch through the autumn and winter when the soil is damper than at other times of the year and then let the worms drag it into the soil for you. Getting the soil in good condition is the single most important thing that gardeners can do to combat drought.

We should also ask ourselves whether it's our fault or the water companies' that April-planted trees and shrubs die for lack of water. Until the advent of garden centres with their container-grown plants, the general time for planting trees and shrubs was the autumn. It is still the best time. Most trees and shrubs are dormant then, although roots continue growing until the turn of the year, when the soil temperature drops.

With no top hamper to worry about, plants can concentrate on getting their roots sorted out, getting the browsing and sluicing systems in place before spring, when everything happens at once. Transpiring through their leaves, newly planted trees and shrubs can lose water faster than they can find it, because their roots haven't had a chance to make close contact with surrounding soil. In cold seasons, you can get away with spring planting because things are held back, leaves emerge later than they usually do.

One huge advantage of autumn planting is that, at that season, you can buy bare-rooted trees and shrubs, dug from open ground, which will have far better root systems than anything grown in a pot. Well-developed roots, snuffling about in well-cared-for soil, is a plant's best defence against drought.

Container-grown plants are generally raised in soilless compost, which creates another potential problem. After their easy life in the open texture of a soilless compost, roots may not be prepared to attack the real stuff. They wander about in the increasingly crowded and starved confines of the pot-shaped bit of compost you have planted and fail to develop a system capable of keeping up with the rate of growth on top. But if they have never been used to the easy life, they won't miss it.

The most common casualties of drought are camellias, azaleas and rhododendrons planted in tubs. That's scarcely surprising. These acid-loving shrubs have surprisingly compact rootballs. That isn't a problem if they are growing – as nature intended them to be – in a woodland setting. There, a mulch of thick leaf litter prevents moisture evaporating from the ground. Overhead trees provide shade and shelter so sun and wind do not dry out the foliage of shrubs growing underneath. Perhaps we should ask ourselves whether we should be risking the lives of such shrubs by growing them in containers, rather than complaining when they die.

Garden makeover merchants treat flowers like scatter cushions to be strewn here and there where the colours will make a good photo opportunity for the next television camera that happens to be passing through. If they die, as they tend to when their owner's requirements are put before their own, no matter; there are more to be had at the garden centre. Garden centres market plants like cans of beans. But gardeners don't have to treat them the same way.

Plants in pots, hanging baskets, Gro-bags or other unnatural places will always need more water than plants in open ground. But a loam-based compost such as John Innes will hang on to moisture and nutrients better than a soilless one. They are not as popular with gardeners because they are much heavier to hump about. If you live three floors up in a building without a lift, that matters. If you don't, use loam-based compost for your containers. Water retaining granules help too. Remember that a pot in full sun will dry out faster than a pot in a shady situation.

Home-grown vegetables suffer in a drought too. This is partly because of the fashion for raised beds, which dry out faster than flat ground. Partly too, it's because tradition dictates that we grow vegetables in rows with a lot of bare soil either side. Bare soil dries out much faster than soil covered with the leaves of plants. This sounds paradoxical, when you think of the amount of water plants take up from the soil. But it's true, as you will know if, during this dry spring, you have slipped your hand under a fat clump of ground-hugging pulmonaria and felt the cool, moist soil underneath.

Broadcast seed, rather than sow it in rows; when vegetables such as lettuces, peas and courgettes are well established, plant marigolds and nasturtiums to blanket the ground round them. Buy a water butt. Buy several. And ponder on the fact that for gardeners, the lack of rain may be an inconvenience, but it is not a disaster, as it is for farmers who have fields full of lambs and no grass to put in front of them.

DROUGHTBUSTERS
Add organic matter to the soil.
Mulch.
Plant trees and shrubs in autumn, not spring.
In containers, use loam-based compost and water-retaining granules.
Match plants to positions.
Soak container-grown plants before planting.
Buy a rainwater butt.

SQUASH CLUB

May is mayhem for vegetable growers. So much stuff needs to be sown, including the crops that will keep you going through autumn and winter: beetroot, autumn and winter cabbage, calabrese, carrots, cauliflower, chicory, kale, salsify, scorzonera, turnips, and the best of them all – pumpkins and squashes. 'Squash never fail to reach maturity,' wrote the American humorist S. J. Perelman. 'You can spray them with acid, beat them with sticks and burn them; they love it.' That kind of dogged determination is an endearing characteristic in a plant. Since you will have to work hard to prevent squashes and pumpkins from growing, you can divert your energy to the question of choice. Which members of this staggeringly varied family – apricot, orange, yellow, green, ivory, or a mesmeric metallic pewter-grey – would you most like to look at this summer?

Choice becomes easier if you divide the family into three different categories. Summer squashes, which include the flat, frilled patty pans, do not store well. Winter squashes such as the beautiful polished blue-green 'Crown Prince' should store right through the winter if the skins are well cured. Pumpkins, which include 'Dill's Atlantic Giant' – at 1,005 pounds the world's heaviest vegetable – will also keep if they are allowed to ripen fully on the vine before they are picked.

Some of the larger pumpkins have the lopsided look of quietly deflating beach balls. Others, like the warty 'New England Blue', bulge intemperately in the middle, tapering off either end like a balloon (there is one in every pack) that won't blow up. 'Marina di Chioggia', striped in grey and sage green, looks just like the streetwise headgear worn by the Capulet gang in *Romeo and Juliet*. Others are avant-garde artworks, customised in patches of apricot and husk-coloured beige.

In essence, growing a pumpkin or squash is much like growing a marrow or courgette. All are members of the same big group, the cucurbits, but some types such as the *Cucurbita moschata* varieties 'Butternut' and 'Harrier' like more heat than others. As with courgettes, you can't put the plants outside until the end of May when temperatures begin to rise.

You can start seeds off in May in pots inside, either on a windowsill or in a greenhouse, setting a single seed on its edge in a 2½ -inch (7-centimetre) pot of compost. Cover the pots with clingfilm and keep them at a temperature of 60–65°F (15–18°C) until the seeds have germinated. This should take no more than a week. The trick is not to get the compost too wet. If you do, the seeds rot.

Later this month, in sheltered spots, you can also sow direct into the ground, setting a jam jar over each seed both to act as a mini-greenhouse and to protect them from mice. Choose an open, sunny site in ground that is rich, well fed but also well drained. Pumpkins and squashes grow most happily where the soil is slightly acid to neutral. Set the plants at least 3 feet (1 metre) apart and away from less robust crops which they may smother.

Most pumpkins and squashes grow on big, trailing stems that may be more than 16 feet (5 metres) long; the well-flavoured pumpkin 'Jack be Little' grows on a more compact plant. In a small plot, the modest fruits of cultivars such as 'Sweet Lightning', the patty pan squash 'Sunburst' or the compact trailing 'Rolet-Gem', which has apple-sized fruits with buttery, firm flesh, will be easier to accommodate than 'Atlantic Giant', a pumpkin that is big enough to take Cinderella to the ball. You can train them over arbours, arches or wigwams of wooden poles, but choose types with smallish fruit. No wigwam will be able to stand the weight of an 'Atlantic Giant' with the bit between its teeth.

Some cultivars, such as 'Sunburst', a very productive bright yellow patty pan squash, and various other scallop and crookneck squashes, should be eaten as soon as they have developed in summer.

Winter squash and Halloween pumpkins mature more slowly and need to be 'cured' in the sun to harden their skins if they are to store successfully under cover through the winter. I especially like the nutty-tasting 'Uchiki Kuri', which has pear-shaped fruit ripening to dark orange. Some nurseries can supply organically grown young plants of this variety for delivery in late May.

Once planted, most of this tribe can be left to their own devices. They will easily smother weeds and their leaves shade the earth so that it does not dry out as quickly as open ground. Butternut squashes sometimes grow masses of leaf and stem but are reluctant to set fruit. Curb this tendency by pinching out the growing tips of the shoots when they've got to about 4 feet (120 centimetres). Butternuts, which do much of their growing at the end of summer, need a long, warm autumn to produce decent fruit. In the States, you see young plants sitting in the middle of low stockades of mounded-up earth, each circle about 3 feet (1 metre) across. The low earth walls stop water running off in all directions when you empty a can over a plant.

In the States too, you often see pumpkins and squashes grown in conjunction with sweetcorn, the long trailing growths winding their way through the tall stems of the corn. This is an economical way to use ground and the combination looks good too. Tomatoes, securely staked, would make an equally good companion crop. Both need sun.

Given the right conditions, pumpkins, once set, fatten up prodigiously fast. They can put on half a kilo a day without even thinking about it, a weight watcher's nightmare, a champion vegetable grower's dream. The yield will depend on the type of pumpkin or squash that you are growing. The little scallopinis or patty pans such as the super-productive 'Sunburst' or 'Yellow Bird' should be cut when they are no more than 5 inches (13 centimetres) across. Cut the summer squashes to use as you need them. Dry off the winter pumpkins until the skins are hard and the fruit sounds hollow when you tap it. Store pumpkins and squashes in a cool, frost-free shed until you need them.

An old book I have says rather intriguingly that young shoots of pumpkin, gathered in summer, are an excellent substitute for asparagus. I've never tried that, but I have successfully toasted seeds scraped from the innards. Clean the seeds off in a sieve under a running tap, let them dry and then spread them out on a baking sheet. Sprinkle them lightly with salt and bake them for about twenty minutes at 190°C/375°F/Gas Mark 5.

CHELSEA SCRUM

For most of the year, Chelsea is a football club. But for one brief, hallucinatory week in May, it becomes a flower show. Since 1913, the Royal Horticultural Society has commandeered the eleven-acre grounds of the Royal Hospital in Chelsea (home of the red-coated Chelsea Pensioners) and filled them with roses and rhododendrons, tents and tea parties. The point of it is its sameness, though within living memory the RHS has introduced a brand-new floral marquee, all extruded aluminium and bright white polyester, in place of the old canvas marquee that had been in use for the last fifty years. It was a great cause for alarm among the old guard, for whom the Chelsea Flower Show is still the first event of The Season. The old tent has been cut up to make 'useful gardening products, stylish garments and outdoor living accessories'. The quote comes from the company that is producing these 'highly valued and collectable pieces'. Poor tent. After outstanding service, it's an undignified end.

'But what's the Chelsea Flower Show for?' asked a Texan friend, who had never heard of it. That depends on who you are. The ruling body of the RHS has always been a bizarre coalition of nobs and nurserymen. From the beginning, the nurserymen used Chelsea as a showcase. The nobs came to London with their head gardeners, made a leisurely tour of the show, and placed orders with the nurserymen for delphiniums, lupins and roses to decorate the herbaceous borders.

But now the nobs ARE the nurserymen and the herbaceous borders have been chased over the horizon by hordes of tropical cannas and bananas in a new enthusiasm for the exotic garden. But some things stay horribly the same, notably the humourless pretension of the flower arranging tent. Here, tortured creations draped in chiffon bear as much relation to the garden as a plastic ketchup bottle. Flower arrangers always refer to flowers as 'material'. They never talk about this sumptuous peony, that scented rose, those wildly suggestive iris. The material has to be 'conditioned', then prodded, pushed and poked in the bossiest possible way to produce arrangements which attract the longest queues in the whole of the show. That must mean that for a large proportion of the 170,000 visitors allowed in each day, Chelsea is about flower arranging.

For the sponsors who underwrite the cost of installing the show gardens – there are usually up to two dozen of them and they are a great feature of the show – Chelsea is about exposure. Sometimes kudos. In the days when newspaper proprietors were also nobs, a great many national papers sponsored show gardens. Now only the *Telegraph* is left in the ring. That is a pity. The newspaper gardens are often the best because they attract top designers. They like the freedom of making a garden that does not have to incorporate the sponsor's product.

Charities have stepped in where newspapers are fading out. Chelsea is a high-profile event and gardeners, by and large, a charitable crowd. Help the Aged has been there, neatly reflecting the RHS membership profile. St Bartholemew's Hospital has been there too, with a Bart's City Lifesaver garden, symbolising 'the chaotic rhythm of the heart during a cardiac arrest'. That's one I'll miss. I garden to escape from chaotic rhythms, not to seek them out.

I think the point of the Chelsea Flower Show is its eclecticism. Even in their new, extruded aluminium disguise, the RHS could never be accused of being modish. Paradoxically, I think this is a great strength. At the show you will find gardens targeted at the most exquisitely tuned Sloane cheek-by-jowl with gardens from the outer reaches of Dunroaminland. You can lurch away from the magnificent tropical splendour of Anmore Exotics, where every plant looks as though it has been dreamed up by Walt Disney, straight into the chaste embrace of the delicate, ancient bonsai shown by Peter Chan of Lingfield, Surrey.

You can buy tractors or terracotta pots. You can sit in the sun twirling an ice cream cone. You can eavesdrop on abstruse conversations about plant genealogy. Nobs, particularly, are as interested in a plant's antecedents as they are in their own, and the rhododendron fanciers are always good value in this respect. Chelsea reminds us that gardening is about more than makeovers. It strengthens and reaffirms a commitment to more ancient values: continuity and renewal.

Tasks for the Month

General

ஆ Be patient with any shrubs you think may have been killed over winter. They may yet show signs of life.

ஆ This is a good time to attack ground elder with a weedkiller based on glyphosate: it is said to be most susceptible just as the leaves have unfurled. More than one application may be needed.

ஆ Mulching will keep down the population of easy annual weeds such as meadowgrass and groundsel.

ஆ If May is warm, greenfly multiply fast. If the ladybirds are not keeping up, spray with a specific insecticide.

Flowers

ஆ Tie in new growths of rambling roses, so that they do not lash about.

ஆ Sow perennials for flowering next year. *Aquilegia alpina* is a fairly dwarf columbine with flowers of a particularly good blue. Sow seed about a quarter of an inch (5 millimetres) deep in a seedbed outside. Plant out in late summer for flowers next spring.

ஆ Continue to clear wallflowers and tulips from tubs and beds to make room for the next plantings.

ஆ Thin out seedlings of hardy annuals that you have sown direct outside.

ஆ Continue to sow annuals such as Shirley poppy, love-in-a-mist, night-scented stock, clarkia and cornflower outside where they are to flower.

ஆ Replant windowboxes and hanging baskets with plants for summer. It should now be safe to put fuchsias and pelargoniums outside in containers.

ஆ Prune wall-trained chaenomeles after it has finished flowering, cutting back each of the previous season's growths to within two or three buds.

ஆ Tie in new growths of solanum.

ஆ Plant out young plants of *Eccremocarpus scaber* at the foot of a sunny wall and give them something to scramble up.

ஆ Trim hedges of *Berberis darwinii* as soon as the flowers are over.

ஆ Sow biennials (such as Canterbury bell, verbascum and wallflower) and perennials (such as aquilegia, lupin, oriental poppy and delphinium) in drills outside.

ஆ Seed of viola, pansies and different forms of primrose and polyanthus can

May

also be sown outside now for transplanting later. Choose a shady spot for these.

- Nip out weak growths in congested clumps of delphiniums.
- Sift fresh soil or compost over clumps of saxifrage to fill in any dead patches.
- Continue to deadhead daffodils, but do not cut away foliage, however untidy, until it dies down naturally.
- Lilies will benefit from a mulch of leaf mould or compost to keep the roots cool. Those in pots will need a weekly feed.

Vegetables

- Set celery plants in trenches, in the bottom of which you should have put plenty of muck, covered by soil. Plants should be about 12 inches (30 centimetres) apart in staggered double rows about 9 inches (23 centimetres) apart down the sides of the trench.
- Sow sweetcorn in a warm, sheltered spot outside. Plant the seeds in a square block in a grid pattern about 18 inches (45 centimetres) apart each way. This helps with pollination.
- Start to earth up early potatoes. Finish planting maincrop potatoes.
- Make further sowings of lettuce, radish and cress.
- Sow maincrop peas and set up pea sticks, netting or some other support for well-advanced early peas.
- Set out plants of broccoli and curly kale.
- Watch out for blackfly homing in on broad beans and pinch out the tips of the plants if they settle.
- Outdoor cucumbers and courgettes can be started off in small pots inside at the beginning of the month. Sow seeds two to a pot and cover with plastic film and paper until the seedlings emerge. Pluck out the weaker of the two seedlings if both have germinated.
- Seed of outdoor tomatoes such as 'Red Alert' and 'Tornado' can also be started off inside at the beginning of the month.

Fruit

- Thin out raspberry canes if suckers are growing very thickly.
- Thin the fruit on peaches and apricots, leaving roughly one fruit for each foot of branch.

❧ Cordon fruit trees, like espaliers and fans, have a habit of throwing out shoots where you do not want them. Pinch out any that are pointing directly into the wall or that are too close together.

Propagating

❧ Make layers of cornus, corylopsis, cotinus, ivy, magnolia and parthenocissus.
❧ Take tip cuttings of abutilon, ceratostigma, cotinus, fuchsia and lilac.
❧ Gradually harden off trays of bedding plants before setting them out.
❧ Plant out well-rooted cuttings of silver-leaved and semi-tender shrubs to grow on in a nursery plot.

A garden in the cathedral close

HOPPING MAD

There was a moment earlier this month when I thought we were almost getting there – that the garden looked knitted together, settled. I walked out early one morning, cup of coffee in fist, to do what gardeners like doing best, mooching about with no particular end in view. I stopped to admire plants I'd forgotten I had, tweaked off the odd dead head, pulled out the odd bit of bitter cress (we've had a bitter cress campaign running since early spring so the stuff doesn't haunt and taunt me in the way it used to).

The old-fashioned pinks grown from cuttings I brought with me from the old garden had spread into big grey mats, full of hundreds of fat buds. The violas ('Spider', 'Belmont Blue') bought earlier in the year from Elizabeth MacGregor of the Ellenbank nursery in Kirkcudbrightshire had spread into deliciously thick clumps and were flowering their heads off. The summer bulbs – blue triteleia, hanging heads of *Allium cernuum* – had successfully pushed their way through the rather denser plantings of spring-flowering species tulips and crocus and were showing masses of bud.

These, together with the black flowers of *Iris chrysographes*, grey lamb's ear, the sprawling arms of *Euphorbia myrsinites*, variegated thyme and self-seeded forget-me-not, fill up the front edge of the flower garden, directly alongside the stone path that we made to snake up the bank. Behind, this year, are clouds of love-in-a-mist, grown from seed I chucked late last summer over the gravelled patch where the yellow *Tulipa sylvestris* grow (I don't want anything too heavy there, so the warmth of the sun can get through to the bulbs underground). Further up the bank are even bigger patches of *Orlaya grandiflora*, which I sowed at the end of August last year. Seed germinates quickly and you can prick out the babies into individual pots and set them out in autumn, by which time they are already sturdy, bright plants.

From a late summer sowing, they are in flower by May before the cow-parsleyish *Ammi majus* which I sowed at the same time. I like orlaya better than ammi. The foliage is more interesting, light and feathery, and the white flowers, in heads about 3 inches (8 centimetres) across, much more intriguing. Each one is strangely lopsided with six big petals ranged round one half and a cluster of little ones round the other. Anyway, it was good to see them fully grown and I liked the way they were spreading to take over the space where the tall bearded iris were coming to an end.

But this week I went out (turn quickly to another page if you can't stand sad endings) and found all the pinks scissored off, the flowers lying all over the path. The violas had been nibbled down to the ground, the tops bitten off the triteleias and the alliums. Rabbits. I'd seen them in the garden, a young litter it looked like, playing around on the lawn in front of the house, but there's plenty of grass for them, and fields and fields of wild flowers all around. We have so many wild things in the garden, the odd rabbit hasn't seemed a problem. Until now.

The problem with rabbits is that they are like a fox in a henhouse. Once they start, they can't stop. If they'd actually eaten all the flowers they'd bitten off, it would somehow have been easier to take. But the delinquent vandalism of their actions enraged me. So they upset me on two counts: first, that I lost so many of the things that were going to sustain the garden (and me) through the summer; second, that they made me feel so aggressive. I've always supposed myself deeply pacifist, upset by violence in any form. Now I find myself hurling stones, the old horseshoes lined up on the outside wall, gumboots, trowels, whenever a rabbit comes into view. And there's another source of irritation. I can't find the trowels afterwards.

Too late, I covered as many of the poor, shorn plants as I could with openwork bamboo cloches (you can get them from Andrew Crace, www.andrewcrace.com) but the rabbits just moved on to the next line of plants and massacred the orlaya and the love-in-a-mist, absent-mindedly beheading the last of the iris while they were at it. Later, I discovered that a splinter group had worked their way along the front of my hut where I have more than fifty pots of bulbs growing on. Nearly all the lilies had been bitten off, the buds lying wilted on the ground; all the roscoeas (four different sorts) had been similarly attacked as had big pots of the dainty gladiolus 'Robinette'.

Ecofundamentalists seem very sure that we must only have native plants (rhododendron, giant hogweed, kill, kill, kill) to satisfy the discriminating palates of our wildlife. But the wildlife itself is evidently not convinced. Why are these wretched rabbits shunning our unimproved pastures full of succulent mixed grasses, gourmet dandelions, pignut, melting sow thistle, and feasting on hybrid pinks and violas instead? I wouldn't mind them in the garden if they helped with the weeding from time to time – a patch of groundsel here, a morsel of fat hen there – but their targets are cruelly chosen.

With a heavy heart, I turned to Graham Stuart Thomas's list of rabbit-proof plants (it's in his *Perennial Garden Plants*, 1990). Alchemilla (yawn), bergenia (never in a million years), cortaderia (I'm not that desperate), malva (coarse beyond bearing), sedum (oh help – I'm saving that for my nineties). No – I'm being unfair. There are some superb plants in the list. I've obviously got to get more of them: crinum, helianthus, epimedium, peony.

And perhaps the natural balance that at the moment seems weighted so heavily in favour of the rabbits will yet redress itself. This morning I walked out of the door and saw a peregrine falcon sitting close by on the gatepost. As soon as he saw me, of course, he was off, curling and curving at amazing speed in a low circle over the yard before speeding down the valley. Will he stay? What will the buzzards and the ravens, so long entrenched, think of him? My bird book says that pigeons are the peregrine's favourite food. But perhaps, just as the rabbits have tuned their palates to favour garden plants, the peregrine too will come to think that a young, fat rabbit might make a splendid breakfast.

COURSON

Style. Exuberance. Verve. Pzazz. I'm talking about the Journées des Plantes de Courson, a kind of gardening fair, held in the grounds of a comfortably sized chateau, twenty-two miles south of Paris. The house belongs to the extended family of Helene Fustier. She and her wildly animated husband, Patrice, arrange the event, which is not quite a show, in the sense that we use the word, but very much more than a plant sale. There is a spring fair, held in mid May, and another one in autumn.

Enterprising English nurserymen have been going there for several years. So have some classy makers of garden furniture and artefacts, such as Humphrey Bowden of Tillington, near Petworth, who was showing off fountains carved in the shape of giant plants. Cravens Nursery of West Yorkshire took fabulous auriculas, just right to show off in a Paris apartment. Since the French seem happy to spend three times as much on a plant as an English gardener would, many English nurserymen return each year.

The atmosphere is laid-back, but it is the kind of laid-back that comes from attention to detail and an enormous amount of planning. Everything works. The chateau at Courson is set in a park, laid out in a way which the French call 'le style anglais', but which isn't really English at all. They choose and place their trees quite differently from us. Around the house are courtyards and barns and cart sheds with wide parkland beyond, all enclosed by stands of magnificent horse chestnuts. During the Courson Journées, stalls are laid out in the buildings, although most are in the park, either in the open or sheltered by white canvas booths.

The first thing you notice is that the French like to buy their plants BIG. Forget plastic carrier bags. Here there are porters with trolleys to wheel sold plants from stalls to car. I watched one of them transferring a rhododendron in full flower to the car park. It was beautifully rootballed in sacking and at least 5 feet (1½ metres) high and wide. The porter eased it over the bumpy grass more carefully than if he had been pushing his grandmother.

One woman was staggering towards the car park with a climbing rose at least 12 feet (4 metres) tall, pink, in full flower, and swathed round with polythene sheeting. She looked as though she was about to toss the caber in some Highland Games, hands locked underneath the pot, face completely lost behind the bulk of the rose's stems. High over her shoulder, the flowers waved to passers-by.

We can do shows very well in England. We can do plant sales too. We can certainly provide settings that might match Courson. But I haven't ever been to an event in England that had the *joie de vivre* there seemed to be at Courson. Nor such good coffee.

The French are much keener on pruning and shaping and training trees and shrubs than we are. You notice this particularly with wisterias, which are rarely shown by English nurserymen grown on a single stem as standards. Many of the ones on display at Courson had been grown this way, the heads beautifully pruned and balanced.

Plant names, of course, are the same wherever you are, botanical Latin constituting a kind of Esperanto which is as easily understood at Courson as it would be in Harrogate or Berlin. Variety names, too, stay the same. At Établissements Cayeux, the inky iris 'Study in Black' did not suddenly become 'Études en Noir'.

In the old stables, orchids dazzled the swallows, who were trying to get on with a spot of nest-building. Spinning over the heads of the visitors, they wove in and out of the rafters like skiers on a slalom, round and round the paphiopedilums, in and out the cattleyas of Vacherot and Lecoufle, the elegant Île-de-France nursery that filled the mangers along one whole side of the stables with their orchids. So if you have time to spare in May or October, head for Courson.

CLEMATIS DILEMMAS

If I was starting again (dread words) I would plant only late-flowering clematis on a pergola, or indeed anywhere else where the clematis was likely to mix itself up with a rose that needed pruning. On paper, the idea of having early, mid season and late flowering clematis on the pergola seemed sound. It would extend the flowering season – something that gardening correspondents are always going on about, even to themselves.

As I tenderly planted April flowering *Clematis macropetala* to surge through the rose 'Easlea's Golden Rambler', as I swathed the incumbent solanum with fresh tendrils of the May-flowering clematis 'The President', I did not realise what complications I was making for myself. Both clematises have gone mad. But the solanum has now died and is impossible to extricate from its suit of borrowed clothes and I can't fight my way through the enveloping blankets of *C. macropetala* to prune the rose when I need to.

If I had planted just late-flowering types of *C. viticella*, all the clematis could have been cut down close to the ground in February and the way would be clear for me to get in and do whatever work was necessary on the host shrubs.

But I didn't. So the solanum will have to stay until some disaster hits the clematis too, when I can get both out of the way and start afresh. It's difficult, though, to limit yourself – even in one part of the garden – to one season of flowering, given a family such as the clematis which can provide flowers in almost any month of the year.

The season starts with creamy-yellow, freckled *C. cirrhosa*, often in bloom by February. It's not such a thug as *C. armandii*, which flowers through March and April. Both those are evergreen, unlike the glorious spring-flowering kinds derived from *C. macropetala* and *C. alpina*. Flowers get bigger as the season advances, so you end up in midsummer with dinner plates such as mid-blue 'General Sikorski' and dark red 'Niobe'. By August and September, when the viticellas are at their best, the flower size has shrunk. In many situations, this is an advantage. Scent is heaviest in the autumn-flowering kinds such as white *C. flammula*, and *C. rehderiana*, which smells of cowslips.

The time of flowering to a great extent governs how you should prune your clematis. An enormous fuss is made about this subject. Some gardeners thoroughly enjoy fussing, so rather than deprive them of hours of profitable worry, I recommend a week with a good book.

In terms of pruning, clematis fall into three categories: those that need none, those that need a light touch and those that respond to butchering. The 'none' option, of course, is the easiest and it is worth remembering that a clematis will not die from lack of pruning. It may flower less than it otherwise would. It may flower at gutter rather than at eye level. But it will not keel over just because you and your flashing Felcos have not been near it.

You need never prune the earliest flowering clematis, such as delicate types 'Frances Rivis' and her friends, vigorous *C. armandii*, *C. macropetala* and the popular *C. montana*, though both this and

C. armandii may need cutting back if they are bullying other plants. If you want to reduce their spread, prune them immediately after flowering. Otherwise leave them alone. I don't prune the yellow autumn-flowering *C. tangutica* either, though some people treat it as a group 3 (hard-pruned) type. Ours mounds itself over a wall, flowers magnificently with no attention, so it gets none.

If clematis do need pruning, then do it in February. Subjects for light pruning include the popular 'Nelly Moser' (mauve with a lilac bar), 'Barbara Jackman', 'Lasurstern' and 'The President', all of which are out at the moment. Light pruning means taking out dead, weak or scraggy-looking stems entirely and cutting the rest of the stems back to the first strong pair of buds you can find. These will already be showing themselves plainly by the end of February.

The clematis that need the toughest treatment are those that flower in the second half of summer: the beautiful purple 'Jackmanii Superba', mauve-pink 'Comtesse de Bouchaud', sky-blue 'Perle d'Azur' and the viticellas (my favourites), such as reddish 'Abundance' and deep purple 'Royal Velours'.

All these should be cut back hard to within 12 inches (30 centi-metres) or so of the ground. This is cathartic and gives you an opportunity each year to train properly and tie in the fresh stems and avoid an unholy tangle of growth. At the same time you can mulch all your clematis with compost or manure to keep the soil moist and the roots cool.

More important than pruning, though, is the position in which you plant your clematis. By nature, clematis are scramblers; they have no means by which they can stick themselves to supports. They are, however, beautifully equipped for hoisting themselves through some other growing thing and this is how they look best. A clematis plant is not in itself a thing of beauty. It has no particular form. Its flowers are its only *raison d'être*.

As it has naturally evolved as a scrambler, clematis thrives best with its feet in the shade and its head in the sun. Grown through some host such as ceanothus or viburnum, these conditions occur without much effort on your part. 'Mrs Cholmondeley', threading its way through an April-flowering ceanothus, will keep decently out of the limelight until the ceanothus has finished its display and then quietly take over a starring role in late May and June. Or you could use the greenish-white *C. florida* 'Alba Plena' with a summer-flowering ceanothus.

Half a dozen little interferences in spring is all it takes to persuade a clematis to range experimentally over a wide area rather than bunch its stems all together in a single matted twist. 'Jackmanii Superba', an especially vigorous variety with sumptuous velvety blooms of deep purple, responds particularly well to this gentle nudging. I have it on a south wall of the house where it wanders among the wisteria. A bush of rue, a peony and other neighbours prevent the sun from shining too hotly on the clematis roots. A thick mulch of muck in late spring also provides insulation – and food, for if the clematis is sharing space with a host shrub, it is also sharing food and drink. Make sure there is plenty of both.

'Jackmanii Superba' is quite happy with this south aspect. 'Nelly Moser' would not be. The flowers, pale mauve with vivid carmine bars running from base to tip of each petal, fade badly in full sunshine. The same is true of the similar 'Marcel Moser' and 'Bees Jubilee'. These are best on east or west walls, but will also flower on north-facing walls, provided that they are not hideously exposed. The elegant white 'Marie Boisselot' is happy with a sunless north aspect. So is the pale blue 'Lady Northcliffe'. Pale clematis shine out in dark corners. Dark purple here would be glum. There is certainly a clematis for every occasion, but you need to make sure you have the right one for your needs.

SLOW GARDENING

I usually see Stonehenge when I'm storming home down the A303 with Eric Clapton pounding in my ears and a half-eaten Mars bar in my hand. It seems disrespectful to flash by it like this. Suddenly, there they are, the stones, and equally suddenly gone. They don't have a chance to speak of their consequence, their gravity, their implications.

You should have to walk a considerable distance to find Stonehenge, to take it in as it slowly rises, naked, from the plain, to watch the rectangles of sky between the monoliths change as you approach. If it is pouring with rain, so much the better. No effort we make to visit this place can rival the effort made by its builders. We demean that by glancing at it idly as we pass by at 70mph.

Travelling at the speed we do, it is difficult for us to capture now those 'peculiar emotions' which the young Joseph Hooker described on seeing new countries for the first time. During his life-time (1817–1911), there were still opportunities for real discovery.

Hooker, who went on to become an influential Director of the Royal Botanic Gardens at Kew, made his first expedition into the unknown when he was only twenty-two. Sailing on the *Erebus*, he left England on 30 September 1839 as official naturalist on a voyage to determine the exact position of the South Magnetic Pole. The Admiralty supplied him with two tin boxes for collecting plants, twenty-five reams of blotting paper to dry and press them and two Wardian cases, like miniature greenhouses, in which to bring live plants back to Kew. Everything else, he had to provide himself.

On New Year's Day, 1841, more than fifteen months after its departure from England, the *Erebus* finally crossed into the Antarctic Circle. In his journal, Hooker described the overwhelming vista of 'snowy precipices covered with an immense bank of broken clouds,

each tinged of a golden colour by the never-setting sun; above
these rose the immensely high peaks of land, towering up against a
beautifully blue clear sky, above which was another canopy of dark,
lowering clouds, their lower edges of a bright golden red colour. It
was one of the most gorgeous sights I ever witnessed.'

Hooker's best-known expedition took him to India, where, close
to the great mountain, Kangchenjunga, he found vast bushes of
Rhododendron falconeri, growing at 10,000 feet with leaves 19 inches
long. In Bhutan he collected sweet-smelling *R. griffithianum*, like a
'fine lily', said Hooker, each pale flower in a truss measuring as
much as 7 inches across.

Painstakingly collecting seeds of these beauties, Hooker packed
them in tins and dispatched them to his father at Kew. Given the
long, slow, arduous process by which these new plants were introduced into cultivation, did gardeners then appreciate them more,
value them more? I think they did. The garden centre, the micro-
propagation unit has reduced plants to commodities, to so many
tins ranged on the shelf. It has, of course, also made them cheaper.

It is only now, too, that through makeover programmes on television, we have been introduced to the concept of gardening against
the clock. Surely, though, most of us garden to escape the clock. At
the very heart of the business is the feeling that, when we garden,
we abandon a timetable constructed around dentist's appointments,
car services and the possible arrival of trains, to plunge headlong
into a completely different timetable, an immense and inexorable
one entirely outside our control, defined by weather, and above all
the seasons.

The Slow Food movement has had some success in increasing
respect for the ingredients with which we cook: good beef, properly reared and hung, decent tomatoes allowed to develop flavour
and ripen without the aid of a man in a white coat. So I'm nominating
this year for Slow Gardening. Chill out. Relax. Observe. Take time to
admire the way a seedling pushes through the earth, its back humped

into a croquet hoop with the effort. Even if it's a seedling of a weed like groundsel, it's still a miracle of tenacity and endurance. Grow something from seed yourself. If it's something useful – basil, coriander, rocket – so much the better. Plant a tree. Train a clematis.

The point of gardening is the doing of it, not having got it done. It's the process that matters, though it is of course directed towards an end result. It's rare now for people to stay in the same place for generation after generation. But continuity produces a tangible effect in a garden: hedges bulge, trees cast ever-longer shadows over a lawn, wisterias send out tendrils to close up the windows.

We live in an impatient age, used to quick results. Because people move around more than they used to, they don't plant things that won't immediately benefit them. This is a danger in gardens. It leads to layouts that, like instant takeaway food, are ultimately unsatisfying. The ingredients are limited and, after the initial gratification, there is no lingering sense of longer pleasures. But a holly tree, though slow, can give you that in spades.

In your garden, you can make a stand against the prevailing trashy mood of the time. The great eighteenth-century landscape gardens were made at a time when their busy agricultural owners were fencing and hedging and parcelling and enclosing land. Capability Brown's idealised landscapes reminded them of a pastoral, dreamy past, before turnips, before corn.

If the mood now is instant, disposable, then our gardens can become places where the opposite things are going on. We should be planting slow, steady, sustaining things. In the garden at least, if in no other part of our lives, we can dream a future.

A satisfying garden is a resonant one. That is easier to recognise than to pin down. A resonant garden has things going on in it that are not of the here and now. Built into it there may be messages from previous owners of the garden and previous uses of the land.

Even after the mammoth building boom of the late twentieth century, fewer people are the first-time occupiers of a house than live in places that others have lived in before. Even if the house itself is new, the space around it may carry hints of what happened there previously. Huge pear trees in suburban gardens round the outskirts of London remind us of the orchards that used to feed the tenement dwellers of the city. Big old bay trees planted close to houses recall the time when gardeners believed quite literally that 'neither witch nor devil, thunder nor lightning will hurt a man in the place where a bay tree is,' as the seventeenth-century herbalist, Nicholas Culpeper, put it.

A holly at the bottom of the garden may be the last remnant of the natural landscape that existed before urbanisation spread over your patch. That is quite a comforting thought – a thread that connects the before with the after. It need not stop you gardening round it, planting cyclamen close to its trunk and ferns to unfold after the holly's berries have gone. Tune yourself into the holly's pace of life. Think slow.

GARDENERS' QUESTION TIME

The late Geoff Hamilton was once dubbed the worst-dressed presenter on television. On the contrary, I felt he was one of the few people in the business who always looked right in his clothes. That was because he made no distinction between what he wore on the screen, when he was the focus of four million pairs of beady eyes, or off it, when he was mooching about the garden of his home in Rutland. He was an unpretentious dresser certainly: jeans slung lowish, checked lumberjack shirts with sleeves rolled up to the elbows, baggy jumpers for winter scenes. His were clothes to work in, not to ponce about in.

That was one of the reasons he inspired such confidence in those (like me) who watched him year after year on his BBC2 programme *Gardeners' World*. You felt he wasn't putting on an act, that you could trust him. When he picked up his spade, he handled it in the easy way of a workman completely familiar with the tools of his trade. The spade is a giveaway. Any hick can flourish a pair of secateurs with convincing assurance, but a spade instantly betrays the failings of those whose boots are made for product placement rather than for digging.

Geoff had an identical twin brother, Tony, both of them born and brought up in Stepney, east London. Tony Hamilton followed an entirely different path. Or tried to. But strangers always supposed he was Geoff and wherever he went, he was accosted by gardeners seeking advice from the only oracle that mattered to them. In the end he found it simpler (and kinder) not to explain the mistake. Whatever the question, he gave the stock reply, 'Cut it right down to the ground.' He said people always seemed to go away satisfied.

Oh! Lucky Tony. Occasionally I get hauled on to panels to answer gardening questions. Events like these are popular around us as a way of raising money for charity, but I never find it as easy as Tony to produce satisfactory answers. The panel on Radio 4's *Gardeners' Question Time* are handed the questions well in advance of the show, so have time to mug up on their answers. When the questions come straight from the floor, you are thinking on your feet and one of the chief difficulties is trying to build a mental picture of the garden that the person grilling you has got.

Many problems in a garden come about not because of pests or disease, but because a plant has been put in the wrong place, or is being treated in the wrong way. But we all prefer to think that our problems are not of our own making. As a panellist, you have to tread carefully. What sort of soil has the garden got? What aspect does the plant have? Has it been frosted or burned by too much sun? How exposed to wind is it? Is the problem plant the kind of thing that performs better when it is regularly pruned? Does it need repotting?

But you can't ask all these questions, because if you spend too long on a response, the audience gets restless. Quite right, because the idea is to get as many questions answered as possible. Panel chairmen are chosen for their ruthless ability to cut you off in mid-flow. Most of the ones round us seem to have been admirals and run a tight ship.

The trickiest questions always centre on bits of crumpled leaf passed up to the panel in equally crumpled plastic bags. What is wrong with this leaf? What is the remedy? Often it's difficult enough to identify the leaf itself, let alone its reasons for ailing. I'm not sure that Tony Hamilton's confident cure-all would work in this situation. But somewhere there must be an equally good response that would carry me safely through these avalanches of pock-marked greenery. All suggestions gratefully received.

ATTITUDE AND ALTITUDE

A roof garden has always seemed to me the epitome of urban chic and glamour; nobody tells you about the stairs. I have been attempting to green up a large balcony, about 17 feet (6 metres) long and 12 feet (4 metres) wide, attached to a third-floor shoe box in London, and I know now that roof gardening is about brawn, not glamour.

It is about carrying things, there being no storage space on balconies of this sort. It is about hauling and heaving and forgetting things that you have left in the boot of your car, parked three streets away. It is about staggering along landings like a pot-bellied Buddha, tubs clasped to your chest.

On the third flight of stairs in this particular building, a sack of compost caught on a banister rail and I watched with fascinated horror as the contents poured down the stairs like lava from Vesuvius. A door opened. A staggeringly chic man emerged and picked his way in shining loafers through the debris, disgust written in every carefully chosen step.

Then, there is the wind. It is far more ferocious and damaging at third-floor level than it ever seems on the ground. The plan for the balcony was modest, depending more on foliage than flowers. Flowers do not seem as important as leaves in this entirely hard landscape where trees wave like drowning swimmers distantly over a sea of rooftops.

Though it probably got me marked down as a voyeur of the worst sort, I found a session on the balcony with field glasses extremely useful in sorting out which plants could cope with roof-garden life and which could not. Rhododendrons were the most obvious casualties. You could imagine how irresistible they must have seemed in spring in full flower in the garden centre. But by nature they are woodland plants. Everything about a roof terrace is wrong for them. They hate full exposure to sun and wind. They hate drying out, which is more likely to happen on a rooftop than not. In contrast, box, clipped into pyramids and balls, held its own remarkably well, marooned three floors up.

My plant list included a claret-coloured vine to train against the west-facing wall, trailing ivy-leaved geraniums with chunky fresh green foliage, and two standard bay trees, lollipops on top of stout trunks four feet high. Evergreens are obviously a good idea in this kind of setting and the formality of the standard bays seemed to suit the unreal surroundings of this small space looking out on chimney pots and attic windows.

The trees started life in large black plastic pots (compromise already, you see) and within the first week, had blown over five times. I substituted even larger terracotta pots, packed with more compost. Though the pots at least stayed upright, the trees, with their neat rootballs, blew out of the pots. I tried guy ropes lashed to house wall and railings, but though that stopped the trees blowing out entirely, they leaned in a pathetic way and the roots, with all the jiggling about, never got a chance to anchor themselves in the compost.

Eventually the trees were reprieved from this miserable existence and came to Dorset. Here, I have learned that heavy flat stones placed on top of the compost either side of the main stem are the best counterbalance to sudden gusts of wind.

This initial disaster forced a rethink. Cobaea, which I had grown from seed for my own garden, proved to be the unlikely saviour. Two plants in a 16-inch (40-centimetre) clay pot have provided all the lushness and leafiness that a starved third-floor shoe-boxer could desire. They have proved surprisingly resistant to the wind, perhaps because their tendrils, coiled tightly like springs, give them such strong handholds.

Planted in the open ground, cobaea, named after a seventeenth-century Spanish missionary called Bernardo Cobo, can easily grow 20 feet (6 metres) in a season. Even in the restricted environment of their pot, the two cobaeas managed to cover the whole of a 12-foot (4-metre) run along one side of the balcony, which is surrounded by plain black railings, about 4½ feet (1½ metres) high.

It has been an easy matter to thread the growths horizontally in and out of the railings. The tendrils quickly anchor the plant where you have put it. Two growths have taken themselves up the cables towards the television aerial on the roof. No enraged addict has yet claimed compensation for an interrupted Vic Reeves show, so I assume the cobaea is not affecting reception. If it were a permanent climber, like wisteria, this exploratory tendency would have to be curbed, but cobaea will be cut down by the first frost and the whole carapace will melt away. That will be sad. In conservatories it will overwinter.

The leaves are held in clusters of six along the main stem, each cluster ending in a terminal curly flourish which is the tendril that gives it its handholds. The stems do not get woody, but are fleshy and pliable, flushed with the same reddish purple that suffuses the leaves. The new growth of the pot-grown plants is quite a dark bronze purple, but the whole thing would be greener in open ground where it would not be so starved.

The flowers come late in the season, starting in late July or August and finishing with the frosts. They are held on fat stems that bob out from the junction of the leaf clusters with the main stem. At first you see a curious pale green calyx with five distinct wings. Then a fat flower gradually blows out of the top of the calyx, like dough rising out of a mixing bowl. At first the flower, a large waxy bell, is pale translucent green, but it soon turns a rich purplish blue. The seedheads are as decorative as the buds and set like long green plums with the frilly calyx making a hat on top.

Cobaea is not difficult to grow but you have to get the timing right as the seedlings grow fast, and like geraniums, should not be set out too soon. May is the general dividing line, but in London, with all its escaping central heating, you could risk it earlier. If plants hang around inside too long, they get very tall and difficult to manage, even if they are staked.

Sow seed singly in 3-inch (8-centimetre) pots. I cover mine with clingfilm and germinate them on the kitchen windowsill. Whip off the clingfilm when you see the seedlings emerge and keep the pots well watered. Harden the plants off gradually before planting them out. I pushed pea sticks into the pot to make an initial climbing frame. Having tested their muscles on that, they were well able to take on the railings.

The plants need masses of moisture all through the season. All the pots on this balcony have big saucers underneath them, which makes it easier to water. Big pots dry out more slowly than small ones and despite the huffing and puffing on the stairs, are in the end easier to manage. Composts based on loam are heavier to carry than coir-based ones, but the extra weight is an advantage in making pots stable. Loam-based composts also hang on to nutrients more efficiently than others.

The pots would be easier still to manage if the entire balcony was covered in old coir matting laid on top of the existing white ceramic tiles. It would act like capillary matting and create a damper envi-ronment around the plants. They would like that. But would the tenant underneath? It might be the loafer man. I could not face another dose of distilled distaste.

Tasks for the Month

General

ٮ The longer the grass, the faster it grows, so mow lawns as regularly as you can.

ٮ Sycamore seedlings sprout as thickly as mustard and cress where they get the chance. Pull them up before they get a hold.

ٮ Indoor plants such as azaleas, pelargoniums, ivies and Easter cactus can be set outside until early September. Continue to feed them as usual.

ٮ Herbs such as tarragon and savory can be cut back hard if they are getting straggly. They will soon produce fresh growth.

ٮ Pinch out flower heads of chives to increase production of leaf.

ٮ Trees and shrubs such as cherries, lilacs, crab apples and medlars which are normally propagated by grafting may start throwing up suckers from the rootstock. As with roses, these must be dealt with quickly. Above ground, cut off suckers flush with the trunk. Below ground, take them back as far as you can to the root system before severing them.

Flowers

ٮ Cut back broom when it has finished flowering, shortening flowered shoots to within 2 inches (5 centimetres) of the old wood.

ٮ Deadhead lilac.

ٮ Cut back *Clematis montana* if it threatens to swamp other plants.

ٮ Shear over clumps of aubretia and arabis to remove dead flower heads.

ٮ Watch for suckers on roses. They always spring from the base of the plant and the foliage often looks different from that of the proper rose. Pull the suckers off before they get too dominant.

ٮ Cut back the foliage of early flowering *Iris unguicularis* so that the sun can warm the rhizomes.

ٮ Lift and divide bearded irises that have finished flowering, though only where the clumps have become congested. Dig them up carefully. Cut out and throw away bare sections of rhizome and replant the newest pieces, each with a hand of leaves sprouting from it and an underpinning of fat, pale roots.

ٮ Cut back weigela after it has flowered. Each year take out a couple of stems entirely, cutting them down to ground level. Deutzia responds well to the same treatment.

ٮ Cut back early flowering oriental poppy to the ground. This gives its neighbours a chance to stretch themselves to cover the space. The poppy will grow a new crop of leaves. The perennial cornflower *Centaurea montana* can be cut back in the same way.

- Clean up candytuft and alyssum by cutting out flowered stems.
- New dahlia plants should be in the ground now, well protected from slugs. Pinch out the tips of young plants as they grow, to make them bushy. Tie in the plants to strong stakes before growth becomes too heavy. A thick mulch will help keep the ground around them damp.
- Pinch out chrysanthemums set out last month.
- If you do not want flowers on your senecio, now is the time to remove them.
- Mildew can be an unsightly problem in hot, dry summers. It attacks roses, of course, but also ornamentals such as acanthus, even pulmonaria. Spray with a proprietary fungicide.
- Cut out some of the old branches from shrubs such as *Rubus tridel* 'Benenden', which has now finished flowering. Cut out as many branches as there are new shoots coming from the base of the plant. If there are none, cut out branches anyway. It will encourage new growth to form.
- Deadhead roses regularly. This will have a great effect on the second flush of roses produced in late summer.
- Deadhead petunias to keep them blooming prolifically.
- Pick over clumps of violas regularly and nip off dead heads before they set seed.

Vegetables

- Plant outdoor tomatoes, providing each one with a sturdy stake unless it is one of the sprawling bush varieties. Bush tomatoes need no pinching out. Others should be looked over every week. Tweak out the shoots that develop in the leaf axils of the main stem. A high-potash feed such as Tomorite helps produce plenty of flowers and fruit. If the plants are short of water, however, too many potash dinners will result in a deficiency of magnesium. Yellowing leaves is usually the first sign of that problem.
- Pinch out the tops of broad bean plants when they have set sufficient pods. The juicy tops are what blackfly most like.
- Leeks can be set out. Make deep holes with a dibber and water a plant into

each hole. Space the holes 6 inches (15 centimetres) apart in rows 15 inches (38 centimetres) apart.

ə♥ Sow beetroot, carrots and a final row of peas.

ə♥ Mulching does a great deal to conserve moisture around thirsty crops such as courgettes, tomatoes and cucumbers. Soak the ground first if necessary and get the mulch on before the ground dries out. Plastic mulches conserve moisture but do not benefit soil structure as bulky organic mulches do.

ə♥ Keep onions hand-weeded as they hate competition.

ə♥ Hoe carefully between rows of carrots, beetroot and other vegetables.

ə♥ Stop cutting asparagus in the middle of the month so that the plants have time to build up some top growth to feed into the roots. Asparagus beds need to be kept clear of weeds.

ə♥ Collars made from old carpet, underlay or roofing felt will prevent cabbage-root flies from having their wicked way with the crop. Cut out circular collars and slit them from the edge to the centre so that they fit round the stems of cabbages.

Propagating

ə♥ Take cuttings of perennial wallflowers. Choose lateral shoots about 2 inches (5 centimetres) long and pull them off with a heel. Push them into a pot filled with a peat/sand mixture.

ə♥ The climbing hydrangea (*H. petiolaris*) can also be increased by cuttings of vigorous side shoots taken this month and next.

ə♥ Take cuttings of African violets. Choose strong healthy leaves and pull them away from the parent plant with about 2 inches (5 centimetres) of stem attached. Sink the stalks into a pot of peat/sand mixture and keep moist and warm (about 65°F (18°C)). When rooted, pot up the cuttings singly to grow on.

ə♥ Take leaf cuttings too from begonia rex, gloxinia and streptocarpus.

ə♥ Stem cuttings of bougainvillea, clianthus, philodendron and stephanotis can also be taken now.

ə♥ Take half-ripe (semi-mature) cuttings from buddleia, camellia, ceanothus, chaenomeles, choisya, daphne, deutzia, hebe, jasmine, lavatera, philadelphus and weigela.

ə♥ Line out heather cuttings in a nursery bed.

ə♥ Take basal cuttings of alpine plants such as alyssum, dianthus and saxifrage.

Old greenhouse, Little Bredy walled garden, Dorset

SEEDS OF THE GOOD LIFE

So far this year, Robert Milne, organic gardener of Brampton Bryan in Herefordshire, has spent 68 hours weeding his vegetable garden, 174 hours on general labour, 72 hours looking after his hedges, 14 hours working in his six-year-old son Henry's garden and 12 hours in his own flower garden. That is what it takes to live the self-sufficient good life these days. It was never like that in the telly series with Richard Briers.

Mr Milne's hours of labour are all jotted down in a big ledger, together with notes of tasks accomplished. On the day I arrived to see the garden he had collected bluebell seed to sow in his little flower garden behind the shed. He had sown a row of spring onions, together with rows of lettuce and radish. He had harvested his garlic (seventy-four heads usable, twenty-one rotten) and had cut some poles out of the hedge to stake his tomatoes. He had hoed the paths between the beds in the vegetable garden and cut a low branch off an apple tree to lighten its load. And that was all before lunch.

He arrived in Herefordshire on his bike after a longish period of not sticking at things. 'I dropped out before I ever got round to dropping in,' he says, by way of explanation. There was a short spell at art school, a bit of teacher training, a spot of archaeology. But now he has made a vegetable garden and the purpose of life has become clearer.

Having found organic growing in the way that other people find God, Mr Milne produces tracts from his shed as pressingly as a nineteenth-century wayside preacher. On closely typed sheets of paper, hand-stapled, you can read his thoughts on Weeding, Hoeing and Bonfires (bonfires are PC – phew!), Compost and Liquid Feeding (with the family's own urine and faeces), Garden Tools and Back Care and many other subjects central to the process of organic growing.

Based as they are on his own, hard-won experience, these are valuable documents, though some gardeners may baulk at the thought of having to go back to an Elsan bucket after the ease of a flushing lavatory. 'Oh, but you must use urine,' says Mr Milne, emphatically. 'Think of all that nitrogen and potassium you would be wasting otherwise. It's the only way to maintain a cycle of fertility – each animal leaving its waste products randomly on the land that produces its food.'

'Can't we make do with farmyard manure instead?' I asked plaintively, but it was as though I had suggested using neat poison on the ground. 'Farmyard manure?' replied Mr Milne. 'I wouldn't touch the stuff. Full of weed seeds. Full of hormones, probably. And spray chemicals.'

You certainly can't fault the family's own product, for from an eighth of an acre of wedge-shaped ground, Robert Milne produces enough fruit and vegetables to keep his family (wife, two children) fed for the whole of the year. He grows potatoes and squashes, salad crops and beetroot, carrots and cauliflowers, artichokes and leeks. Walnuts and hazels are planted next to the house and the front garden is full of willow, for he wants to start basket-making as soon as he has grown enough of the withies.

And when did he start thinking organic, I enquired, imagining a kind of Pauline conversion as Mr Milne was pushing his bike along the Herefordshire lanes. 'Oh, I've always taken that for granted,' he replied briskly. 'You know you're doing the right thing, don't you?

It's a kind of altruism, saving all those fossil fuels and packaging and transport. Everything I do, I ask myself, can I justify this. Once you are aware of the adverse consequences of any other way of life, this is all you can do.'

For a man living as he does, June is the hungriest month. Last year's stored crops have finished, this year's have not come on sufficiently to be harvested. And this year, said Mr Milne, he gave away too many leeks. And the spring cabbage failed because he transplanted it and that encouraged it to bolt.

But he has got on top of the root fly. A friend advised him to plant thyme in all his cabbage beds and he says it seems to work. He had purple sprouting broccoli up to his chin. Having got the brassicas called to order, the carrots have been misbehaving. Germination has been a problem. He blames the weather: too hot and dry. He sows late as his patch is cold and wet, using a variety such as 'Autumn King' which goes in in early June.

The vegetable garden, across the road from his cottage, bounded by beautifully maintained hedges, is a model one. It is divided by straight earth paths into five plots and each plot is further divided into a series of long beds, each about four feet (just over a metre) wide. If you make the walkways permanent, he explained, you don't waste precious compost and liquid manure on the paths. His five-plot rotation (each set of crops moves along to the neighbouring plot each season) is worked out according to the vegetables' own likes and dislikes. Some need a more acid soil than others and these are grouped together to be grown in the same plot.

Big 'Hubbard' squashes are a staple winter food and Mr Milne saves the seed as they eat the squashes, cleans it and sells it back to a seed company. The revenue from that pays the rest of his seed bill. 'Ideal, you see. Tucked away out here, there is no danger that the squashes will get cross-pollinated by any other type of pumpkin.'

The ground at his cottage works hard, with some plots producing three or four crops a year. Catch crops such as radish and rocket fill the ground when slower growing crops such as potatoes have been lifted. After harvesting the garlic, Mr Milne was planning to sow vetch, partly to act as a soil cover, partly to use as a green manure. He leaves the vetch to grow as long as possible, then hoes it off with a sharp spade so that the roots with their nitrogen-bearing nodules stay in the ground to feed the next crop, which will be brassicas. The vetch haulm is carted off to one of the compost heaps.

'Do you get pleasure from all of this?' I enquired anxiously, after we had criss-crossed the paths through the vegetables like pieces on a chess board. Mr Milne seemed to be so busy counting the hours of labour (120 hours weeding in 1988 – a bad year for weather), I was worried that the delights of gardening might have passed him by. Fortunately not. '*Enormous* pleasure,' he said. 'It's cerebral as well as manual. And what can be more worthwhile than growing your own food?' With that, I heartily agree. But he's never going to get me converted to the Elsan.

EXTRAVAGANT BEDS

One of my most memorable birthday treats was a two-day visit to Paris, where, having flown for free as it were, on Air Miles, we stayed with unprecedented extravagance at the Hotel Lancaster, rue de Berri. Big square pillows. Linen sheets. Dinner at the Brasserie Lipp. And a whole day at the Bagatelle garden in the Bois de Boulogne.

We walked there from the hotel, round the edge of the Arc de Triomphe, all the way down the avenue Foch and through the Bois de Boulogne, by a footpath which trickles along the side of a slightly dank stream. The way is not difficult to find, bossed along as you are by concrete maps that sprout up like giant mushrooms by the paths, with a '*Vous êtes ici*' and a pulsating arrow in the foreground.

Bagatelle is the only house in this huge park which survived the Revolution. Napoleon hunted there. Lord Seymour, the Marquis of Hertford, gardened there, building grottoes, an orangery and a pleasantly dotty pagoda (all the rage in the 1840s). He also built the stable block, now organised as a restaurant where you can get outrageous ice creams.

In 1905, Bagatelle was acquired by the Paris city council and came under the powerful influence of Jean-Claude Forestier, curator of the city's parks and gardens. He is commemorated by a vast statue in the iris garden, flanked, when we were there, by tubs of apricot daturas. Forrestier's face did not persuade me that he would have approved of the daturas. Too dangerously seductive.

Coming from the Bois de Boulogne, the entrance to the garden is through magnificent blue and gold wrought-iron gates. The path takes you past a very strange maze mound with a grotto underneath. If you veer to the right you come to the house, with its formal entrance court. If you steer left instead, you will eventually come upon Bagatelle's enormous rose garden. Between the two is the head gardener's house and my favourite part of Bagatelle, the area rather strangely called the Presentation Garden.

This is a long thin area bounded down one long side by a tall boundary wall. There is a path running down the middle of the garden broken at regular intervals by hooped arches swamped with climbers. Serpentine box hedges wind down the areas on either side of the central path, creating a series of bays, crammed with flowers. The whole effect is brilliantly exuberant, very Edwardian.

Yellow is the predominant colour, used with lime-green and white. At the back of the biggest bays were clumps of enormous sunflowers, with heads big enough to knock you out, should they happen to fall your way. Some of them were double. The foreground planting was made up mostly of annuals in the white, yellow and lime-green theme, used in slightly different combinations in each bay.

Lime-green nicotiana was one of the stalwarts, growing at its proper height, rather than in a dwarfed state. White cosmos was another, the clean simple flowers set against surprisingly good foliage. There are not many annuals noted for their leaves. Both these flowers are easy to raise from seed and go together well, the tobacco flower's stodgy foliage relieved by the featheriness of the other. With these two came tall acid-yellow African marigolds, the whole lot laced together with creeping tendrils of lime-green helichrysum.

In other bays, the white came from frilly petunias and snapdragons, planted again with the lime-green nicotianas and a foreground of *Sanvitalia procumbens*. This is a low-growing daisyish sort of plant, small single yellow flowers with prominent black centres. They are more recessive than marigolds, and make good fillers amongst noisier plants.

Sometimes grey helichrysum bobbed up instead of the lime-green, with yellow snapdragons and seed-raised bedding dahlias. The gardeners at Bagatelle were using a pretty dahlia called 'Suzette', the colour of rich Jersey cream. Sometimes English marigolds were used instead of the African and French kinds. Tall yellow and white zinnias were underplanted with alyssum and *Nierembergia* 'Mont Blanc'.

At the top end of the garden were two almost rectangular beds, edged in box, but the box was cut at an angle so that it sloped up from ground level to the exact height of the plants massed inside. It made not so much a hedge as a border. The bed was divided into a trellis design by bands of clipped grey santolina, the shapes made by the santolina filled with lime-green coleus. Six tall standards of Paris daisies with grey foliage and white daisy flowers stood at the outer corners of the trellis diamonds. The effect here was intensely formal and restrained, in contrast with the wildly luxuriant planting of the flowering bays beyond.

Plants such as the coleus, which we think of more as conservatory or house plants, were used throughout the planting schemes in Bagatelle. A triple row of spider plants rather surprisingly filled in the gloomy space at the foot of a yew hedge. In the formal garden in front of the house, the polka dot plant *Hypoestes phyllostachya* was used very effectively as a filler in the long narrow borders of standard roses and penstemons.

The master touch here was the use at regular intervals of the airy *Gillenia trifoliata*. This is a perennial that looks as if it might be a bulb. The foliage is sword-shaped and during the second half of summer it sends up long flowering stems which explode at the ends into a branching series of small white flowers, the calyces a marked reddish brown. It is a most elegant plant and without it, the penstemon and polka dot brigade would have looked too congested. It grows just over 4 feet (1 metre) tall and does not seem to be fussy about soil or position. I have seen it growing in widely differing situations with no histrionics.

There is little left now at Bagatelle of the *jardin anglais* laid out here in 1777 for the Comte d'Artois by the Scottish gardener, Thomas Blaikie. Blaikie spent most of his working life in France, promoting the English style and importing vast numbers of Scots gardeners to work in the gardens he laid out. He survived the Revolution and died in Paris in 1838.

When the Marquis of Hertford took over, at about that time, he almost doubled the size of the garden, adding all the ground that lies beyond the formal garden with the standard roses and penstemons. A path takes you down to a lake overhung by a stupendous weeping beech. Forestier, who was a friend of Monet's, added the waterlilies.

The path curves round the back of the lake, leading you into the grotto planned by the Marquis and built from massive stone boulders. You make your way through the grotto on stepping stones set in the water, which reflects flickering patterns on to the stone roof.

Between the stepping stones were flocks of fish, all pointing in the same direction as though they were posing for a curtain design. Water trickles gently down over the front of the grotto roof in a fall, so that you look back across the lake to the house through a fractured veil.

When you look back at the grotto from the other side of the lake, you would scarcely know it was there, for the roof is disguised with mounds of ivy and a huge green-leaved smoke bush, *Cotinus coggygria*. Dr Johnson was grumpy about grottoes. Fit only for toads, he said. I disagree. There are several good ones at the Bagatelle garden, which is open daily (9–5 in winter, 8.30–6 in summer). You will find it at the junction of the allée de Longchamp with the allée de la Reine Marguerite. If you don't want to walk, the nearest Metro station is Pont de Neuilly.

HEAVEN SCENT

The easiest herbs to grow are the permanent ones: rosemary, thyme, sage, tarragon. You buy a plant, stick it in the ground and away it goes. To these you could add winter savory (*Satureja montana*), which, like tarragon, is perennial. In a mild season it stays in leaf all winter. If it doesn't cooperate, grow it in a pot and bring it under cover. Then you can be sure of a constant supply of leaf to use in bean stews. It's a compact plant, no more than 12 inches (30 centimetres) tall, 8 inches (20 centimetres) wide, and in summer has a crop of lippy pink or white flowers. In my last garden, I used it as an informal edging in one part of the herb patch. It's not as neat as dwarf box, but more productive. Like many Mediterranean herbs, it does best in poorish ground and needs plenty of sun. If you've never tasted it, think thyme or marjoram. It has the same kind of tang.

A more unexpected perennial herb, in this country at least, is lemon grass. I potted up some I bought in a supermarket and to my surprise, it grew. It's not hardy, of course, so when the nights began to get chilly, I put it in the cold frame. There, it still gets plenty of light, but can be kept free of frost. The top growth died down, but new shoots pushed out in spring and it has kept us in fresh leaf all summer. When it gets colder, the pot will have to go back in the cold frame, but I'm hoping it will resurrect itself again when the days begin to get longer.

India is its home, but I first came across it in Guyana, where it grew in vast clumps like pampas grass underneath the canopy of the rainforest. At that time, my husband and I were making regular expeditions into the most inaccessible areas of Guyana with a small group called Remote Area Medical, set up by my Guyanese sister-in-law. She's a doctor and her idea was to try and bring help to some of the most scattered Amerindian communities – Macushi, Waipashana and Wai-Wai – living in the rainforest. We'd only go where we were invited and we'd only do things that didn't get in the way of their own very successful medicine. But a course of antibiotics can stop a child dying from a septic piranha bite. And, in a culture where the bow and arrow is paramount, a pair of glasses means that a hunter can continue to feed his family.

So with guides provided by the headman of each small community, we walked from village to village through trackless, mapless rainforest. As well as medical supplies, we carried all our own food, so we wouldn't be a burden to any group we stayed with. One time, on a three-week walk, our basic supplies (cassava, rice, beans) began to run out. All we had left was sugar. For four days, we lived on sugar and boiled water, flavoured with the leaves of lemon grass. On particularly tough sections of the trail, even that began to seem as desirable a treat as a four-course dinner at The Ivy.

So I'm rather attached to lemon grass and a few leaves chopped up in a glass with honey and hot water remains my favourite drink.

You can chuck chopped leaves in a bath too, and get the same slightly oily, pungent smell around you as you wallow. That was a nicety we never got round to in the rainforest. Bathing there, in river pools and under waterfalls, you were more concerned about cayman and piranhas than you were about aromatherapy. Lemon grass is said to be a good anti-depressant, but that wasn't a concept familiar to the Macushi. They used it to ease stomachaches and fevers.

It may have been beginner's luck, the fact that the stems I bought rooted so easily. But if you look at the faintly bulbous sticks packed in their transparent bags, you can sometimes see slight swellings or bumps at the base of the stalks. These are the growing points from which roots and shoots may come. But as with a daffodil bulb, if the cut has been made too far up the swollen base, there's no hope that it will be able to make roots and grow.

You can also stick the stems in a glass of water and hope they will root in the way, for instance, that mint will. It may be four or five weeks before you see these developing. When you do, lift out the stems and pot them up. Don't be tempted to use too big a pot. In our cool climate, the plants are prone to rot and too much damp compost sitting around the roots only increases the danger. You can try growing lemon grass from seed too, but germination is slow and erratic, even if you manage to maintain a temperature of 68–86°F (20–30°C), which is what the seed requires. Potting up stalks is much easier.

If you're using lemon grass in a stir fry or to make Thai fish cakes, you need the bulbous bottom end of the plant, rather than the leaves. With a sharp knife, it's easy enough to wiggle a stem free from the clump and cut it right down at the base. But you can't do this too often. The rate of growth in our climate isn't as vigorous as it is in the tropics.

Once the plant is established in a pot, there is very little you have to do except cut down the top growth when it dies down in winter. During this dormant period, lemon grass needs very little water. When the plant starts into growth again, start to water and feed it using a liquid fertiliser high in nitrogen, which will boost leaf growth.

You don't need a garden to keep yourself in lemon grass. Or winter savory. A sunny windowsill can be the Mediterranean and the Tropics all in one.

SLUGGING IT OUT

I like plants that are spooky, slightly sinister. And I particularly like arums with their handsome arrow-shaped leaves and menacing spathes. Our native arum, called cuckoo pint or lords and ladies if you are in polite company, has a pale green spathe, like a cowl drawn up to protect the purplish spadix inside. Later in the season, the leaves disappear, leaving a spike of poisonous red berries.

Arums grow from fleshy tubers and the islanders of Portland in Dorset used to boil them up and strain them to produce starch and a kind of arrowroot to thicken sauces. It was big business (though hell on the laundresses' hands) and in 1797 Mrs Jane Gibbs won a gold medal and thirty guineas from the Royal Society of Arts for the perfection of her arum starch.

So when I saw *Arum nigrum* from the Balkans and Northern Greece advertised in Paul Christian's rare plant catalogue, I had to have it. He describes it as 'strong and robust, with large, strong plain green leaves and great big, pure, unbroken, satin-like, jet black spathes around a jet-black spadix in May. Fully hardy and one of the most remarkable and striking garden species.' Who could resist? So last October, I planted my one tuber in a pot, where I could keep track of it, and then in early spring, when the first green shoots came spurting through, transplanted it to the garden.

It grew lustily and during April and early May, I began hovering over it, anxious for the first sight of the satin spathe and the jet-black spadix. Like a tightly rolled umbrella, the spathe shot up with astonishing speed. 'Tomorrow,' I said to myself. 'Tomorrow it's going to unwrap.' So I made the pilgrimage which had by now become a twice daily event, and found the spathe lying on the ground, felled at the base like a tree.

A web of mucus connected the fallen column with its fleshy stem. Even the hapless Watson could have deduced that the culprit was a slug. Or a snail. For a positive identification, I'd need Sherlock Holmes too. But why, when there were several hundred native arums growing scarcely a snail's pace away, did the target have to be this particular plant? Curses on all molluscs. The plant won't produce another spike this season. There's a whole year to wait until I get another chance to see it.

So, given the number of gardeners that at this very minute will be ranting over their chewed hostas, weeping over the mangled remains of their sweet pea seedlings and lamenting that they forgot to protect the emerging shoots of their French beans, it is not surprising that, according to Andrew Halstead of the Royal Horticultural Society, slugs and snails still top the list of Britain's most hated garden pests.

It's a grisly top ten, this one, with lily beetle, vine weevil, leatherjackets, chafer grubs and mealy bugs all jostling with the slugs and snails for pole position. Why aren't there more things that eat slugs and snails? Where are the hedgehogs when we need them? Unfortunately, I know the answer to that one. They are squashed on the roads while ambling quietly about their business. And against the vast numbers of pet cats intent on trouble, thrushes don't have a chance.

I'm not squeamish about stamping on snails and where I see them, that's what I do. It's a quick death, which is what I'd wish for myself, if only I could fix it. Slugs are more unpleasant to deal with.

I used to chuck them in one of the water butts, until I realised that, as well as being hermaphrodite, they are also amphibious. Through the water, they crawled up the inside of the butt and then over the top and out, to start munching on some fresh treasure. Now they get dropped into a tub of water mixed with a lot of salt, which pickles them quite efficiently.

But hand-picking is only effective if you make daily (or rather nightly) patrols, and even then, you'll catch only a tiny proportion. Both slugs and snails are active from early spring to late autumn and if winters get warmer and the growing season extends, they too are likely to prolong their attacks. Biological control with the parasitic nematode *Phasmarhabditis hermaphrodita* only works when the soil is damp and reasonably warm. In a biggish garden it's a prohibitively expensive option. Copper bands, which set up a static charge as the mollusc crawls over it, work well round pots, but are not so easy to set in place round particular plants in a crowded border. In cold frames, packed in spring with exactly the kind of fresh young shoots that slugs and snails like most, you could use slug pellets, as no other birds or animals will be able to get at them. But there is no complete answer to the problem and the wretched things know that we, as gardeners, will never be vigilant enough to keep on top of them.

A new entry on the pest list is the rosemary beetle *Chrysolina americana*, which has zoomed straight in at number four of the top ten. Despite its name, it's not from America, but from southern Europe, and was first seen in southern England in the late 1990s. Like the lily beetle, another pest quite recently introduced from abroad, the rosemary beetle is now spreading steadily through the country, helping itself to man-sized portions of lavender, sage and thyme as well as rosemary.

In its adult form, it's a pretty-looking little insect – only a third of an inch (8 millimetres) long but glistening in iridescent bands of purple and gold. Adults mate in late summer, and the larvae, grubby-looking things of greyish-white, also fill up on herbs before disappearing into the soil to pupate. Fortunately, like the lily beetle, the rosemary beetle is slow on its feet and easy to see. Gardeners in Norfolk and Leicestershire, as well as those in the south of England, are likely to know about them already.

Andrew Halstead says that insecticides, if you are thinking of using one against the rosemary beetle, are likely to be most effective in spring or in late summer and autumn, when you can interrupt the life cycle of the pest. But if you use these herbs for cooking, then obviously you shouldn't spray. Once again, picking the beasts off by hand will be the only way to control them.

'Oh,' said an organic friend airily, when I complained about pest attacks in the garden. 'It's easy. You just double up on everything: one plant for the pest, one for you.' But I don't seem to be the only gardener cursed with pests that can't count.

FULL OF BEANS

The score in the kitchen garden is pigeons – six, gardening correspondent – one. They have got the peas, the French beans, a seedling row of black kale, purple cabbage, rocket and Brussels sprouts. I have got the broad beans. Our place has always been massively overstocked with birds. The rooks cause little trouble. Although they sleep here, they have the decency to eat elsewhere. It shows initiative. And I like the way they clatter about as they come back in the evenings after their expeditions. They are slow to settle down. Occasionally, little groups of avian Hell's Angels swoop out of the trees and plummet at vast speed straight towards the house. At the last minute they pull out of the dive and climb fast back up to the top of the chestnuts, shrieking 'Chicken' to each other. It's pure show-off stuff and very engaging.

I like the woodpeckers, too. A pair of them (green) fuss about nervously on the lawn outside the sitting room. Whatever it is they are eating – ants, leatherjackets – I'm sure I'm better off without it.

The same goes for the robins that flick in suicidally close to the edge of my spade to snatch up grubs. They are bossy little boots and pour out streams of vitriol if another robin comes close. Unadulterated aggression. The red chest says it all. How on earth did they con their way on to the front of Christmas cards – the season of supposed good will? A robin has as much good will as a traffic warden on Monday. But as they are small, the aggression is hilarious rather than troubling.

The pigeons are another matter. They are heavy, slow, clattery flyers. They don't go anywhere. They just sit about in the trees, waiting for the next meal to be put in front of them. They sing outside the bedroom window in croony, insincere voices. And they have wiped out my French beans, two long rows of lustrous 'Purple Teepee'.

French beans are now available in a staggeringly diverse range of varieties, bush or climbing. 'Purple Teepee' is a bush bean that holds its pods way up above the foliage. Unfortunately the gorgeous colour drains away when you cook the beans, but the taste is excellent. And they are stringless.

The prettiest of all are the borlotti beans, the pods splashed with red on a cream ground. They don't bear heavily but they are versatile. You can use the beans as flageolets (half mature), or let them grow on to become fully fledged haricot-type beans. 'Borlotto Lingua di Fuoco' is the one to look for. It will need support as it is a climber, but it is a pretty enough bean to grow up a tripod in the flower garden.

French beans aren't actually French at all. Like runners, they are New World beans, brought back to Europe by the Spanish conquistadors. These beans, wrote the early herbalist, John Gerard, 'boiled together before they be ripe, and buttered, and so eaten with their cods, are exceeding delicate meat, and do not ingender wind as the other pulses do'.

The most important thing about French beans (apart, that is, from protecting them from pigeons) is not to be in too much of a hurry to sow. The end of May or beginning of June is usually about right, but this is a notoriously capricious time of year. By nature, French beans are fast-growing annuals and it is a waste of seed to put them in cold, dank ground. Sow at regular intervals, starting in late spring, when the soil temperature has reached about $55°F$ ($13°C$). The climbing types will need support, but the compact bush varieties will crop without any propping up, even in pots and Gro-bags.

They like rich, light soil, but are not fussy about whether it is neutral or acid. They do best in a sheltered position. You can sow them in individual pots in a greenhouse or cold frame, or set them in compost in a deep apple box lined with newspaper and then transplant them out when the weather warms up. This system offers some defence against the perils seed faces in the open ground, but the shock to the system holds back transplants and indoor sowings may crop no sooner than seeds sown outside. If you sow direct, set the seed about 1 inch (3 centimetres) deep and about 9 inches (23 centimetres) apart in the rows.

In exposed situations – where this can't be avoided – you can earth up the stems of young plants as they grow, to give them extra support. Provide canes or other supports for climbing French beans. Keep the soil moist throughout the growing period, but especially when the plants come into flower.

Expect about 9 pounds (4 kilos) of beans from a 10-foot (3-metre) row. For fresh beans, pick the pods while they are still succulent. For dry haricot beans, leave the pods and pull up the whole plant at the end of the growing season. Hang them under cover until the pods have dried off. Then shell the beans and store them in airtight jars.

In Ecuador we often saw climbing French beans planted among sweetcorn, so that they could use the strong stems of the corn for support. The traveller Samuel de Champlain noted exactly the same symbiotic relationship in his journeys in Brazil in 1605. It's a partnership that we could easily copy. The two crops like the same kind of situation. From various caches of beans dug up in caves in central Mexico and Peru, archaeologists reckon that South American Indians have been cultivating beans since at least 6000 BC.

I'm still working my way slowly through the French bean archive (any decent catalogue will now offer at least thirty different kinds) but I have enjoyed eating 'Purple Teepee' (purple-podded), 'Slenderette' (green-podded) and 'Sonesta' (yellow-podded). 'Slenderette' is slightly slower to crop (seventy to eighty days) than the other two (sixty to seventy days). Among the climbing French beans I've liked 'Blauhilde' (purple flowers and beans), various borlotta types, striped and streaked with red, 'Helda', which crops quite early, and 'Neckargold', a vigorous variety which bears juicy yellow beans.

WIZARD TOOLS

It is a wonderful relief to leaf through gardening magazines and realise that there are so many things I don't want. No, it's stronger than that. There are things that, even if they arrived free, shining, and with a five-year guarantee, would still be put straight in the boot of the car and driven to the nearest Oxfam shop. Gadgets and me don't have a long history. I expect them to go wrong and, obligingly, they do.

Multi-task tools seem to me the worst. Does it really make my life easier to have one stick and three interchangeable heads, each of which do different things? I don't think so. If I want a rake, I like to reach out my hand and pick it up. I don't want to scrabble round with levers and locks, fiddle with clip-on–clip-off devices to build my own rake from what had previously been a hoe.

The tools you really need in a garden are so few, so well defined, you can understand why manufacturers get frustrated. It doesn't give them much opportunity to expand their markets. The basic kit is the same one that John Evelyn described in the seventeenth century: spade, fork, trowel, line, hoe, rake, something to cut with. For him that would be a beautifully made pruning knife. For us, it's a pair of secateurs. Now that was a breakthrough.

Do I want a gas-driven weed wizard, with a butane gas cylinder fastened to a long handle? Fire up the flame. Burn off the weed. No, I don't. The thought makes me feel sick. Not because I have sympathy for the weed (I'm battling against them all the time) but because the method speaks of industrial estates, ugliness, harsh environments, techniques from a factory world that have nothing to do with the world I am trying to pull together round me in my garden.

And why go to such a lot of trouble for a weed? With a decent knife, you can quickly hook even long-rooted perennials such as dandelions and docks out of paths or paving. You haven't consumed any energy, except your own. You couldn't use a butane killer on a lawn, or anywhere else where the weed was growing close to something you didn't want to kill.

Garden vacs? No, NO! 'Take the effort out of tidying up, just zip around with the latest in garden gadgets,' trilled an advertisement I read recently. Why turn gardening into housework? Vacuuming the carpets is a sad necessity, given the number of feet that tramp about our place, but the stuff that lies around outside is not dirt displaced. It's what is meant to be there. It is potential humus, the lifeblood of your soil.

The vac is noisy too, but perhaps that could be forgiven (though not by me) if the contents of its bag were tipped on to a compost heap or used to build a leaf clamp. But it seems they are mostly not. They are bundled up and driven to the tip; two lots of energy needlessly consumed. And think of the poor beetles, the ladybirds and other insects sucked into that undiscriminating maw.

Legs broken, wing cases smashed, they hurtle through the whirling maelstrom, their poor bodies shattered in the vacuumed debris that they so trustingly thought was home. The environment? We've never heard so many people blabbing about it. And we've never been surrounded by so many people who think that if they put a bottle in a bottle bank once in a while, they've done their bit for the planet.

I feel myself getting cross. That wasn't what I wanted. Lighthearted, I said to myself at the beginning of this piece. But having got the garden vac out of the way, I think I'll be all right now. To me, it represents the worst of the wrong directions that gardening can go in. Crushed car windscreen – the New Look gravel – raises the blood pressure too, so I'd better not write about that. How can you look at that stuff and not think of car crashes, ambulances, police sirens, anger, anguish?

Gloves? No, never. But then I've never kept a pair of Marigolds under the kitchen sink either. My skin is still there. So are my nails sometimes. The fact that nifty Japanese inventors can mould textured latex palms on to elasticated polycotton gloves does not make my heart sing. Having rotten circulation, I'd like to find a way of keeping my hands warm while gardening in winter, but gloves just get in the way.

Hand-painted stone table? 'Unique and elegant,' its Italian makers assure us. But heavy too, I should think, and the thing about tables, especially ones outside, is that you are always moving them to catch the sun or miss the wind or escape the smell of the next-door neighbour's barbecue. They need to be portable. And if I was looking for a painted table, I'd be thinking wood, not stone.

Yippee, an irrigation system, another thing I don't need. 'An automatic irrigation system is no longer a luxury. It is an absolute necessity.' That is salesmanspeak and it is bunk. Water IS a luxury. It has been expensively sucked out of rivers that might have had better things to do with their offerings, and has been even more expensively purified and piped to our door. Great waterfalls have been silenced so we can turn on a tap.

And we are fortunate in living in a country where enough rain falls out of the sky to give our gardens all the water they are likely to need. Yet it takes just one dry summer to put us into a state of complete lunacy about the stuff. The end of the world as we know it, we were told, after a dryish summer a few years ago. Then last winter it never stopped raining and the doom merchants' torrent of articles on Britain – the new Sahara – came to an end.

Think, before you put in that seep hose, that pop-up irrigation system, or instal those catheters in the borders, that more things die from drowning than they do from drought. Unlike us, plants have mechanisms to cope with thirst. Think too of what watering systems are doing to your bulbs (especially your tulips), which depend on a dry, hot summer baking to initiate the flower buds for the following season. By irrigating all summer long, you are murdering them in their beds.

Oh! how heady this all this. No to butyl pond liners, no to 'How to' garden videos, no to striped patio awnings, plastic compost bins, battery-operated wheelbarrows, Father Time weather vanes, soil cables, polytunnels, HT roses … You might think that this has been a story of negatives, all noes, no yesses, but not for me. I'm so pleased to find all these things that I don't need, I'm going to order a case of champagne to celebrate. Champagne – now there's a real necessity.

Tasks for the Month

General

❧ Gather herbs such as rosemary and thyme and hang them in bundles to dry in a cool, airy place.

❧ Trim hedges regularly – especially if they are privet. Untended hedges tend to become bare at the base.

Flowers

❧ Cut down flowered stems of aquilegia and sweet rocket before they spread seed all over the garden.

❧ Continue to deadhead roses.

❧ Keep picking sweet peas, if you grow them. They will soon stop flowering if they are allowed to run to seed.

❧ Sow Brompton stocks, pansies and perennials such as alpine and Iceland poppies in seedbeds outside now for flowering next year.

❧ Cut out flowered stems from mock orange (*Philadelphus coronarius*), leaving the new shoots to flower next season.

❧ Continue to deadhead violas to encourage them to produce new flowers. Clumps that have got very leggy can be sheared down close to the ground, which will encourage bushy new growth.

❧ Wisterias need two prunings a year. Do the first now, the second in February. First choose the growths that you want to keep to fill extra space and if they have not started twining round any support, help them on their way. Shorten all other growths, leaving five or six pairs of leaves intact.

❧ As soon as you can get hold of them, start to plant autumn-flowering bulbs such as colchicum and sternbergia.

❧ Cut back helianthemums.

❧ Delphiniums may give a second late show if you cut down the first stems as soon as they have finished flowering.

❧ Evergreen ceanothus can be pruned if it has grown out too far from a wall. Cut back flowered sprays to within a few buds of the main branch.

❧ For the biggest dahlias, you need to disbud plants, taking off the two side buds that generally appear on either side of the central boss bud.

❧ Gather fresh seed from astrantia, campanula, foxglove, hollyhock, honesty, hellebore and polemonium.

July

- Pinch out the tips of home-grown wallflowers to make plants bushy and compact.
- Regular deadheading extends displays in pots and hanging baskets. Pay particular attention to ageratum, marigolds, cornflowers and pansies.

Vegetables

- Support runner beans with poles.
- Transplant cabbages and broccoli from seedbed to final position while the ground is still damp.
- Thin kohlrabi plants so that they are not less than 6 inches (15 centimetres) apart.
- Thin young beetroot. Baby beets are delicious steamed whole with butter and a scattering of grated orange peel.
- Sow more lettuce and radish for continuity of supply. If the weather is very dry, water the seed drill before you sow the seed.
- Transplant purple sprouting broccoli, making a deep hole with a trowel and setting the young plants deeper in the soil than they had been in the seedbed. Water them liberally into the holes and then firm down the earth hard around them.
- If you like exotics, try a row of Chinese radish. Sow seed in pairs at 6-inch (15-centimetre) intervals, then thin out the weaker seedling in each pair.
- Lift garlic as soon as the leaves begin to wither and allow the bulbs to ripen on netting outside as you would onions. They can then be cleaned off and hung up in bunches.
- Lift early potatoes as the haulms begin to die down.

Fruit

- Keep an eye on strawberry runners which quickly play havoc with a neatly laid-out strawberry bed. Leave the two strongest on each plant and nip out the rest. When the season has finished, tidy up beds by cutting off old leaves and removing straw.
- Pick whitecurrants and redcurrants regularly.
- Apple and pear trees trained in espaliers, cordons and fans may need summer pruning. Do this gradually, so the tree does not suffer too much of a shock. Leave the leaders at the end of all the main branches

untouched. Prune back the new side shoots that have been growing so that you shorten each one by a third.

- Cut out old raspberry canes as soon as fruit-picking has finished. Tie in new canes, leaving no more than eight or ten to each plant.
- Prune stone fruit such as plums and cherries, cutting out diseased and dead branches and thinning out over-vigorous growth.
- Plant new strawberry plants, setting them at least 15 inches (38 centimetres) apart in rows 30 inches (75 centimetres) apart.

Propagating

- Take cuttings of pinks, about 3 inches (8 centimetres) long, and stick them in pots filled with a mixture of peat and sand. Firm the soil down well around the cuttings.
- Take cuttings from cistus, using non-flowering side shoots.
- Layer border carnations. Choose young side shoots that have not flowered and nick through the joint at the base of each shoot. Do not cut it completely. Bend the side shoots down and peg them firmly into the ground with a bit of bent wire. Cover the split stem with fine, damp soil and keep the plant well watered. The layers should have rooted by early September.
- Increase stocks of hybrid berries such as loganberry and tayberry by tip layering. Bury the tip of a shoot about 6 inches (15 centimetres) in the ground and firm down the earth around it. By next spring it should be well rooted.
- Layer azaleas, choosing shoots that are growing close to the ground. Make a slight nick with a sharp knife on the underside of each branch that you want to layer. Scrape out a hollow in the ground under each branch and bury each one in its own little trench, pinned down with bent wire. Remove any flower buds that form on the layer next spring. They should have rooted by autumn next year.
- Take stem cuttings of hydrangea, ceanothus, hibiscus and evergreen viburnum, by choosing sections of healthy strong stems and trimming them down to about 4 inches (10 centimetres). Root them in a pot filled with peat/sand mixture. Cover them with a polythene bag supported on sticks, so that it does not snag against the leaves. Keep the pot out of direct sunlight. When the cuttings start to show signs of fresh growth, pot them into individual pots.

The medlar tree

SWEET PAIN

One of the nicest jobs in a summer garden is tying up sweet peas. Most of ours grow over a hazel tunnel which straddles a grass path in the kitchen garden. It's a home-made structure, built with hazel poles cut from the garden and stuck into the ground either side of the path, about 18 inches (45 centimetres) apart. They are long poles, bent over and tied together at the top to make a series of arches. When all these were in place, we tied more hazel poles horizontally between the uprights so that we finished with a tunnel made in an 18-inch (45-centimetre) square grid. If you have the hazel to hand, as we do, such structures are relatively quick and easy to make. But the hazel must be used fresh and green so that it bends without snapping.

The sweet peas are the old-fashioned kind, smallish flowers but with a scent that is swoonier than any other smell in the garden. I've been saving seed for six years now, gradually honing our own strain of sweet pea, a very dark voluptuous mix, some magenta and purple, some all purple, some all magenta, some almost mahogany. If a particularly good flower emerges, different from any that I've already got, I put a twist of wire round its stem to remind me to let it seed at the end of the season.

Saving sweet pea seed is not a complicated business. The pods ripen very fast and become buff-coloured and dry. I try and leave them on the vine as long as possible, then gather the pods and spread them on a table in the shed to finish drying. Shelling them into a container (they are the size and colour of black peppercorns) is a pleasing late autumn job. It's a job that lets you dream. From these minuscule orbs, as hard as shotgun pellets, will come 10-foot stems, loaded with summer. In late autumn that's a good dream to have.

The sweet peas were first planted in mid March, seven seeds to each 5-inch (13-centimetre) pot. They germinated on the kitchen windowsill, then went quickly out into the cold frame. They are best grown cold and hard. We planted them out from their pots at the beginning of May and they were in full production by the third week in June. The first ones had wonderful long stems. Gradually the stems get shorter and shorter, but the smell remains as ravishing.

I feel in a weird way that I owe my life to that smell. While the sweet peas were blooming, a few years ago, I went into hospital to have various bits of cancer cut out. When you are through the intensive care bit, the bit where you are not really alive at all, they start giving you morphine. But morphine makes you retch. When your lower body has been well done over by a knife, retching is not what you want to do. It is excruciatingly painful.

So I stopped taking morphine and concentrated instead on the smell of the sweet peas by the side of my hospital bed. They were our own sweet peas and my husband brought a fresh bunch in every day. He knew they had to be kept on top of. But what neither of us knew was how crucial they would become to my recovery. The sweet peas became the most important reason to get the hell out of that horrible place and get myself back into the garden.

When the pain was more than tiresome, I screwed up my eyes and concentrated on the smell of the flowers by my bed. Who needs aromatherapy from a bottle, when the real thing is at hand? But I learned that mind over matter works, if the matter becomes worth getting your mind over. The sweet peas gave me two lifelines. First, they allowed me to lift my mind away from my body, its ludicrous state and its pain. And they gave me a most pressing reason to recover, so that once again, I could wander down the garden, through the tunnel, to bury my face in their generous petals.

BUTTERFLY BALL

Cool, cloudy, wet summers are even worse for butterflies than they are for us. Deprived of holiday picnics on the beach, we can at least loiter in pubs and cafés instead. Butterflies have fewer options open to them. Even the buddleias, the butterfly's motorway service stations, attract only a few dazed-looking peacocks. The good news in a wet summer is that there are fewer cabbage whites on the greens.

The things that butterflies seem to like in our garden – the old hollies, the ivy, the elms, the wild grasses – have happened by accident rather than design, so I have no reason to get worked up by their absence in an unsuitable summer. But Philip Bowler takes the whole thing very personally. When he and his wife moved to their house in Heage, Derbyshire, he worked single-mindedly to turn the whole of his half-acre patch into a Shangri-La for butterflies.

For a few summers he was in ecstasy. The small skipper settled in his Yorkshire fog grass. The large skipper laid eggs in the cock's foot. Caterpillars of the green-veined white fed contentedly on his honesty, the progeny of the small skipper munched his sorrel. Late broods of the Holly Blue sipped nectar from the ivy that covers the gable end of his house and small coppers flocked in to feast on his ragwort.

But in a bad summer, he comes close to a nervous breakdown. Despite his working every spare hour left over from his job to make his home (named after a variant type of the silver wash fritillary) the crème de la crème of butterfly stopovers, scarcely one shows up when skies are dull. He minds. Telling him that it is all the fault of the weather doesn't help. He thought that the butterflies that flocked in in huge numbers for several years had come because of him, not because it just happened to be sunny and warm.

There is more to pleasing butterflies than planting the odd buddleia, as you understand when you walk round Mr Bowler's garden. Nectar is the butterflies' fuel. It keeps them flying. But if you want them to stay in the garden, you have to provide a comfortable place for the females to lay their eggs and five-course meals for the caterpillars.

The nectar bit is relatively easy in a garden. As well as the buddleia, you need alyssum, aubretia, catmint, golden rod, honesty, lavender, Michaelmas daisies (mauve seems to be the preferred colour here), sweet william, thrift, valerian and *Sedum spectabile*, whose fat juicy flowerheads fill the September gap when the buddleia is over. If there is a choice, use single flowers rather than double, which get butterflies' tongues in a twist.

The small square of garden immediately outside the kitchen window at Mr Bowler's place is filled with these sorts of flowers. Outside that it is wilderness – carefully managed wilderness. In fact the wild part of the garden is far more difficult to keep on the right track than the proper garden. Wild flowers will not stay where they are put. Bush vetch this year has made a takeover bid for the entire hillside.

And it took him a while to realise how fussy butterflies were about grass. At the beginning, he used to have a big clean-up in the wild garden before winter, cutting the grass short, burning the rubbish. Then he learned that the eggs of the small skipper butterfly overwinter on the Yorkshire fog grass, tucked neatly into the sheath made by the leaf as it coils round the grass stem. His clean-up was doing them no good at all.

Most of the wild part of the garden lies on a steep hillside which falls away from the house. The soil is relatively poor, which is a help, as wild flowers generally favour starved ground, where they are not crowded out by the coarser type of grass. There is plenty of ragwort (horse-lovers will hate that), tawny-coloured fox and cubs and bird's foot trefoil, which provides food for the caterpillars of the common blue.

Mr Bowler has also planted masses of alder buckthorn to try and lure in the brimstone, a wonderfully sulphurous butterfly with a small orange spot on each of its wings, the colour of sherbet lemons. Although to us, the buckthorn seems an unremarkable tree – the flowers are infinitesimal, the leaves are no more than leafish – to the brimstone it is heaven. It can pick one out as though it had a neon light flashing over it, 'Cheap Eats'.

Butterflies generally favour open, sunny sites, but they also need protection from the wind, which in the Heage garden is provided by a shelter belt of elm suckers. There is a butterfly called the white-letter hairstreak which is entirely dependent on elm and populations crashed when Dutch elm disease arrived in this country.

In our garden, we lost thirty elms when the disease first struck in the mid seventies, and the suckering regrowth only seems to be able to get to a certain size before it is reinfected. Mr Bowler is watching his anxiously. The hairstreaks only use the tops of elm trees, so they are not easy butterflies to study and nobody is yet sure whether sucker growth is going to be good enough for their discerning palates.

Few gardeners are going to be as single-minded as Mr Bowler in his pursuit of the butterfly, but gardens have an important place in the web of habitats that butterflies need to survive. Simplest to provide are refuelling stations, a good range of nectar-producing plants. Mr Bowler would add plants such as marjoram, dandelion, hemp agrimony, devil's bit scabious and sweet rocket to the list of garden flowers that I gave earlier.

It is more difficult to persuade butterflies to stay with you on a permanent basis. Nettles are not necessarily the answer. They are important food plants for the caterpillars of the peacock, the comma, the summer-visiting red admiral and the small tortoiseshell (which is the most common butterfly in British gardens), but a survey carried out by Dr Martin Warren of Butterfly Conservation showed that butterflies rarely use nettles in a garden setting, preferring those on roadside verges and other wild places. There is no shortage of nettles and the butterflies that use them are wandering species, well equipped for long flights if they are properly tanked up.

Dr Warren considers ivy to be the most important plant that gardeners can provide for butterflies. This supplies food for the second brood of the holly blue and a place to overwinter for the brimstone. Of all the species of butterfly, the holly blue is the one that Dr Warren thinks can be most helped by gardeners. The first brood feeds on holly, which is a handsome if slow garden tree, and they also take to dogwoods and the snowberry *Symphoricarpos albus*, both useful garden plants.

But I am worrying about Mr Bowler, brooding over his ragwort and scanning the tops of his elms with his binoculars, waiting for a hairstreak. I wonder, if I were to capture the two mothy red admirals that came to our buddleia this morning and drive them up to Derbyshire, whether it might cheer him up?

PLUM PASSION

Feast or famine is the rule with plums. Even when it looks as though it is going to be a feast, there is still the war of the wasps to be won. But if early frosts do not strike and bullfinches find some other garden to raid, you might find yourself looking, as I did one August, at four plum trees all of which have prolific crops.

In the case of 'Coe's Golden Drop' prolific means fourteen plums. The position of each of these fruit on the map of the tree is as vividly memorable to me as the sequence of stations on the London Underground. The loss (cause unknown) of no. 15 plum was more shocking than the disappearance of Gloucester Road from the Circle Line.

The variety is named after Jervaise Coe, a market gardener in Bury St Edmunds who raised it at the end of the eighteenth century. He was never sure who the parents were, but thought they were most likely to be 'Greengage' and 'White Magnum Bonum', which grew side by side in his nursery.

The fruit has the melting sweet flavour of a perfect greengage, but intensified threefold. It matures late at the end of September and is lemon-shaped, with a characteristic little bump at the stalk end. It has yellow skin and rich golden-yellow flesh. But it is what is euphemistically known as 'shy-fruiting', the meanest of all plums. That is why fourteen can be interpreted as a triumph rather than a disaster.

Planted on its own, it would bear nothing, for 'Coe's Golden Drop' is one of several important plums that need a pollinator, a plum of a different variety nearby, in order to set fruit. 'Rivers' Early Prolific', 'Jefferson' and 'Kirke's Blue' are equally hopeless on their own. But the self-fertile types, even the paragon 'Victoria', do not have such a good flavour. And they, too, set better crops if they have other plums as neighbours.

Climate also makes a difference. Generally, they are more difficult in the western counties of Britain than in the rest of the country. They like hot summers, hard winters and a late, short spring. The Caucasus and the countries round the Caspian Sea are their home and they have not forgotten it.

Situation matters, too. They need shelter from wind and as much protection as possible from late frosts. Late-flowering varieties such as the dual purpose 'Oullin's Gage' have a better chance of escaping frost than the early flowering 'Jefferson'. The most succulent fruit comes from fan-trained trees planted against south-facing walls. Plums are too prolific in growth to make cordons or espaliers.

As with apples, trees are grafted on to different rootstocks which control their relative vigour. The most common is 'St Julien A'. Grown on this a 'Victoria' plum will spread at least 16 feet (5 metres) after about ten years. Dwarfing rootstocks are less common with plums than with apples, though there is one in use called 'Pixie'. It cuts down the eventual size of the tree by two-thirds or a half, but the tree needs richer soil and more cosseting than the same variety growing on 'St Julien A'.

Grafting is the horticultural equivalent of a piggyback. The graft borrows stronger legs than its own to do what it needs to do. But when you are planting, you need to be sure that the graft, which usually shows as a bump or a bend or a slight swelling on the trunk, is well clear of the soil. If you bury it, the top graft will try to grow its own roots and so lose the benefit of the piggyback from its stronger companion.

There are still more than eighty different varieties of plum available to anyone who has space to plant. Compare that with what is on offer in the shops. Where there is room for only one tree, I suppose it would have to be 'Victoria'. It is not as fussy about its position as some other plums and it crops well and regularly.

In fact, it has a tendency to overcrop, and if you let it, it will then want to rest the following year, like an enervated actor after a particularly stressful run of *Hamlet*. Thinning is the way round this problem, leaving no more than one fruit every 4 inches (10 centimetres). The tree sheds some fruit itself, usually in June, when the stones are beginning to harden.

Where there is room for more than one tree, you must work on setting up the right relationships. A spread of early, mid-season and late varieties seems a simple option, but check that you have chosen varieties that have the same or overlapping flowering times. This is vital if you are including varieties that are not self-fertile. Kind nurserymen include all this information in their catalogue, leaving you free to drool over the descriptions.

There are a few stumbling blocks to avoid. 'Jefferson' and 'Coe's Golden Drop' will have nothing to do with each other, even though their flowering times overlap. 'Cambridge Gage' will not help common greengage.

And then there is the pruning … First of all, if you want a fan, forget all those complicated strip cartoons that tell you in various shades of green which bits of the tree to keep and which to cut off. You can buy fans already beautifully trained with eight straight arms. Fix eight long bamboo canes to fan out from a centre point on your fence or wall and tie the branches on to those. Keep them tied in as they grow.

You can allow other shoots to grow into more branches if you have space to fill, but all the rest of the shoots sprouting from this main framework need to be nipped out. Do this in two stages. In July pinch back all side shoots to about six leaves. These will be the shoots that will bear fruit the subsequent summer. When they *have* fruited, cut back these side shoots by half, to about three leaves. Any shoots that are pointing directly into the fence should be rubbed out entirely.

Fans are decorative and take up space in just two dimensions rather than three. But because growth is restricted, you cannot expect more than 30 pounds (15 kilos) of fruit from each fan. A free-standing tree will produce more: 50 pounds (25 kilos) after ten years, twice as much again when it is mature.

Ordinary trees require very little pruning. Just take out dead wood and thin growth if it becomes overcrowded. Any cutting should be done in late spring or summer. This reduces the risk of silver leaf spores infecting the tree.

Silver leaf is the most serious of the plum's problems and there is no cure. You can cut out infected branches and hope, but if more than a third of the tree is blighted, you will be lucky to see it recover.

Bullfinches are at least a more decorative problem and not terminal – except to your hopes of an epicurean dessert. Robert Fish, head gardener in the 1860s at Putteridge Bury Park in Bedfordshire, was not so forgiving about bird damage. He sprayed all his fruit trees with a thick wash made from soot, lime, clay, cow dung and salt. This, he reported laconically, 'sticks on pretty well by the help of the clay and the cow dung'.

'So long as the buds are thus crusted,' he continued, 'the buds will hardly be touched by any bird.' It's the thought of the heavily crusted junior gardeners who had to carry out this spraying that worries me.

GONE BULBS

'Hay or antiques?' asked the woman who came out to meet me as I drove into a Lincolnshire farmyard recently. A woollen hat was pulled firmly over her head. Below its rim, a row of flat grey curls marched along her forehead as though they had been glued in place. I wanted to say 'Hay' and establish my rural credentials. But it was the peeling 'Antiques' sign that had pulled me into the yard.

'You looked more like hay,' she said, unlocking the barn that had 'Antiques' painted on the door. 'We've sold a lot of hay today. It's the weather for it.' The barn smelt of damp Sundays and was piled high with sad things: china mugs, old mantelshelf clocks, plywood chairs with plastic seats, little dishes that had spent previous lives nestling on dressing tables with lace-edged doilies.

I no longer hope for wild discoveries in barns like this. *The Antiques Roadshow* has made everyone an expert now. I did once find a mahogany Queen Anne chest on a Wantage scrap heap, but it has never happened since. Whenever I polish it, I remember the way the bottom of my stomach turned over the first time I saw it, beached among the washing machines and old cars of the dealer's tip.

It takes a while to get your eye in, in this kind of place. It's partly because of the muzzled light, and partly because you are fighting the melancholy ingrained in these remnants of other people's lives. There were big, cast-iron saucepans there, and mangles and flat irons. There were rat traps, and a small sofa covered in uncut moquette. There were kitchen cupboards with chrome handles and pictures mottled in mould.

In a corner on the floor stood a small, galvanised tub, about 9 inches (23 centimetres) high and 12 inches (30 centimetres) across at the top. It had a nice, weathered feel about it and I could see it standing on our kitchen table, planted up with hyacinths. The owner saw me looking at it. 'Plenty more in the next barn,' she said and unlocked another door.

Through that door lay the most extraordinary collection of artefacts: vast riddles, baskets, bunching boards, buckets, clay pots, rakes, wooden boxes stamped with growers' names, all the detritus of the bulb-growing business which was once a big thing in the Fens. It started with Elizabeth Quincey of Fulney, who in 1885 sold snowdrops locally at the price of a penny a bunch. By the late 1930s, almost 10,000 acres of Fenland were planted with bulbs, producing at least 200,000 flowers an acre.

The silty, well-drained soil in this part of Lincolnshire suited bulbs very well and the increase in demand for cut flowers in Britain's industrial cities was matched by a growth in the railways. Without the means to get their flowers to Covent Garden market, the bulb growers of the Fens could never have built up such a demand.

Piled in uneven towers were hundreds of the galvanised tubs. 'We used to put the flowers in them, in water, when we'd bunched them up,' explained the old lady. 'Then they told us we hadn't to do it any more.'

'Why?' I asked.

'I don't know,' she replied. 'I expect it was because they could get the blooms to market quicker. They didn't need their drink first.'

I bought half a dozen of the tubs at £2 a throw and managed to persuade myself that I did not need a bulb basket with a wire grid bottom or a riddle that measured 4 feet (1 metre) across. I could not think of a use for them and these things deserve to be used, not strewn about as set dressing. I'm very glad to have my tubs, but I would be gladder still to see the bulb fields (now reduced to a measly 300 acres) bloom again in the naked landscape of the Fens.

A CORSICAN CLIFFHANGER

Our summer holiday is usually spent sailing, but fortunately, the friends we sail with are as keen on walking as they are on navigating the waves. This time we picked up the boat, a Bavaria 42, in the Maddalenas, a scattered group of wild islands that lie off the northern tip of Sardinia. The forecast was for a good steady blow from the east, so we couldn't resist the chance to zip up once again to the stupendous red cliffs of Corsica's west coast.

This was the fourth time we have headed to these waters. Corsica's rocky coasts provide some surprising anchorages, if the wind is kind, and whenever possible, we drop anchor and overnight in some quiet bay. Cala di Tuara in the Golfe di Girolata (though Corsica is French, many place names are confusingly Italian) was a new discovery: no houses, no lights, no road, though we could see one of the island's long-distance footpaths dipping down to the shore and then climbing steeply on to the north.

So we had the place pretty much to ourselves and in the late afternoon rowed ashore to explore the dried-up river bed that disgorged on to the steeply shelving beach. Corsica is a good place for plants; nowhere else I've wandered gives such clear lessons on habitat. One particular set of plants (sweet chestnut, cyclamen, *Helleborus corsicus*) lives high up in the cooler air of the mountains. Another set (arbutus, myrtle, sea buckthorn) is what you'll find in the hot, dry maquis. On the shore are the dead, matted rhizomes of *Posidonia oceanica*, a strappy monocotyledon which grows in great meadows on the seabed. Bulbs on the shoreline are most likely to be sea squills or sea daffodils. Bulbs growing in poor pasture will probably be asphodels.

But the first plant we saw on the stony dried-up river bed was something I'd never encountered before: a shrubby kind of perennial, four to five feet high, thin leaves, small clusters of creamy flowers, not very conspicuous, towards the top of the stems. Its most outstanding characteristic was its seedpods, extraordinary comma-shaped capsules, up to two inches long, green and covered with soft bristles. When they dried, they split to shed a mass of soft thistledown.

So where do you start when you want to identify a stranger such as this? I've got three flower books that cover the area: *Flowers of the Mediterranean* by Oleg Polunin and Anthony Huxley, *Mediterranean Wild Flowers* by Marjorie Blamey and Christopher Grey-Wilson and *Wild Flowers of the Mediterranean* by David Burnie. Constraints of space on board mean that I usually take only two of the three.

Trained botanists may well start their search with the identification key: flowers spurred or not spurred, flowers in umbels or distinct heads, petals free or fused, leaves heart-shaped or linear, ovary below tepals or underground. But this is too daunting a task for most of us, who take a lifetime even to understand that wild-flower books are not laid out alphabetically but according to the age of the family in question. So my Mediterranean flower books start with pines, which, according to the fossil records, are the oldest group of plants in the region, and finish with families such as the thrifts, olives, gentians and bedstraws, which, in geological time, evolved much more recently.

But I'm not a trained botanist and my way in is much more random. Sometimes the general habit and style of a plant will suggest a family – spurges, perhaps, or geraniums. The plant in front of me on the river bed didn't do that. By far its most arresting and decorative feature was its extraordinary seedpod, and I wondered whether this might have led to a common name which highlighted this feature. So when I got back to the boat, I flicked through the various bladder plants listed in the indexes: bladder campion, bladder senna, bladder vetch, but it certainly wasn't any of those.

After that, I had to depend on good pictures, and in this respect David Burnie is by far the most helpful. His book uses photographs, not drawings, and the illustrations are always alongside the text, not clumped in separate sections. Flicking laboriously through the first 176 pages, I found my plant, the bristly-fruited silkweed *Gomphocarpus fruticosus*, because it was so well illustrated, with details of leaf, flower and seed capsule pictured alongside a stem of the plant itself.

But if I'd pursued my first approach a little further, I might indeed have been able to track this plant down by its common name. When I picked a sprig to take back to the boat, the stem produced a milky sap, like a spurge. The plant is in fact one of the milkweed family and milkweed in the index would have led me straight to it. It turns out it's not actually a native at all, but was introduced into the Mediterranean as an ornamental plant from South Africa. It was particularly pleasing to read – the final positive identifier – that its preferred habitat is rocky watercourses.

From Calvi we made a favourite trip up to Corte, a university town in the wild, craggy centre of the island, to walk part of the Mare a Mare path through the mountains. At first this is maquis territory, drifting into chestnut where watercourses provide sufficient for the trees to drink. The best way to get to Corte is on the train which hauls itself from east coast to west on a track that defies all laws of gravity. But the train people were *en grève* and the buses that got us to Corte then decided to join them. So we got back to our boat thanks to a magnificent taxi driver determined to prevent anyone from overtaking her – ever.

In high-speed French, with much waving of hands, sometimes both at the same time, she gave us the local news. There had been a big flood at Bastia. Her Mercedes was washed away. Pouf! A landslide had crushed a lorry, just here, on the road. Pouf! A new hotel had been built in the town we were passing through. An outsider. Said he didn't think much of the Corsicans. The next day, Pouf! No more hotel. So, just to get this absolutely clear, I LOVE CORSICA.

FIVER FRENZY

Instant gardening does not come more instant than at the Columbia Road street market in east London. Dreams of pots and hanging baskets materialise in front of your eyes. The recipes are familiar ones: two trays of lobelia and half a dozen pink trailing geraniums, a tray of purple petunias with a tray of pink verbena, two standard fuchsias and a couple of pots of helichrysums.

The place had acquired mythical status before I ever paid my first visit. You do not get further than five minutes into conversation with any London gardener before Columbia Road is mentioned. I had to see what it was like.

It is not difficult to find. In fact the process is rather like a paper-chase. The first clue came in Old Street Tube station. A crop-haired man in black leathers was trying to manhandle a large kentia palm and a couple of trays of petunias through the ticket machines. Further along Old Street, I passed two girls almost entirely disguised by monster rubber plants. Then there was a pushchair with a load of marigolds balanced on the hood, the baby underneath peering anxiously through large fronds of maidenhair fern.

The fourth clue was a brilliant red rhododendron parked by a bus stop, in full strident bloom among the empty drink cartons and sheets of yesterday's newspapers. By the time I got to the road itself, I felt as though I had been swept into the final scenes of *Macbeth*. Forests of Dunsinane greenery passed me by: climbing ficus, cordylines, passion flowers, fuchsias.

There isn't much carrying room in Columbia Road. People clutch potted plants to their chests, using them as gentle battering rams to forge a way through the crowd. The flowers and leaves wave around above head height, in constantly changing combinations. This is a novel way to view plant associations. Cordyline with red geraniums? Or perhaps better with the yellow marigolds coming in from the left. Then the cordyline disappears down a side street and sheaves of lilies come wobbling into view.

As far as value is concerned, Columbia Road is astounding. Big trays of bedding plants, busy lizzies, lobelia, verbena are available at giveaway prices. Herbs are a snip. Fine osteospermums are cheap, cheap, cheap. So are shrubs such as choisya and climbing hydrangea. By one o'clock the prices are even keener. That is when the market is supposed to close down. The trading becomes even more frenetic: two big trays sold for the price of one, seven geraniums in a box rather than five, azaleas clashed together in hastily marked-down pairs.

I was hoping in the general fiver frenzy to get hold of a couple of superb standard bays, but they remained firmly stuck at their starting price. Compared with what you would pay elsewhere, they were still pretty cheap, but in the end the vision of the man on the Tube with his kentia palm put me off. I could not see myself handling the escalators very well with a brace of 6-foot (2-metre) bay trees as luggage.

The flower market in Columbia Road has been established for more than a hundred years and has fortunately survived a recent threat to its future on this site. There was a faction ('vested interest,' they said darkly in the market) which thought it would be a good idea to move to the new Spitalfields development. Residents and traders called in the Electoral Reform Society to conduct a proper vote on the matter. The result was a resounding victory for the market. More than 90 per cent wanted it to stay where it is.

How it got there in the first place, nobody could tell me. This is a narrowish, ordinary sort of street, old shops lining it along one side, many turned into flowerpot shops and craft shops: extraordinary one-off garden ornaments, excellent dark green watering cans with brass roses, square clay seed trays (they make good containers for sempervivums and alpines), clay Long Tom pots, old clay flowerpots with enough patina to satisfy the fussiest designer, solid stainless steel handforks and trowels. Much of what you see in the shops here is made to order, with some particularly good ironwork: rose arches, tall twisted iron supports that you could use for roses and clematis.

As for plants, anything that had a bloom buried somewhere in its genes was blooming in Columbia Road. I even expected blooms on the rubber plants. The fuchsias were bulging with flower, shipped in directly from Holland, it seemed from the boxes, stamped with the logo of Bloemen Veiling.

All the bedding plants were flowering fit to bust. 'Do you have any petunias that aren't in flower?' I asked a stallholder with a ginger hat and a profile like a Roman emperor. He looked at me as if I was mad. 'You having me on?' he asked suspiciously and returned to the chanting roar of his sales pitch. So much for the endlessly repeated warning that bedding plants already in flower will not bulk up so well as plants that are set out before they come into flower.

Generally, the plants were in good condition, though I would not buy any bedding plants without looking underneath the trays to see how many roots were trailing out of the bottom of the container, and poking a finger into the compost to see how dry it was. French marigolds shoot up to flower very quickly if they are stressed by lack of water. Unfortunately, they then think their job in life is done and make no further growth or flowers.

The fuchsias represented staggeringly good value, especially the mop-headed standard kind, which take quite a long time to train. I would not be worried about setting these out immediately. If you were buying early in the season, you would have to spend some time hardening them off gradually, for until they emerge blinking in the Columbia Road, they will have spent their entire lives in humidity-controlled, everything-controlled Dutch greenhouses.

There were a cheering amount of twenty-somethings shopping for plants in the market. I am an unashamed eavesdropper on these occasions. I like listening to other people's debates about whether they should have a broom or a hydrangea on the left as they go in at the front gate. 'That's the thing that died in the frost,' said one half of a couple, pointing accusingly at a plant. 'But it's very pretty,' said the other. 'I know what it is now. It's an osteospermum.' And you think, 'There's another gardener hooked.'

Although I had to leave the bay trees behind, I could not resist the Paris daisies. A fiver of course. Produced in Italy. How can they grow plants 24 inches (60 centimetres) across, beautifully trained and pinched out, covered in bud *and* send them from Italy, all for a fiver? 'Don't ask,' said the trader. 'Just buy.'

Tasks for the Month

General

ᘒ Trim evergreen hedges such as holly and yew and reshape topiary if necessary. If you trim too late, new growth is knocked back by frost.

ᘒ In sultry, overcast weather, top up the water in pools to bring much-needed oxygen to gasping fish. Thin out pond weed if growth becomes too dense.

ᘒ This is a good time to prepare sites for new lawns to be sown next month.

ᘒ Horsetail is particularly difficult to eradicate, but research suggests that it absorbs weedkiller more effectively if lightly trampled before spraying.

Flowers

ᘒ Shear alchemilla down to the ground to prevent plants from seeding: mounds of fresh new leaves will see you through nicely until autumn.

ᘒ Cyclamen corms that have been resting can be started into growth again. Do not bring the plant inside until at least six flowers are in bud.

ᘒ Cut out the old growths of rambler roses as soon as they have finished flowering and tie in the new sappy growths, fanning out the stems as much as possible. If no new shoots have appeared, cut out one old growth entirely and prune back the side shoots on the rest.

ᘒ Thin out some of the old wood on rampant honeysuckles.

ᘒ Do not cut back stems of lilies after flowering. Like daffodils, lilies suck back the goodness of the stem into the bulb to build themselves up for next season.

ᘒ Trim out tired flower heads of *Stachys byzantina* and of other plants such as *Geranium psilostemon*.

ᘒ Cut everlastings before they come into full bloom.

ᘒ Plant bulbs of forced hyacinths if you want them in flower for Christmas. A few bowls now, followed by a few next month, will give you a succession of blooms. Use bulb fibre or compost in the bowl and set the bulbs so that their noses are just above the surface of the compost. Water them well. Store the bowl in a cool place (not more than 48°F (9°C)) for eight to eleven weeks. Bring the bowl into the warm when the flower buds are pushing out from the bulbs. Flowering should be in full swing three weeks after the bulbs come into the light.

August

Vegetables

- Harvest baby beets, lettuce, French beans and carrots.
- Make further sowings, if you need them, of mustard and cress and radish.
- There is still time to sneak in a last sowing of carrots which will provide fresh roots in autumn.
- Pick cobs of sweetcorn when the silky tassels on the ends have begun to wither. The kernels should still be soft enough for you to stick a thumb-nail into them. White milky juice will ooze out.
- Clear away peas and beans that have finished cropping. Compost the haulms.
- Pull up onions and leave them to ripen on top of the ground until the green tops have withered away.

Fruit

- Early apples such as 'Discovery' and 'George Cave' should be picked as soon as the stems part easily from the branch.
- Peaches may also be ready to pick. Do not leave peaches to ripen fully on the tree or they may drop. A day in a warm kitchen will finish them off more safely.
- Cut out old fruited stems of loganberries and tie new canes in their place.
- Summer pruning of trained trees such as apples and pears encourages fruiting spurs. Shorten all mature side shoots to within three leaves of the base cluster of leaves. New shoots springing from existing shoots should be treated even more harshly. Cut them back to one leaf.

Propagating

- Take cuttings of zonal and ivy-leaved pelargoniums.
- Choose 3 to 4-inch (7 to 10-centimetre) cuttings from non-flowering shoots of lavender and stick them in a pot or a shady cold frame in sandy compost. Keep them watered.
- Take cuttings of *Artemisia arborescens*, senecio and other grey-leaved shrubs.
- Cut back hard any particularly good violas and pansies that you want to

increase and cover the crown of the plant with a finely sifted mixture of sandy soil. This will encourage some good new growths. You can pull these out with a few roots attached and pot them up as fresh plants.

- Take tip cuttings of indoor plants such as coleus, tradescantia, zebrine and busy lizzies. When the cuttings are rooted and growing away, pinch out the tops to encourage bushy growth.
- Take cuttings of rosemary, thyme and sage, pulling off shoots about 6 inches (15 centimetres) long with a good heel and lining them out 2–3 inches (5–7 centimetres) deep in fine, sandy soil. Firm down the soil around the cuttings and keep watered.
- Take cuttings of slightly tender perennials such as penstemon, Felicia and argyranthemum. These will need protection through the winter.

The Old Rectory garden, Puncknowle

AMAZING MAZES

When I met David Goff Eveleigh, he had just come back from a Mad Hatter's tea party in Shropshire. 'Ah!' I said carefully. 'And what do you do the rest of the time?'

'Alchemy,' he replied, looking me straight in the eyes. 'Clowning about. Being Lord of Misrule. I create and control chaos. It's a wonderful thing you know, chaos. The lord of chaos is master of all. I deal in fire and water. Fire and air.'

'Ah,' I said again.

'Now I'm into earth,' he added helpfully. 'I'm earthed at last. I was once before. I had a smallholding. A big organic patch. Grew veg. Very pretty. I had chickens. A performing goose. A cockerel called Sir Henry Oake who used to play the drums. And the piano.'

Just then I was very tempted to write an entire article on training cockerels to hit the skins. Suddenly, it seemed so boring being a gardening writer. A new life as circus correspondent glittered before me. But it was not to be. Mr Eveleigh remembered that I'd come to see a maze. Maze-wards we went, tramping through the parkland of an old estate called Penpont, just west of Brecon.

Penpont had recently been taken over by Gavin and Davina Hogg. 'The whole maze thing started because we had an incredible crop of beech mast,' explained Gavin Hogg, an arboriculturist by training.

'All over the woods these little beech trees started springing up. We wanted to find a use for the trees. And we wanted to do something for the millennium. First we thought of an avenue in the park, but that wouldn't have used many of the beech. Then we got into mazes.'

This maze is extraordinary. It lies on gently sloping ground at the edge of the parkland and represents the Green Man, a potent figure in Celtic mythology. Most of the outline is traced in beech, but the curling lips are made of yew, clipped in billows, the nose is a bank of lavender tumbling from a tumulus of stone and the chin is a pool, mostly filled with a jagged upturned tree trunk.

The goal at the centre of the maze is a standing stone, set round with wild flowers. 'I wanted the goal to be simple,' explained Mr Eveleigh. 'Very much a quiet place of nature.' At the heart, there is also a holly tree, symbol of the Green Man. Either side are the Green Man's eyes: one modern, set with intricate patterns of stone, the other a Renaissance eye, not matching. Above are eyebrows of yew.

Everything of course is tiny. The trees were only planted last year. All through the last winter, the maze was Twig Man, rather than Green. Now the beeches have flushed and the whole place has come to life. The brief – insofar as there was any – was to incorporate as many materials from the estate as possible. There are intricate patterns of sandstone cobbles brought up in buckets from the River Usk that runs below the house. White quartz stones were carried from the Wye. The cobbling, not easy to do well, is superb.

Stone paving came from a quarry at Coed Major below Hay Bluff. 'I liked the stone so much I bought the quarry,' said Mr Eveleigh in the American accent of the shaver man on the telly commercial. And it's true. He has. Incorporated in the design are two thrones made from stone from his quarry. 'For seraphims,' said Mr Eveleigh simply. Of course. I should have known.

But how do you start on a maze like this, I wondered? 'I dowsed the site,' said Mr Eveleigh. 'Dowsing made the decisions for me. I pegged it out on 16 December 1998 at the time of the winter solstice. Then I discovered that the sun set right down the centre of the Green Man.' He dug into the ha-ha to prepare an entrance to the maze. And there, precisely where he'd planned his entrance over a new wooden bridge, he found two stone pillars from some previous, much older bridge. It's all good, spooky stuff, but I glazed over when Mr Eveleigh got into sacred geometry mode. 'Chartres Cathedral. The Pyramids. Cell structure. You know.'

No, I don't, but Mr Eveleigh says it underpins the whole of his design. The distances between things and the proportions are all worked out according to certain principles, a geometry that has nothing to do with Euclid. Certainly, it feels right. Mr Eveleigh puts it down to necromancy. I'm happy with the feeling that it's what happens when someone works instinctively with the lie of the land rather than against it. Intuition as much as geometry.

The idea of the maze or labyrinth has been around since before the Minotaur. As garden features, they developed later in sixteenth- and seventeenth-century Europe. Four mazes were recorded at the Villa d'Este in 1573. In Tudor England, they first appeared in the form of knot gardens, low hedges of shrubs or herbs twisted into intricate designs round in-fillings of coloured gravel. The maze as we now think of it, made of tall hedges, laid out as a puzzle, developed during the seventeenth century. The best known is the one at Hampton Court Palace, which dates from about 1690.

So in this wonderfully precarious existence of clowning, creating fire festivals, building wickerwork giants, what is he going to do next, I wondered? 'Well, I've always wanted to go on an epic horse journey,' he replied. 'But there's the question of where you sleep on a horse. So I bought rather a nice chicken house. And an old tractor. I'm going to drive 3,000 miles to Georgia to see some friends. The tractor will be so much easier than a horse. Higher. And at the end of the day I can just switch it off. I'll sleep in the chicken house.'

'With chickens?' I asked.

'Of course with chickens,' he replied. So if you happen to be in Europe and see a man in a tractor towing a chicken house, wave. It's bound to be Mr Eveleigh.

GIANT VEGETABLES

To the outsider, there is a magnificent lunacy about giant vegetables and the wildly competitive shows at which they are pitted against each other. Carrots are turned into Gorgons' heads, whirling nests of bright orange snakes. Pumpkins look like mounds of slowly sinking dough. All giant pumpkins have the same saggy, flattened, run-out-of-steam look, the look of a vegetable that has been pushed to the limit. In the process of getting big, most giant vegetables also get ugly. Only giant onions retain their svelte sleekness. And there are sometimes wondrous cabbages, symmetrical, grand, carved, although they may be more than 4 feet (1 metre) across. At the Bay Tree Nurseries, Spalding, which regularly holds giant vegetable events, I once saw a cabbage that weighed 116 pounds. It was almost as heavy as its owner, Ken Dade of King's Lynn.

The growers at these shows stand around in knots, arms folded, shirt sleeves rolled up, leaning back slightly from the waist, the stance of men who know where they fit in the great scheme of things. The conversation is only of vegetables. 'I've not done it on the sub-laterals. That's where I've slipped up.' 'I fancy he's lost a bit of weight overnight. I'm not happy about him.'

Only the novices look at all nervous, worrying that at the last minute an unexpected parsnip or tomato might turn up on the show bench and smash their dreams for ever. The old hands know who has won long before judging has even started. At the tail end of the season, many of the vegetables – onions, marrows, parsnips, giant radish – are already old troupers. They have done shows in Scotland, won prizes in Wales, travelled the pubs of the north-east where the leeks and the onions gather.

Wherever two or three growers of giant vegetables gather together, you will find arguments about rules and standards. Forget GATT. Forget CAP. Nothing that goes on in Brussels could be more serious and impassioned than an onion grower's plea for standardisation of the neck-trimming procedure *re* onions. 'It's a minefield,' says Bill Rogers, an old hand. You can lose an all-important quarter of an ounce with a bad trim.

'Why do you do it?' I once asked a trio of growers, rudely interrupting a conversation which had consisted entirely of tales of onions past, dreams of onions future. I may as well have asked 'Why sleep?', 'Why eat?'

'Well,' said one of them eventually, scratching the knitted back of his cap. 'I was looking for something to do.' Courtesy demanded an answer and these are kind, courteous people.

The expertise needed to produce these monster vegetables, the love and care lavished on them, is self evident. But why is bulk so much more interesting than quality? Because it is measurable, say the people who grow them. Incontrovertible. It's a mine-is-bigger-than-yours situation. No argument.

Of course you won't find men like these poncing about with

courgettes or petit pois, though it is surprising that no one has yet found a way to persuade a potato to abandon its sensible way of life and take its place among the giants. Anything these people take on has to have the capacity for mammoth growth: swedes, leeks, beefsteak tomatoes, beetroots, watermelons, cucumbers. They have been quick to see the possibilities in mooli, the Japanese white radish. I've seen radishes that could double as truncheons.

And I like being amongst people who have expertise, however esoteric it may be. I liked watching Ian Neale of Newport, Gwent, when he presented the world with its biggest ever beetroot, forty and a half pounds of inedible fibre, which he lifted as a shot putter might, the vegetable balanced menacingly in his huge hand. It was forty-two and a half inches round the waist, he told me proudly. I am of course hooked on the idea of exhibiting my own giant vegetable one day at the Baytree Nurseries, Spalding. The recipe for success is daunting. First take forty tons of muck and dig it in well ...

A MASTER OF PLANTS

Regulars arrive at Bob Brown's Worcestershire nursery with the self-satisfied smile of people let in on a secret. New customers each have different tales of where they got lost and why. I chickened out and asked for directions at the Spar shop in Badsey, where there are stacks of nursery postcards with maps on the back. Bob Brown seems rather to enjoy the fact he's difficult to find. 'Keeps away the people who aren't particularly keen,' he says.

Persevere. It's worth it. At the nursery itself, there was no difficulty in finding Bob Brown himself, stocky, bearded and dressed like a Hawaiian surfer in very bright shorts with a yellow bandana wound round his head. I ate his home-made cake and dropped crumbs on the nursery catalogue – long, thin, no pictures, packed with information. Like the schoolmaster he once was, he marks each plant out of ten. I haven't found the teacher's pet yet, the one that gets ten out of ten, though *Euphorbia characias* 'Purple and Gold' comes close with 9.5.

He bought the ground where his stock beds now wave with verbena, crocosmia, rustling pampas and agapanthus, in 1989. Two years later, he got his first write-up. 'It was in *Gardening Which*,' he said. 'I had twelve enquiries, one sale. Typical *Which* reader. He complained.' Although he could have gone anywhere, the nursery ground wasn't a random acquisition. Being a geographer by train-ing, he made all sorts of calculations about population centres and worked out where he would be most likely to find customers. That brought him to the junction of the M5 and the M6, where nobody would ever wish to live or work. But Badsey is close. 'And close to Hidcote too, which is closed in the mornings.'

So, I thought, underneath that Hawaian surfer disguise, a beady businessman lurks. He also got his timing right. Although there are shrubs and climbers in his catalogue, his speciality is perennials and they have been booming over the last ten years. 'Yes,' he said, with a pleased smile. 'I find myself always a bit ahead of the game. It's called being perceptive.'

He doesn't claim to have made the fashion for perennial plants. That, he attributes to the Hardy Plant Society and the arrival of *The Plant Finder* (Dorling Kindersley, £15.99). But even as a child, he'd fallen in love with perennials and with black and white photographs of forgotten phloxes and Michaelmas daisies in dusty gardening books of the thirties and forties.

'I had a mission,' he says, with all the zeal of a religious convert. 'But I also had a lot to learn. Especially about propagating. I thought I could divide *Salvia nemorosa*, fool that I was.' But the stock beds grew, polytunnels sprouted, and now there are more than 1,700 plants listed in his catalogue. He's got administrators to handle the increasing paperwork so that he can go on doing what he likes doing best. Which is digging.

The soil is uncompromisingly heavy, though sustaining for plants whose roots can fight their way through it. Hostas, he says, hate it. That doesn't trouble him too much. 'Nobody should have more than three hostas in their garden,' he says firmly. 'It's quite enough.' Coloured-leaved heucheras are dispatched with equal verve. 'Fifty of them around now. It's ridiculous.' But still, he lists thirty in his catalogue. He's got a business to run, after all, and customers like them. But only two of them rate nine marks out of ten: 'Helen Dillon', which has leaves speckled with cream, and 'Raspberry Regal', with dense spikes of flower the colour of crushed raspberries.

Had he seen much change in his customers since he opened, I wondered? He had. Customers, he said, know much more now and are less frightened by Latin names. They are more eager to buy flowers that are different. And that suits him fine because he's got plenty to offer: *Carex petriei* ('my favourite dead grass,' he says in his catalogue), *Campanula persicifolia* 'Pride of Exmouth' ('robust but suffers from rust'), *Ligularia* x *palmatiloba* ('cut leaves particularly where mollusc populations are high').

He's also aware of changing fashions in plants. Penstemons have come and gone in the last ten years but are about to come again. There has been a slow but steady increase of interest in daylilies. Same with grasses. Eryngiums started coming up a couple of years ago. Gladioli are down and shouldn't be. Pyrethrums are down and should be. Monardas, despite the fuss made over them by Continental nurserymen, are never likely to succeed in our milder climate, he explained. 'They come from the North American prairies, where the cold weather locks them up in winter. Here, it's not cold enough for them so they get covered in mildew.'

Umbellifers, he says, are going through the roof. They are the flat-headed, cow-parsleyish kind of things such as selinum and *Seseli gummiferum*, which is certainly the best plant to have come into my own garden this year. Bob Brown gives it 8. I'd give it 9, despite the fact that it's a biennial and slightly tender. It's out now, looking stunning, with a stem that kinks at each leaf axil, finely cut grey foliage and flat heads of flower, densely packed in pink buttons.

The ground in our garden is dry and cracked – clay at its worst – and it is a ridiculous time to try and plant. But I still came away from Bob Brown's nursery with two carrier bags full of plants. It's that kind of place. With a pickaxe I've managed to plant three witchy arisaemas (another group of plants which is poised to take over the herbaceous border) and two grasses. I've been slow to take to grasses, mostly, I think, because I've seen too many of them dumped in grass gardens, with only themselves for company.

In flower, at this time of the year, they are at their most appealing. I picked up *Eragrostis airoides*, a relatively low-growing grass with bright green leaves and creamy green oatish heads. Its partners in the garden will be *Aquilegia rockii* and eucomis. I've just looked up eucomis in Bob Brown's catalogue, wondering whether he liked it or not. Guess what? Eucomis 'Sparkling Burgundy' is teacher's pet. Ten out of ten. Wow!

CLOSE TO THE HEDGE

We've spent several holidays sailing along the south-west coast of Ireland, between Kinsale and Dingle. If you are lucky with the weather you can scarcely find a better cruising ground: slow-drawn Guinness and scallops ashore, fine, solitary anchorages and the landscape like Sibelius, rising in a stunning crescendo as you goosewing your way up the long reach of the Kenmare River.

On beached Valentia Island, which once hoped, thanks to Marconi, to be the buzzing hub of a new transatlantic telecommunications industry, we bicycled ourselves silly, hauling up the long hot hills to zoom down the other side between tall hedge banks of fuchsia. There's nothing like a bike for giving you a sense of ridiculous speed.

The banks themselves were show-stoppers. The fuchsia (plain green-leaved *F. magellanica*) was in full flood, with sheaves of orange-flowered crocosmia filling in underneath. Where the banks had ditches running alongside them, feathery plumes of meadowsweet were added to the mix, together with fronds of the royal fern *Osmunda regalis*. Small knobs of blue sheep's bit scabious bobbed up at intervals along with the sherbet-yellow stems of toadflax (*Linaria vulgaris*) and purple vetch.

Plodding up the hills through the enfilades of fuchsia (I've never quite got the hang of fifteen-gear bikes) I was thinking about the difficulties of using wild flowers in the garden. Wild-flower meadows, so fashionable and so much written about, are extraordinarily difficult to manage properly, mostly because, in gardens, they are made on ground that is too good for them. Bullies thrive at the expense of the flowers one was hoping to encourage.

But the hedge bank has the inbuilt advantage of being a much more starved environment, encouraging to certain decorative plants, discouraging to nettles, docks and hogweed. There is no reason why you could not adapt the idea to make a garden boundary, running perhaps along the back of a garden. The Irish hedge banks were first thrown up with stones cleared from the fields they surrounded. In the garden, it would be a way of getting rid of all the pieces of broken concrete, brick, clinker and other detritus that you find when you first clear a place that you have just taken over.

The best way to make it would be to sandwich layers of stone and rubble with layers of old turf (the kind of stuff you might strip off a garden in order to make a new lawn), and a thin layer of soil to keep everything level. The layers should taper to a top that is narrower than the base. It may take time, but that doesn't matter. Despite television's desire to turn everything – archaeology, cooking, gardening – into races against time, the point of gardening is that you *don't* have to do it against the clock. It should be a release from and a panacea for all those things in life that *do* require endless clock-watching.

The hedge itself should be planted along the top of the finished bank in a channel of soil that you have incorporated between the two faces of stone. Don't try to start with big plants. They won't settle fast enough to be able to sustain themselves. I would guess that the original Irish fuchsia hedges were set with semi-hardwood cuttings, side shoots with a 'heel' of old wood, torn off in autumn and stuck straight into the ground. This is a cheap, low-tech way of increasing stock, the method that our old neighbour always used to make extra plants to thicken his flowering boundary in Dorset.

The fuchsia, of course, is naturalised in Ireland. It isn't a native wild flower, any more than the crocosmia is. To some xenophobic naturalists, this matters. I don't think it does. We've developed a taste for sun-dried tomatoes and lemon grass. Why shouldn't butterflies be allowed a sip of buddleia and bumblebees their fuchsias?

But the point of the garden hedge bank is that it should seem natural, even if it contains a mix of native and naturalised plants. To that end, avoid incorporating any plants that are too gardenesque. Fat, fleshy-flowered fuchsias would not be right in this situation. Use *F. magellanica* or its hybrid 'Riccartonii', which does not grow so tall. If you plant in early autumn, the newcomers will have time to settle themselves in before there is any question of drought. The roots will have the opportunity to travel down between the stones to gather up water where they can.

The same goes for crocosmia, which, if you want to emulate the Irish effect completely, you ought to plant in the sides of the bank. Forget the posh hybrids such as brilliant 'Lucifer' or the stunning

bronze-leaved 'Solfaterre' and go for the tough old cottage garden
plant that often goes under the name of montbretia. The corms can
be worked into pockets up the sides of the bank, again planting in
autumn rather than spring.

Western Ireland is generally wetter and warmer than most of
England apart from Devon and Cornwall. Bear this in mind if you
plan to make a hedge bank yourself. You should already have noticed
if you live in the kind of place where fuchsia crumples up in winter.
Even if it does, established plants will generally spring new shoots
from the base. They will make more than 4 feet (1 metre) of growth
in a season.

Truly wild flowers such as vetch are probably best introduced as
'plugs' – small plants with good rootballs – in spring. The Irish one
we saw was the showy tufted vetch *Vicia cracca*, with long spikes
of bluish-purple flowers drifting up to a more pinkish purple at
the tips. It is a beauty and flowers over a long period from June
to August, scrambling by way of its tendrils over all sorts of other
vegetation in the hedge banks. It is a more telling plant than either
the common vetch or the bush vetch. Bush vetch has bigger individual flowers but fewer of them. It's better in shade, though, than
the tufted vetch and that is a useful attribute.

The toadflax is like a snapdragon shrunk in the wash and the colour
is acid and sharp, the best sort of yellow to see against the magenta of
the fuchsia. Don't fuss too much about colour combinations, though.
The core concern of gardening in the wild style is to choose plants
that will appreciate and thrive in the particular habitat you are providing. Adopt nature's own magnificent unconcern about the supposed
solecism of yellow getting into bed with magenta.

Other wild flowers to try in the hedge bank might include pink
sainfoin, greater stitchwort for spring, red campion, the greater
celandine (a medicinal herb in medieval times), jack-by-the-hedge
(*Alliara petiolata*), wild strawberry, herb robert, hedge bedstraw and
hedge woundwort.

SIGN OF THE TIMES

A new load of tin arrived in our valley to celebrate the millennium: bright blue signs with red numbers on them, not big but very eye-catching. Each has a bicycle on it; the Sustrans bicycle network has given us its blessing. In principle I like the network idea, but haven't any of these people heard of maps? Is the prospect of getting lost in West Dorset so dangerous that seven of these signs need to be put up within the space of a few miles?

At every junction now, through this pleasantly ramshackle valley, blue tin winks out from the hedgerow, brightly alien, shinily modern. I have always thought of cyclists as an intrepid bunch. Do they really need directing every inch of their rides? If you go walking in a patch of country you don't know, you're considered an idiot if you don't have a map. But here we are, with a lot more tin, and a little more initiative taken away from us.

Tin has been increasing at a great rate recently. It started with a sign announcing the name of our village. At a parish meeting, a newcomer protested at the lack of any evidence that he was living in the right place. Nobody else was worried by this, but at the same time, nobody could think of a logical argument why the village shouldn't be named. So now there are signs at every entrance – large and prominent, as signs must be, if they are to be there at all.

It was not long before the village sign was joined by another larger one underneath: 'Please drive carefully through our village'. The sage chairman of the parish council – gone now, alas – pointed out that it was not strangers who sped. It was locals. Strangers are far too worried by the narrowness of our lanes and the possibility of scratching the paintwork of their cars to do more than crawl. But the sign stays, and the tearaways tear away to the bright lights of Weymouth just as they've always done.

Then a third piece of tin arrived. It was inevitable, for the same tripartite welcome is now common in most rural areas. It was the one that reads 'This is a Neighbourhood Watch Area'. Again, no logical argument can be raised against it. But it is sad that such a thing needs to be said at all. Neighbourliness should be taken for granted. The real problem is a lack of neighbours. Fewer people are actually in village houses, pottering about, any more. Twenty-two houses in our small village are second homes.

Our old neighbour, now dead, was a complete neighbourhood watch on his own. He never moved further than he could walk from the place where he was born and like most old countrymen, noticed everything. Once, he tried to turf out a friend who was using our house while we were away. 'He had a beard,' our neighbour explained later. I nodded, understanding the ramifications. 'He's a writer,' I said, trying to excuse the beard. But the fault was mine. I should have told our neighbour what we were up to.

It was a long time before we ever put up a house sign and when we did finally get an old piece of slate lettered, it was set in by the gate that nobody ever uses. The ivy is obscuring it nicely now. I can tell you the name of the ivy though – *Hedera helix* 'Boscoop', a Dutch cultivar, as you'd guess by its name. It has fat, slightly frilly leaves, tough as leather.

So in the matter of signage and labelling (as in almost everything else), I'm schizoid. I hate not to be able to put a name to a plant in the garden. It seems inhospitable, as a host, not to be able to introduce them to friends when we amble round the garden, coffee mugs in hand. But there again, I don't want the label staring me in the face. I've tried burying labels in the ground at the three o'clock position, a system recommended by a gardening friend. But she can't have such ferociously determined blackbirds or moles as we have. The labels disappear.

Tying on labels would make them too prominent, so now I do without them altogether. The name of each plant goes into a card index, with the date, the person I got it from and a rough note of where it is in the garden. It works as long as I know whether I'm looking at an abelia or an abeliophyllum. Then the index can remind me whether it is *Abelia* 'Francis Mason' or *A.* 'Edward Goucher'. But sometimes a plant comes up in spring that I can't ever remember seeing before. Arisaema? Asarum? I don't know where to begin to look.

'What you need,' said a friend who is deeply into retrieval systems, 'is another card index of parts of the garden, cross-referenced with the first …' But she saw from the look on my face that it was never going to happen. The garden will continue to be an occasional bran tub of surprises.

HYDRANGEA HEAVEN

The plant hunter Ernest 'Chinese' Wilson set out on his third expedition to China at the end of 1906, the party consisting of 'eighteen carrying coolies and one head coolie, two chairs, two handymen, an escort of two soldiers, my Boy and self', as he noted in his diary. From this trip, he brought back the first regale lilies, though his entire consignment rotted on the sea journey home. They had been packed alongside raw animal hides, which did them no good at all.

Stoicism was the thing in those *Boy's Own* days, and Wilson's upper lip was so stiff he could scarcely speak. He could write, though, and his diaries provide the underpinning of some splendid biographies. His third trip, funded by the Arnold Arboretum in America, produced *Lonicera nitida*, cardiocrinum, the brilliant blue *Ceratostigma willmottianum*, which flowers in August and September

and my favourite hydrangea *H. sargentiae*, named after Charles
Sprague Sargent, the director of the Arnold Arboretum.

After reading about Wilson's travels, you look at such shrubs
with new respect. I ordered my *H. sargentiae* years ago from Hilliers
nursery near Winchester and it arrived, neatly wrapped, on a lorry.
Wilson got his from the slopes of a mountain in western Hupeh.
The weather was appalling, the terrain tough, accommodation even
tougher. 'Dingy and damp', he writes of a Buddhist temple where
they found shelter one night, 'a wretched hovel', of the charcoal
burner's hut into which he and his party crept the following day. On
4 and 5 July they spent the night in a piggery.

All you can say is 'Thank you'. By September, *H. sargentiae* is
usually overtaken by *H. villosa*, but at the beginning of August, it
was the best thing in the garden, with huge paddle-shaped leaves
the texture of sharkskin. The flower heads are flat, about a foot
across, filled in the middle with tiny mauve flowers. Each has bright
blue stamens. Haphazardly arranged around the edge are the sterile
florets, quite a stark white, tinged with mauve.

These great flower heads are held on stiff, hairy stems and the
whole bush has a rigid, formal look. It needs space about it. It also
needs fairly deep shade to look its best. Mine grows under the shade
of an old Portugal laurel. This kind of overhanging shade may draw
the shrub up more than if it were growing in the shade cast by a
building, but for the moment it seems happy.

It is no good trying to cram a hydrangea such as this into a dust
scrape. It needs rich, well-fed ground and blankets of mulch each
year to keep the soil moist and cool around its roots. *Hydrangea villosa*
needs similar conditions, though it is not so fussy about being in
shade. This stands higher than *H. sargentiae*, though some of the once
upright growths on my specimen are now leaning on the ground
on their elbows, peering out from a ground cover of ginger mint
and hostas. The leaves are long, narrow, hairy, softer in texture than
H. sargentiae. The flower heads are deeper in colour, though made

up the same way with a big central mass of tiny flowers, surrounded by a showier ring of sterile florets. The overall effect is deep mauve, though when you look into the flower, you see there is a great deal of blue in it.

To get the best from hydrangeas, you need to spend time preparing their quarters, enriching the soil with manure or compost if necessary before planting. Chemical food is no substitute. Only hydrangeas forced to live in the more cramped conditions of a tub need this kind of artificial boost. Although by nature they are woodland plants, growing in dappled shade, they do remarkably well in tubs in full sun. In this situation, the showier mopheads look more at home than the delicate lacecaps.

Neither *H. sargentiae* nor *H. villosa* would give of its best in a tub. They grow too big. They are insufficiently domesticated. Grow them in a shady corner of the garden with Japanese anemones for company. These are excellent plants which never need spraying or staking or fussing over and they come at just the right time for the hydrangeas. White varieties, such as the old 'Honorine Jobert' raised in the 1850s, shine out more in shade, but the common silvery-pink types give a more subtle combination of colours. The anemones will cope with quite deep shade, although they do not flower there as freely as they do in sun.

So far, I have been disappointed by *Hydrangea quercifolia*. It has a lot to live up to, being in the same border as *H. villosa* and *H. sargentiae*, but its habit is lax and stooped and the leaves, though an interesting shape, seem to weather badly. The flowers are cream and droop down in rather shapeless long panicles. The way the other two hold their flower heads is so much better. They present them like waiters swirling into a dining room with plates poised high on their fingertips.

If I had soil that was a little more acid I would have gone for *Hydrangea paniculata* instead, perhaps the cultivar 'Kiushiu', which I remember looking good in a woodland garden in company with the blue flowers of a hibiscus. This has wonderful glossy leaves and huge pyramids of cream flowers. Some forms can get up to about 12 feet (4 metres) but 'Kiushiu' is generally more compact. Unfortunately it would not be happy in my garden, but it is a shrub I would like to grow. I might try clouds of blue willow gentians round its feet. I have not succeeded with those either, though they are said, unlike most of their family, not to be fussy about soil.

Although they are widely planted, the mophead hydrangeas, like *H. paniculata*, seem to be happiest in soil that is on the acid side of neutral. It is well known that on limey soils, mophead hydrangea flowers are pink, rather than blue. That does not matter, but limey soils often make the hydrangea leaves horribly chlorotic as well. The combination of yellow foliage with the pink flowers is not a pretty one. A dose of chelated iron helps improve the condition, but it is so much easier to garden with rather than against prevailing conditions and throw away the medical props.

The first hydrangea I ever had charge of was a large pink mophead that grew outside the gate of our cottage in West Sussex. Following the forcible edict of a neighbour who came patrolling regularly down the lane to see what I was up to, I cut the whole thing down to the base every autumn. It takes a new gardener, as I was then, years to shake off basic misapprehensions such as this. I wondered for several years why I got strong growth but never any flowers.

A book gave me the answer. 'Time to cut that hydrangea down,' shouted my neighbour that year over the wall. 'I thought I'd leave it alone this year,' I answered as boldly as I dared. 'It won't flower,' he said with chilling finality, as he stalked on down the lane. He evidently had not noticed that it had never flowered anyway.

So, do not cut your hydrangea to the ground every year. This is a good technique for rejuvenating old overgrown hydrangeas, but most need only occasional thinning. Cut out two or three stems

from the base of the plant, choosing growths that are lax or unpro-
ductively twiggy. This is a job that is best done in spring, when
you take off the old flowerheads. These provide some protection
against winter weather. They also look good when rimed with
frost.

Tasks for the Month

General

ℰ Repair damaged lawn edges by cutting a rectangle of turf behind the edge and then re-laying it round the reverse way so that the worn edge is on the inside. Sift a little earth over the join.

ℰ Spike over-established lawns to aerate them and top-dress them with a mixture of compost and sand.

ℰ Rooted sections of chives, mint and marjoram can be gently levered away from clumps in the ground and set in pots of compost for a winter supply of fresh herbs.

ℰ Clip Virginia creeper back from windows and haul it out of gutters.

ℰ Mulch wherever you can with whatever bulky material you can get hold of. Mushroom compost is excellent. So are home-made compost and grass cuttings with fallen leaves mixed with them.

Flowers

ℰ Annuals such as poppies, calendula, larkspur, limnanthes, love-in-a-mist, clarkia and cornflower will make an early show next year if they are sown outside now where you want them to flower. Protect them with netting against marauding cats and birds. Leave any necessary thinning until next spring.

ℰ Continue to plant prepared hyacinths for indoor flowering; 15 September is the last possible day for planting if you want them showing by Christmas.

ℰ Some dwarf tulips also make good potted plants, but must have at least twelve weeks buried or kept in a cool, dark place before they are brought into the warm.

ℰ Start planting daffodil bulbs, which always look better in large groups. If planting in grass, choose a spot where their dying leaves and the lengthening grass will not irritate you to the extent that you mow too soon.

ℰ Cut off and dry seedheads from leeks, alliums, Chinese lanterns, honesty and opium poppies and hang them upside down to dry for winter decoration.

ℰ House plants need less food and water as growth slows down for winter.

ℰ Start to clear out summer bedding plants to make way for autumn plantings of wallflowers, sweet williams and tulips. Choose wallflowers with the growing tips pinched out to make compact, bushy plants.

September

- Mildew often affects Michaelmas daisies at this time of year: the spores overwinter on stems and leaves. Cut out all diseased stems after flowering and burn them, and control mildew by using a systemic fungicide. Start spraying in the spring and continue at fortnightly intervals. Old *novi-belgii* types are particularly prone. Replace them instead with *Aster* x *frikartii*.
- Biennials and perennials grown from seed can be planted out in their permanent positions.
- Clear rotting leaves of iris and water lilies from garden ponds.
- House plants that have been standing out for the summer should start to come indoors again. Remove dead and damaged leaves, check staging and watch for pests such as whitefly, which multiply in the more encouraging indoor climate.
- For a spring display, sow seed of a hardy pansy. Scatter seed thinly in pots of compost, cover with more moist compost or vermiculite and wrap the pots in clear polythene covered with newspaper. Remove the covers when the seeds have germinated (usually about a week). After about three weeks the seedlings should be ready to prick out into individual small pots. Plant out in late February or March.
- Set colchicum bulbs to flower inside on saucers of small pebbles. Keep the bulbs well watered, but not drowned. Within a few weeks they will show their long-necked, crocus-like flowers.
- Clean out ragged old flower heads of climbing hydrangea, making the cut where the stem joins the main branch.

Vegetables

- Plant Japanese onions now for an early crop next summer. They fill the gap before other onions come on stream.
- Spinach can be sown now to overwinter and give an early crop in April next year.
- Lift potatoes and store them away from the light.
- Clear runner beans and French beans from the vegetable plot.

Fruit

- After the last of the peaches and nectarines have been picked, wall-trained trees will need pruning and the new shoots tying in to replace the old fruited shoots. Cut out entirely any shoots that grow straight out of the front of the tree at right angles.

❧ Morello cherries fruit on growth made the previous year, not on older wood. Dissuade them from fruiting only on the outer fringes by cutting away one or two older branches now, to a point where a strong new shoot has broken out.

A corner of the garden

THE ANSWER LIES IN THE SOIL

Soil isn't sexy. It's sad but it's true. Gardeners may sigh over their salvias, worship their wisterias, but soil, they take for granted. In gardening books you can bet that any chapter on soil will be illustrated with a hefty boot doing impossibly tiring things with a spade. I have sympathy with readers who may already be turning away in droves from this page, fearing that it is all going to be about double digging, bastard trenching and the like.

I have the same problem with anything to do with DIY. All those instructions about preparing walls before you paper may be music to some ears. Not mine. I'm more interested in the final effect than the underpinning. But soil is different from inert commodities such as plaster and Polyfilla. It is a living thing that needs to be treated with consideration and respect. It is not inexhaustible. It gets tired and hungry and sick. If it only ever gets chemical medicines chucked at it, it turns into a kind of addict, only able to function with stronger and stronger doses of drugs.

Soil is a mixture of bits of rock, water and organic matter such as rotted leaves. Sandy soils are made from relatively large bits of rock, clay soils from small particles. One is called light, the other heavy. The essence of success in gardening lies in getting the right balance between the two, the right structure. For that, you need the proper ratio between earth crumbs and air pockets. On heavy clay soils, there is not enough air. Plant roots keep bumping their noses on the underground equivalent of brick walls. On light, sandy soils, there is too much air and the fine, hairy rootlets that absorb nutrients are unable to clutch at what they need.

Between the two there is a perfect soil. This is the fabled loam, and you can magic it into being by adding humus to your soil at every possible opportunity. The easy way is by mulching heavily over the surface of the soil, leaving the earthworms to drag the humus underground. Humus opens up heavy soils and adds bulk to light ones. Few remedies work with equal success on diametrically different problems but humus is, as I said, magic.

In natural habitats, soil is replenished with a litter of dying vegetation and animal droppings, gradually pulled down into the earth by worms and insects. The garden, though, is an unnatural habitat, where we whisk away dying vegetation like dirty coffee mugs from the sitting room. That's why gardeners have to compensate by blanketing their plots with compost. Anything bulky and organic will do: mushroom compost, spent hops, home-made compost, farmyard manure.

In town gardens, where there is often no access from front to back garden except through the house, this is easier said than done. But done it must be. You do not expect a building to last unless it has decent foundations. The same goes for plants. If the roots are happy, the rest of the plant will mostly take care of itself.

Before plants can take up food, they need roots which can find it. Plant roots need passages along which they can run and from which they can absorb the nutrients necessary for healthy growth. Humus helps create these vital passages. Chemical fertilisers don't.

The minerals that plants need for healthy growth are generally lumped together under the heading trace elements and include boron, copper, iron, manganese and zinc. In fertile soils, they are present naturally, but lack of them shows up in plant deficiency diseases. Organic animal manures are rich in trace elements, and if you use these regularly, you are unlikely to have problems.

Magnesium deficiency (leaves turn brown and wither) is more prevalent on acid soils than alkaline ones. Chlorosis is more likely on limey soils: leaves that should be bright, pulsating green turn a pallid, sickly yellow. The plant cannot absorb the minerals it needs from the soil because they are locked up by too much lime.

Acid and alkaline are terms that apply to the pH (the potential of hydrogen) in the soil. The pH scale runs from 1 to 14 with neutral somewhere in the middle. Above that dividing line, soils are said to be alkaline, below it, acid. Most vegetables grow best in slightly alkaline soil. Rhododendrons need acid soil, between 4.5 and 6 on the pH scale. Kits, with all the charm of toy chemistry sets, are available to tell you whether you have one or the other. Happy gardeners go with the flow and grow plants that like their soil.

Megalomaniacs find this a difficult precept to accept. They dig pits in their gardens and fill them with a different kind of soil, hoping to hoodwink plants into believing that everything is as it should be. For a while this works. But gradually, the soil's true constituents leach into the pretend patch and take it over. Or the plant's roots wander outside the cordon sanitaire and choke on the unfamiliar food. And there is nothing more miserable in a garden than a miserable rhododendron, panting in a sea of lime for its fix of acid.

Prepare beds for planting during autumn, winter and early spring, working only when the soil is dry enough not to stick to the soles of your boots. On heavy ground, you need to dig to throw up clods of earth so that they can get broken up by frost (you soon learn in gardening not to do jobs that others, such as frost and worms, can do for you). You also dig to get air into compacted soil and to bury weeds or other organic material.

But digging no longer has the heroic status it once had, along with bastard trenching and double digging, which is twice as backbreaking as the ordinary kind. Only masochists now make digging loom large in the gardening calendar. On light soils, you can often get away with not digging at all.

Heavy ground, or places which have been used as throughways, need more attention. Digging improves drainage and introduces air into earth which has been hard packed by feet. Heavy clay soils should be dug at the beginning of winter, light soils as late as possible in spring. Light soils do not need to be broken down by frost. The main problem here is hanging on to water and nutrients. By leaving a light soil firm over winter, you will be helping it to hold as much water as possible.

If you are making a new bed on light sandy soil, you can kill off the weeds with a non-residual weedkiller, mulch it heavily and then plant direct into the ground. Mulches break down into humus at different rates, depending on what they are made of. Leaves of ash and apple disappear very quickly. Leaves that contain resins, such as pine needles, or have waxy finishes, such as holly, break down very slowly.

The rate of breakdown depends on the ratio of carbon to nitrogen in the living plant. Grass has a low carbon to nitrogen ratio, about 5 to 1, and so breaks down fast in the soil. In pine needles, the ratio is much higher, about 100 to 1, so deterioration is much slower. In the autumn, a mature tree will provide at least five pounds of leaf litter for each square yard of ground under it. That's nature's way of conditioning and feeding the soil. Match it if you can.

HIGHLAND FLING

Reading the suggestion book left in the cottage we rented recently in the Highlands had the voyeuristic quality of eavesdropping on other people's conversation. Notes, suggested the owner of the cottage, might cover such things as excursions, restaurants and improvements to the cottage itself. But the book ranged far wider than that. Several pages, for instance, were filled with a treatise on the price of petrol, which included details of every garage within a fifty-mile radius of the cottage. The cheapest fuel happened to be twenty-seven miles away, but it was worth the round trip, said the writer firmly. He proved it by a complex calculation of mpg versus pap (price at pump).

I read all this with the same incredulous, fascinated attention that I read agony aunt columns. Why did this man bother to come on holiday, if the price of fuel remained the overriding concern of his fortnight in this remote, extraordinary place? Out of the back door of the cottage stretched fifty miles of hill with nothing in it except red deer, heather, golden eagles and orchids. No houses. No roads. No aeroplanes. No people. Absolute silence. And he thinks about petrol?

The book showed that foodies were frequent visitors to the cottage. In this Highland heaven, epicures can buy the freshest of fresh scallops, steaks of Aberdeen Angus beef, goat's milk cheese, obscure malt whiskies. There were enough shopping tips to keep a holidaymaker in feasts for a month. Serious cooking evidently mattered, especially to the man who suggested that the kitchen saucepans (aluminium) might be better replaced by ones of stainless steel.

Often the suggestion book became a place of dialogue, especially on the question of restaurants. 'Brilliant,' one entry would read. 'Dire,' would be the response of the next person who tried the place. Sometimes it became not so much a place for suggestions as challenges, some more subtle than others. Overtly aggressive was the curt 'Best time to Loch an Iasaich 34mins 2.5sec.' Then the killer, 'There and back.' Now there was a bristling gauntlet thrown down on the muddy track that led to the loch and its dour conifer plantations. I loved the .5sec bit. That must have been a serious stopwatch he was using.

Other entries concentrated on the various Munros that were within reach of the cottage: best routes, best views, potential hazards. As one who has been reading mountaineering books since the age of eight, I devoured all that. It let me off climbing the peaks myself. One entry described a walk recommended by a couple of Munro bashers as suitable for a 'rest day'. With admirable precision they laid out their route, grid references, points of interest along the way, ending with the phrase 'and only 27 miles'.

This being Scotland, there were plenty of suggestions about occupying children on rainy days. Of these, the train ride on the two-coach train that shuttles between Inverness and Kyle of Lochalsh was hot favourite, with or without a break for sticky buns at Plockton. There's a proper station at Plockton but many of the other stops are by request only. 'Making flags to stop the train at the halt occupied our children happily one rainy day,' I read as I sat by a delicious log fire on another day of rain.

A familiar miasma of guilt enveloped me. As our children never tire of pointing out, we never had the craft knives, the right kind of glue or staple gun for this kind of activity. Every airing of *Blue Peter* was cause for new recriminations. They stopped watching it in the end. It was too embarrassing to confess to their classmates that they lived in the only house in Britain without double-sided Sellotape.

THE APPLE OF MY EYE

Apples will always be mixed up in my mind with air-raid shelters. No bombs ever fell near our home in the Welsh borders but my godfather built a shelter, just in case, and much later it became an important landmark for us, the prison for captives in the massive games of chase that we played through the summer and autumn.

If you were captured, you were locked inside the shelter, which, by then, my godfather had turned into a fruit room. Polishing up an 'Egremont Russet' or a 'James Grieve' on your sleeve, you munched and waited for a member of your tribe to come crawling through the undergrowth and rescue you by touching your hand through the iron bars of the window.

Damp and cool in this underground cave, the apples kept in mint condition. But if you don't have a store and are short of growing space, an apple that you can pick and eat straight from the tree is perhaps a better bet than one that needs a few quiet months at 40°F (4°C) to get its gastronomic act together.

'George Cave' is such an apple, a summer fruit, bright and shiny as you could wish, which I planted fourteen years ago as an espalier, part of a screen along a path in the vegetable garden. Later, it was provided with a post and wire support. It should have been the other way around, of course, support before tree, but the cash for the posts and wires kept dribbling off into the black hole that we call the roof of the house.

By the time the wires, neatly strained at 9-inch (23-centimetre) intervals between 4-inch (10-centimetre) square posts, came on the scene, the fan had grown exuberantly into a can-can petticoat, swirling off in all directions. What I could tie in, I did. The rest I sawed away.

Now that the structure has been re-established, and each of the seven wires has a branch tied horizontally to it, the tree can be pruned properly each year. With espaliers (and fans and the like) you need to take off excess growth in early August. Excess means anything that you cannot train in as part of the basic shape. It includes shoots that poke out at the front or the back of the trunk and the new growth that zooms up from the horizontally laid branches of an espalier. You have to cut these back, leaving three pairs of leaves.

If you start cutting too early in the summer, you find that the tree sprouts again and you have to do the job a second time. I generally spread this summer pruning over a couple of weeks, feeling, anthropomorphically, that this will be less of a shock for the tree.

'George Cave', which is usually at its best in mid August, was raised by Mr Cave in Dovercourt, near Harwich, Essex in 1923. Was this the same George Cave who was at Kew in the 1890s and then went out to India to work in the botanic gardens at Calcutta and Darjeeling? I like to think of him in retirement, raising apples in Essex. His papers are kept in the botanic garden at Edinburgh. One day I will find the answer.

His apple is crisp, juicy, fine-textured and smells faintly of strawberries. Like all early dessert apples, it quickly loses its crunch and its flavour. That is why these early varieties can so rarely be found in shops, which is another good reason to grow them.

The fruit is smallish (an advantage if you have smallish children), the green flushed and streaked with red. The tree grows cleanly and vigorously without any sprays. Its only fault is that it lets go of its fruit as soon as they are ready. If you are not around to catch the apples as they fall, the slugs beat you to the feast.

'Beauty of Bath' was the early apple of my childhood. It never found its way into the air-raid store because, like 'George Cave', it must be eaten straight from the tree. I don't have it now, but I remember it as a highly scented and coloured apple, the flesh sometimes flushed pink under the skin. It was juicy, but quite soft. It was my grandmother's favourite apple and we used to bring the first of the crop ceremoniously to her on one of her favourite china plates.

This is an older apple than 'George Cave', introduced in the 1860s by George Cooling, a nurseryman in Bath who actually specialised in roses. Early gardening books recommend that you put mattresses of straw under it at fruiting time, as the fruit has the 'George Cave' habit of falling rather suddenly off the perch.

'It pays for liberal treatment,' says Edward Bunyard, whose *Anatomy of Dessert*, published in 1929, is the best book on fruit ever written. He does not tell you *how* to grow fruit, but gives you a thousand reasons *why* you should. He was a howling snob, gastronomically. 'The man who cannot appreciate a Blenheim [apple] has not come to years of gustatory discretion; he probably drinks sparkling Moscatelle ...' he wrote, but you forgive him this for his fire and ardour − especially where apples are concerned.

Because they are of limited commercial value, early apples have not been much developed by modern breeders. 'Discovery' is one of the best of the modern varieties, a cross between a 'Worcester' and a 'Beauty of Bath'. It is hardy but rather slow to start fruiting and the apples, though pretty to look at, heavily flushed with crimson red, lack the evocative smell of 'Beauty of Bath'. But when it does start to fruit, it is generous, for it bears on tips and spurs. Most apples favour one or the other but not both.

'Laxton's Epicure' is one of a whole string of excellent apples which bear the name of the Laxton brothers, nurserymen in Bedford at the turn of the century. It smells faintly alcoholic and is a pretty apple, striped and streaked in russet-red. It is at its best from late August to mid September. The trees are hardy enough to survive in cold areas and are smaller, perhaps no more than 8 feet (2½ metres) across, than any of the others I have mentioned. The apples need thinning if they are to grow to any size.

Apples (and other fruit) are much better bought as bare-root trees than as container-grown ones. The root system of a tree that has grown in the open ground will be far better developed and far better able to support the head above than roots that have seethed and coiled inside a pot.

This means buying and planting in early winter. The traditional lifting time is Guy Fawkes Day, but much depends on the weather at the time. If you can get a tree in the ground in November, the roots will be well established before they have to set to work dragging up food and drink for the new leaves in spring.

If you order fans, espaliers or cordons, they will automatically be grafted on to rootstock that has a dwarfing effect. You need to souse the vigour of a tree that is growing in a restricted shape. The disadvantage of dwarfing rootstock is that the dwarfer it is, the fussier it is. You need to keep the trunks clear of competing grass. You need to feed and water them, mulch them with compost.

For general planting, I like half standards. They are slightly slower to fruit than dwarfer types, but they make superb garden trees, easy to mow under, easy to plant under, undemanding, long-lived. A half standard is a tree that has at least four clear feet (a metre) of trunk before the branches start branching. There will be plenty of room for a deck chair in the shade under its branches, where 'Beauty of Bath' apples can fall straight into your lap.

PUTTING ON THE STYLE

Fortunately, despite the best efforts of the style police, English gardeners remain anarchists. We garden in a million different ways, depending on where we are, who we are and what we think our gardens are for. Those who don't know who they are, employ garden designers to tell them.

Despite that, if you look back over the last five decades in Britain, you can see there have been very particular fashions and trends. The fifties were about HT roses, the sixties majored in island beds and dwarf conifers (the garden was the only part of the sixties that didn't swing). In the seventies there was a mass identification with Sissinghurst – mad because nobody had Vita's army of gardeners to stake the herbaceous borders. The eighties saw the beginning of adventurous exoticism – a love affair with New Zealand spikies, which stayed and grew through the nineties. By the end of the nineties, style began to overwhelm content in gardens. Glass, zinc, polished steel, water, bamboo screens, decking, black slate chippings predominate. In today's stylish garden, hard landscape is the thing, with perhaps sixty blue fescues dotted around the slate chippings. There may be a palm or a series of box balls, but not much else in the growing line.

The exotic style (bananas, dahlias, castor oil plants, echeverias, cannas) is perhaps the most fashionable now among gardeners who actually like plants. But it is hard work as so much stuff is tender and has to be overwintered somewhere frost-free. Minimalism, though, will always be cool among urban trendies, who don't want to commit to plants. They prefer cut flowers inside, or pots of orchids scooped up for a ridiculously low price at the Sunday morning Columbia Road market in London.

But what about the so-called German style of planting, favoured by a trendy group of influential plantsmen in England? It's a style that was honed in Germany's public parks: big loose groupings of perennials and grasses – echinaceas, monardas, miscanthus, especially – unstaked and set out in enormous bold, interlocking shapes. But we're warmer and wetter than Germany or the Netherlands. Plants grow taller, lusher, and consequently flop unless they are staked. Monardas get mildew. It's not a style that always translates successfully to the rich, heavy ground that underpins many of our gardens.

I garden voraciously but not in any one particular style. Growing fruit and vegetables, training fruit in fans and espaliers, gives me perhaps more pleasure than anything else. There is certainly a resurgence in kitchen gardening now. Is that a style thing? More a desire for decent food, I'd say, reflected in the fact that the one magazine in the UK devoted to the kitchen garden has increased its circulation dramatically. But style can dictate the way you arrange your vegetables. The best plant combinations in our garden often come from the kitchen garden, where the lustrous cabbage 'Red Rookie' with its swirling skirts of pewter-purple is set against a backdrop of purple and magenta sweet peas.

Gardeners now are far more interested in perennials, annuals and bulbs than they are in HT roses or shrubs. The passion for hardy perennials was first fostered by the Hardy Plant Society and it was they who pioneered the publication of the first *Plant Finder*. More than 700 different daylilies and 1,500 different primulas are listed in its close-packed pages. We take these riches for granted because we have the advantage of living in an equable climate which accommodates the needs of a vast range of plants.

We grow grass very well and the lawn can become a fetish for gardeners, especially men, who like the boys' toys that go with it – the mower, the spiker, the edger, the fertiliser spreader, the strimmer. Gardeners are constantly being urged to drag up their lawns and make gravel gardens instead. That had point while the doom merchants were predicting rising temperatures and drought, but after winters when vast tracts of the UK have been submerged under floods, permanent drought seems an unlikely scenario. The lawn will survive.

NORTH WALLS

Drainage is not a sexy subject. It is one of life's greyer areas, like the workings of the Inland Revenue. You just hope you never have to grapple with it too closely. I only have once before, when no. 2 child was about four years old and posted enough extraneous items down the lavatory to gum up the entire system.

The local plumber came to the rescue and retrieved an impressive number of objects from one of the drains. He found trees, gates and several cows from a model farmyard, a small stuffed cat, a sock, two doll's dresses and enough Lego to build a prototype of the Taj Mahal.

Why had she done this, I asked our daughter. To see where they came out, she replied. Now you know, I said. Fortunately the exercise was conclusive enough for her to be able to tick off drains as a subject of enquiry. And I, too, had learned something about the subterranean geography of our house.

Unfortunately, not enough to prevent the recent deaths of a series of plants all growing in one corner of the courtyard, where a stone wood store butts on to the west wall of the house. First to go was a huge old T-shaped pear tree on the west wall. I put it down to age, possibly hastened by honey fungus, which is endemic in old gardens. It was a great loss, but not a surprising one, given the tree's girth.

But then, the *Parthenocissus henryana* I'd planted on the north-facing wall of the wood store died too, and that was a shock. It's a beautiful ornamental vine, with dark green hand-shaped leaves, veined in silvery white. Like most of this tribe, it colours spectacularly in autumn, vivid orange-scarlet. The dour store, stone with a slate roof, blazed for this season, because the vine, having covered most of the wall with its self-clinging stems, had wandered all over the lean-to roof as well. I loved it.

Finally, in the cataclysmic storms we had around Christmas, water started gushing out of a grating in the drive that I'd never taken much notice of. Drain problems again. The drain from the grating led back to the courtyard and the outflow from the kitchen sink and dishwasher. For some time soapy water had been seeping out underground, evidently poisoning the roots of the plants closest to the outflow. Now the drive has been dug up, the drain remade and I've got a bare north wall to cover.

When you first start to garden, the whole palette of plants is open for you to try. You quickly employ the usual sacrificial victims for north walls: jasmine, ivy, pyracantha, various parthenocissus (but not the rampageous Virginia creeper), honeysuckle, climbing hydrangea. All are excellent, especially the climbing hydrangea *H. petiolaris*, with peeling tan bark and big heads of creamy white flowers, arranged like a lacecap hydrangea.

And there's the rub. Because I've already used these excellent climbers and wall shrubs elsewhere in the garden, I'm looking for something new. I could, of course, use a different kind of pyracantha, a yellow-berried one instead of the two red-berried ones I already have. And, in a lifetime of planting, you could scarcely run out of ivies; there are at least 350 different kinds to choose from. But there is already a variegated ivy covering the wall behind the now dead pear. So ivy is not an option. We'd be ivied to death if I planted another so close.

Lurking in the wings are the wall shrubs and climbers that have never yet set foot in the garden. Why? It's the same why that hovers over the choice of a jersey. Or curtain material. It is what makes the way we dress, our houses and our gardens so completely different from each other, despite the best efforts of style gurus to turn us all into clones.

Take the tassel bush *Garrya elliptica*. Except that I wouldn't. It is one of a whole group of shrubs suggested for north walls, that never even gets to the first interview. It is a drab shrub, with leathery leaves of greyish green. In late winter it produces catkins, up to 5 inches (13 centimetres) long, of a slightly paler grey-green colour. That is the supposed high point of its existence. Then the catkins drop bits all over the leaves, so for weeks the shrub looks tired and dusty. When rain has washed that debris away, the tassel bush sits, gloomy and unchanging, until it is tassel time again. It is one of the most depressing shrubs I know.

There's another group of climbers that will put up with north walls, though they may do far better in other places. In this case, you have to decide how much worse the performance is likely to be and whether you are going to feel sorry for the poor plant each time you pass it by. The Noisette rose 'Mme Alfred Carrière' is often recommended for north walls and I have seen some good specimens growing in this situation.

It's an old rose, introduced in 1879, with small double flowers, pinkish in bud, opening to creamy-white. And they smell lovely. Its only disadvantage is that it will be too big for the space in question. 'Mme Alfred Carrière' will quickly reach 15 feet (4½ metres) high and at least 10 feet (3 metres) across. The wall is no more than 8 feet by 6 feet (2½ metres by 2 metres). And perhaps a rose isn't the best idea for a wood store that we visit in pitch darkness most nights of the winter. However well trained the rose, there would always be a stray thorn or ten to catch in one's hair.

Some clematis will grow on north walls. Feet in the shade, head in the sun, is the usual recipe for success with clematis. In this situation, there would be no problem with shady feet. And if the clematis grew profusely enough, it could scramble up on to the lean-to roof, as the parthenocissus did. There, it would find sun, as the roof slopes to the west. But, in its eagerness to reach the roof, would it leave me behind, looking at a wall of chicken wire support thinly traversed by a few straggly stems?

'Nelly Moser' will do on a north wall and has large, pale pinkish-mauve petals, striped with a darker bar. Each flower has a boss of reddish-brown anthers in the middle. It flowers in late May and June, but often produces a second crop in late summer and early autumn. Like other May-flowering clematis, it needs very little pruning and is actually best in some shade, because full sun bleaches the flowers.

'Lasustern' has creamy yellow anthers surrounded by big, blue-mauve petals. It, too, produces its main crop of flowers in May, with another, lesser show later. I might even be able to persuade 'Marie Boisselot' (large white flowers, beige anthers) to call the wood store home. White looks good, shining out from shady corners.

Clematis, though, always look best rambling through some other shrub, which disguises their own lax, lank stems and provides the foliage and substance that they themselves lack. The answer, I think, will be to plant another *Parthenocissus henryana* for the sake of its beautiful foliage and startling autumn performance and, in the same generous hole, add a clematis at the same time. Then I have the comfort of things staying the same, together with the excitement of them being different. I hope it works.

THE OLD VICARAGE AT EAST RUSTON

Part of the reason we garden and visit gardens is to escape: from ugliness to beauty, from tension to tranquillity, from noise to peace. The mobile phone is changing all that. On the gorgeous day in late summer when I went to The Old Vicarage at East Ruston, Norfolk, the garden was full of the mindless diddledada, diddledada, diddledada DA of telephones, full of hideous summonses to the outside world that the garden's owners, Graham Robeson and Alan Gray, have tried so carefully to exclude. By a vast brugmansia, in extravagant apricot bloom, a woman in red shrieked, 'You're breaking up, Malcolm, you're breaking up.' Out of the extraordinary great fronds of the tree ferns in the North Garden came a shrill voice, 'Quick, quick. I'm running out of credit.' Fortissimo from the other side of an ilex hedge, 'I'm losing my signal. I'm going to have to call you back.' It's difficult to commune with the spirit of place, or whatever it is we're looking for in a garden, with these crescendoes of panic erupting all over the place. They pierce through the amiable conversational buzz of gardeners on a spree like thorns in flesh. They are impossible to ignore.

I've given up supposing that the one designated quiet carriage on the train from the West Country to London will actually be quiet. Even at half past six in the morning, aggressive suits step into it, shouting into their mobiles. I've got used to being run down on pavements by people peering intently into the postage stamp screens of the latest in Nokia technology. But in a garden, the poison of mobile phones is even more intrusive, as carefully crafted illusions are shattered by the banality of computer-generated ring tones.

But what about the garden itself, which has grown hugely both in size and reputation, since the owners acquired the empty brick house and two acres in 1973? Well, it's rather extraordinary, wildly theatrical, a garden made now as much, it seems, for public performance as private pleasure. If I lived closer, I'd get a season ticket because there's far too much there to digest in a single visit. I was dizzy with images after only ten of the thirty different 'happenings' that now cover more than thirty acres.

Graham Robeson and Alan Gray's great achievement has been to create shelter in this vast empty landscape only a few miles from the North Sea. They planted huge boundary belts of Monterey pine to filter the worst of the wind, with eucalyptus and Italian alders as additional defences inside. They've also created the illusion that land rises and falls within the garden, although when they took over, the plot was as pancake flat as the rest of the corn prairies that surround it. In early homage to the late Christopher Lloyd at Great Dixter, they excavated a sunken garden near the house and created an Arts and Crafty brick pergola.

A series of aerial photographs displayed in the pavilion that terminates the Kings Walk shows what happened once (from 1989 onwards) they started acquiring extra land. The long borders became even longer. The land beyond the pavilion was bulldozed into a series of curving terraces backed with red brick walls. A vegetable garden appeared between sheltering hedges, rows of cabbages and parsley alternating with flowers to cut for the house. An area of meadow became a New Zealand garden, planted with strangers from the Southern hemisphere.

On the southernmost boundary, they excavated a hugely ambitious desert garden, making an Arizona landscape of flints and boulders and gravel planted with agaves and aloes, strange puyas and spiky beschornaria, washed over and between with masses of self-seeding orange eschscholzia (Californian poppy). The soil here is light and fast draining, which means that a surprising number of tender exotics overwinter in the ground. The dryness of this part of the country helps. Many so-called tender plants can survive cold. It's the combination of coldness and wetness that does them in.

Robeson and Gray have made a highly structured garden: hedges, allées, topiary, gazebos, pedimented entrances and exits from the Dutch Garden to the Holm Oak Walk, from the Tree Fern Garden (tree ferns underplanted with bright blue monkshood) to the Green Court, from the Autumn Garden to the Acacia Avenue. It's been a massive undertaking and it hasn't stopped yet. Curving crushed bark paths meander west into what will one day be a vast woodland garden.

But it's rare to find garden makers who are as interested in the technicalities of carving up space as they are in filling it with flowers. The Arts and Crafts-style detailing on their new walls and pillars is enchanting. The brick they've used, though, seems disinclined to weather and in some areas, such as the curved south-facing terraces of the Mediterranean Garden, the hard elements overcome the soft and the plants seem hardly able to compete with the harsh texture of the red brick walls that contain them.

My two favourite areas both contained unusual, exotic plants, though they were very different in terms of atmosphere and tempo. Adjoining the house to the north, close to the original entrance, is a small walled courtyard thickly planted with succulents that give the impression of growing straight out of the gravel. The handsome black aeonium 'Zwartkop' flourishes here like a small, stubby tree,

three or four feet tall, each branch ending in a waxy rosette of leaves.
Echeverias and cotyledons lumber over the ground between clumps
of spurge, strappy variegated phormiums, eucomis and the pleated
fan leaves of Chusan palms. There are also clumps of agapanthus,
but the emphasis in this closed-in court is on foliage. It is an arresting piece of planting and beautifully balanced, restrained even.

My other favourite was the Exotic Garden, where the borders
that march down either side of the two central pools are huge and
uninhibited. The space is closed in at the top end by a roofed platform that looks like something from the Borneo jungle, swathed
in creeper. Down either side, backing each of the borders, are tall
hedges of escallonia and holm oak. Everything in here is over-scaled:
vast clumps of bananas march down the borders, surrounded by
purple perilla, masses of cannas, dark-leaved dahlias, suckering rhus
and a variegated form of the giant reed grass, striped in green and
white. The colours are hot, the effect stupendous. And the half-
hidden paths along the backs of the borders are not to be missed.
Creeping through here, squidged between monster hedge and
monster banana, I found a delicious phone-free refuge and listened
to the banana leaves cracking open in the sun.

Tasks for the Month

General

- Lay new turf now so that the grass can settle during the winter.
- A collection of different mints can be difficult to control. Punch or burn holes in the bottom of a number of big square ice-cream or margarine containers and plant a different mint in each box. Sink the boxes under the earth.
- Wash the shafing off the greenhouse and insulate it with bubble polythene.
- Gather up autumn leaves and stack them in an enclosure of wire netting to rot down into leaf mould. This makes a superb mulch.
- Leaves in garden pools are a bad thing. Catch them as they fall by stretching netting over the pool.
- Trees are best planted any time between now and Christmas.

Flowers

- Continue to plant daffodils, scattering bonemeal into the planting holes. A long-handled bulb planter that takes out neat plugs of earth is the easiest tool to use when planting daffodils in turf.
- Puschkinia and *Anemone blanda* will both naturalise successfully and should be planted now. Puschkinia can be planted in short grass, rockeries or in the front of a border.
- Finish planting spring bedding such as wallflowers, polyanthus and forget-me-nots. The latter make an excellent undercarpet for tulips, especially the dark mahogany 'Abu Hassan' or the lily-flowered 'White Triumphator'.
- Martagon lily is a hardy, lime-tolerant, basal-rooting species that will thrive in sun or shade. Plant the bulbs about 4 inches (10 centimetres) deep and 9 inches (23 centimetres) apart on a sprinkle of sharp sand to deter underground slugs. Mulch in spring with compost or leaf mould.
- Start to overhaul herbaceous borders, changing any groups of plants that have set your teeth on edge during the summer. Split up congested clumps and replant them in soil refreshed with compost or bonemeal.
- October is a bad month for gales, so check the ties on wall shrubs and climbers.
- Some alpine plants, particularly those with woolly leaves, need protection from excessive damp during the winter. A dressing of stone chippings will help rain to drain away fast.
- Leave dahlias and begonias in the ground as long as possible before lifting:

tubers do most of their growing in the short days of autumn. Lift them only when the foliage has been blackened by the first frosts. Cut the stems off about 4 inches (10 centimetres) above the ground and stack the tubers upside down in boxes to dry out. Store them in a frost-free shed.

- Frost also stops tender fuchsias in their tracks. Shift them in their pots into a frost-free shed or porch for the winter.

- Lift pelargoniums that you want to keep and stack them in boxes of peat in a cool, frost-free place. Do not water, but allow the leaves to die off naturally. Wrap the rootballs in polythene bags with a little damp peat. Tie the bags in bundles and hang them up until spring.

- Windowboxes need clearing of summer displays ready for planting with winter pansies or bulbs such as low-growing crocus and irises. Variegated ivies are excellent gap-fillers for winter months.

Vegetables

- Lift maincrop carrots, if the veg patch is inconveniently far from the back door. They store well in bags of slightly damp sand or peat stacked in a cool place.

- Cut down the dead brown stems of asparagus fern and clean up the beds. Put markers in any space where you may need fresh plants.

- Spread muck thickly over at least a third of the vegetable garden after ground has been cleared and roughly dug. The muck can be dug in during the spring months when it has weathered.

- In a greenhouse, continue to sow special winter-hardy lettuce.

Fruit

- Clean up the ground between strawberry rows, getting rid of weeds and unwanted plants that may have rooted themselves. Mulch between the rows with well-rotted compost or manure.

- Many apples and pears are now ready for picking. Temperature is the most critical factor in successful storage. It should be 36–41 °F (2–5 °C). Somewhere dark and slightly damp is ideal.

- Put grease bands around the trunks of fruit trees to trap the crawling, wingless, winter moths whose progeny may cause havoc among the fruit next season.

Propagating

ֶ❧ Pot up rooted cuttings of zonal and ivy-leaved pelargoniums, so that the plants have a chance to develop a decent root system before winter sets in.

ֶ❧ Take cuttings of gooseberry, redcurrant and blackcurrant. Use pencil-thick growths, about 12 inches (30 centimetres) long.

Eggardon

BLUE SKIES AND GREEN FINGERS

Gardeners (and there are 27 million of us in the UK) have a vested interest in the climate and vivid memories of the cataclysms that have been unleashed on our beloved gardens. In the sixties, millions of supposedly hardy plants died in the savage winter of 1962–3. The seventies were marked by the extraordinary drought of '76, when plantsmen baled out their weekly bath water to save rare rhododendrons and hydrangeas. In the eighties we had the great gale that felled an estimated 15 million trees in southern Britain alone. Those of us in the West Country, which had escaped the worst effects of the 1987 storm, had our own replay in 1990. I remember roaring encouragement to the great beech trees in our garden, a lunatic, powerless figure, wearing the tin hat my father had as an ARP warden in the last war, as I shouted to them to hang on, hang on. Why the hat? Because flying slates, branches and bits of our neighbour's greenhouse were skimming through the garden like slingshot. In 2000 and 2001, the threat was not drought, but flooding. Rivers could no longer contain prolonged and torrential rain, burst their banks and stormed through homes, leaving gardens buried under a mulch of sludge and mud.

These events are unsettling and always have been to us humans. Gilbert White, the great eighteenth-century naturalist of Selborne in Hampshire, wrote of the 'amazing and portentous' summer of

1783, a season of 'horrible phaenomena' such as meteors, thunder-storms and a weird smoky fog that lasted from 23 June to 20 July. 'The sun, at noon,' he wrote, 'looked as blank as a clouded moon ... but was particularly lurid and blood-coloured at rising and setting. All the time the heat was so intense that butcher's meat could hardly be eaten on the day after it was killed; and the flies swarmed so in the lanes and hedges that they rendered the horses half frantic.' In the following summer, Selborne was hit by hailstones three inches across, which broke the windows of White's house as well as all the glass in his cold frames. It was followed by floods so violent that the lane to Alton was blocked by falling rocks, some of them weighing more than two tons apiece.

These events, though recurrent, will always be seen as extraordinary and memorable. More insidious are slow changes in climate. The Central England Temperature record, which collates information from several sites in Britain (some records date back to 1659), shows that the average temperature in central England rose by 1 °F (0.7 °C) between 1750 (which marks the beginning of the Industrial Revolution in this country) and 1900. It went up by another 1.5 °F (1 °C) in the hundred years of the twentieth century; two-thirds of that rise happened from the 1970s onwards. Five of the six warmest years since 1659 have been 1989, 1990, 1995, 1997 and 1999.

As temperatures have gone up, frosts have decreased. Gardeners of the 1880s could expect at least fifty-five frosty days in their gardens in central England. A hundred years later, the thermometer showed just thirty-five. So are we going to see olive groves in Oxfordshire, peaches in Peebles? Will the plants of Tresco, already blooming happily in the gardens of Tunbridge Wells, charge on up to Teeside? Much depends which climate scenario you fancy. UKCIP (the UK Climate Impacts Programme, funded by DEFRA and based at Oxford University) has developed four models, ranging from bad to worse. In the worst-case scenario, temperatures increase by 3.5–5.5 °F (2–3 °C) in winter and 4.5–9 °F (2.5–5 °C) in summer, and rainfall decreases by up to 10 per cent. Levels of carbon dioxide are already rising at a rate of 1 per cent a year.

As always, these scenarios put us at the centre of the picture. Because we depend on oxygen to survive, we see an increase in carbon dioxide as a threatening prospect. Plants have an alternative view. They thrive on the stuff. Photosynthesis – the process that drives plant growth – depends on a fusion of carbon dioxide, which the leaves absorb from the atmosphere, and water-borne nutrients, which the roots gather in from the soil. Sunlight provides the energy and we benefit from the oxygen which the plant releases as a waste product. But the whole process is carefully weighed against temperature and day length. Some plants, such as garlic, will never continue to grow after the longest day, no matter how warm the summers become, or how extended the growing season. Their clocks are set in a particular way, regulated by a particular gene, and at a certain point, they stop ticking.

But commercial growers have known for years that if they increase the levels of carbon dioxide in their greenhouses, they will get better crops of some (not all) flowers and vegetables. Doubling the CO_2 can increase yields of carrots by 50 per cent, provided they have everything else they need. Under this regime, roses bear more flower buds than normal; they also come into bloom earlier. A report in the Forestry Commission Bulletin suggested recently that tree growth in the UK may increase by 40 per cent as extra carbon dioxide allows trees to photosynthesise more efficiently.

But only if, and it's a big if, they have enough to drink. That is, in large part, our responsibility. We are shockingly selfish in our use of water – topping up water features and swimming pools, watering lawns (which they very rarely need), showering twice a day, turning on the washing machine to wash a single shirt. Consider the poor trees. As the water table drops, their roots can't find what they absolutely must have. Being tuned in to their environment in a way that we are not, they desperately try to cut consumption, drop all their leaves and stand stark naked in August, as they did in the summer of '76.

Provided there is sufficient water for them to draw on, a 1.5°F (1°C) increase in the mean temperature will also suit many plants. It gives them a longer growing season: as much as three weeks in the south-east, ten days in the cooler north-west. Since the mid 1960s, Mary Manning has been recording the first flowering date of the flowers in her garden in East Anglia. Forty years ago, aconite flowered around 11 January, hazel around 3 February. Now both tend to flower in mid December. But for most gardeners the 2006 season was different: a long, cold haul through February and March set flowering clocks back to a more normal pattern. Winters in both 2009 and 2010 were Arctic in their severity.

If the UKCIP models are accurate, wine growers at least may have something to celebrate. Buds will burst from the vines a couple of weeks earlier than they do at present, which will give growers a better chance of ripening their crops in autumn. But I'm not expecting to produce our own Chablis or press extra virgin oil from our own olive grove.

It's not that olive trees can't grow in this country. They can and do. Reads Nursery in Loddon, Norfolk, sells a couple of hundred of them every year. In the Chelsea Physic Garden, London, there's an olive tree that is already 33 feet (10 metres) across, probably planted sometime in the 1880s. But the garden is very sheltered, and the tree is tucked away in the warmest place by the glasshouses, on very well-drained, sandy soil.

London, though, is a heat island, wrapped in wasted central heating and car fumes, insulated by heat-absorbing tarmac and concrete. The temperatures there bear little relation to what's going on in the rest of the country. Gardeners in Sussex may be shivering in a climate 23°F (13°C) lower than that in Notting Hill.

Then there's the critical question of winter wet. Mediterranean plants die here, not because they are cold (so is France, away from the coast) but because they are wet at the roots. They rot, rather than freeze. All the UKCIP scenarios predict wetter, even if warmer, winters. Only on well-drained soil, such as gardeners have at the Chelsea Physic Garden, do tender Mediterranean plants have a chance of seeing more than their first birthday.

Gardeners in this country now have access to more than 70,000 different kinds of plants (our native flora numbers a measly 1,500 species) but growing exotics is not a new thing. Lord Burghley, Queen Elizabeth I's Chancellor, was at it way back in 1561. 'If the prise be not too much', he wrote to Thomas Windebank in Paris, 'I pray you procure for me a Lemon, a Pomegranate and a myrtle tree.' Windebank did his stuff and sent the trees. The lemon cost Lord Burghley fifteen crowns.

A hundred years later, the diarist Samuel Pepys went off to see oranges growing in Hackney. He pulled one off and ate it, when the gardener wasn't looking. That was in 1666, two years before the coldest period ever recorded in England. Then, for twenty-one miserable years, frosts came in August, and winters lasted for all of eight months. In the winter of 1683–4 the Thames was frozen solid from November all the way through until April. That year, the diarist John Evelyn noted that there had been widespread damage to 'sipris' (cypress) trees.

Despite a trend towards global warming, there are still going to be sudden frosts in this country which will have a devastating effect on tender plants such as trendy tree ferns and bananas. On two succeeding nights in the nineties, the gardeners at Crathes Castle in Scotland recorded temperatures of -7.6°F (-22°C), which caused the worst damage in living memory to the trees and shrubs growing in the sheltered walled garden there.

And Mike Nelhams, head gardener at the famous garden on the island of Tresco, will never forget the destruction caused by the January frosts of 1987, when 80 per cent of his rare plants were killed. Tresco, until then a frost-free paradise of tropical,

Mediterranean and Australasian plants, suffered temperatures of -3 °F (-25 °C). Even long-established plants, such as Norfolk Island pines, 80 feet (24 metres) high, were massacred in the unaccustomed freeze. Just one blip like that, even if it runs counter to a well-established trend, can mean death for marginal plants.

Self-preservation, not altruism, is at the centre of our concern with global warming. Plants are exquisitely adaptive creatures, and will survive things that we cannot. Largely, they are destroyed not by climate change but by human greed. When we have gone they can once again get on with what they were doing for a hundred million years before we ever arrived on the scene.

NOTE: *Gardening in the Global Greenhouse* is written by Richard Bisgrove and Paul Hadley of the School of Plant Sciences at the University of Reading. It documents the likely impact of climate change on gardens in the UK and is available free from UKCIP, Union House, 12–16 St Michael's St, Oxford OX1 2DU. Tel.: 01865 432076.

SHEDDING

The urge to throw things away doesn't come upon me very often, so when it does, I take full advantage of it. I had a go at the cutlery drawer in the kitchen the other day. That was relatively easy. Nozzles from a cake icing set? Out. I know now that I will never ice a cake again. I'm still baking them – just. But icing, no.

For years, season after season, I made vast Christmas cakes with tooth-rotting amounts of crystallised fruit soaked in brandy. I made my own marzipan, whipped up royal icing with egg whites, traced spidery patterns and a drunken Merry Christmas on the top with my icing set. The cake was part of the ritual of preparing for a family Christmas, but nobody ever wanted to eat it. First, they were too full after lunch. Then, when the children got older and we switched to an evening feast, they said they were saving themselves for the turkey. Finally, I got the message. The cake was redundant.

It wasn't difficult either to throw away the four sets of chopsticks, wedged dustily at the back of the drawer. When I first came to London after university, I joined a friend in an ill-equipped flat in Kensington. There were a few teaspoons, but nothing else by way of eating irons. The logic is hazy, I know, but we invested in chopsticks to make up for the lack of knives and forks. Given my sheltered upbringing in the Welsh border country, it seemed an amazingly cosmopolitan thing to do.

They have been redundant for years and years, those chopsticks. So why haven't I got rid of them before? It's mostly because of the baggage they carry. The chopsticks are among the few things I still have that link me back to that attic flat and my first door key. We didn't have keys at home. Consequently I was always forgetting it. You could get yourself back into the house by leaning on the doorbells of other flats in the building. And we discovered that by balancing on the top banisters over the stairwell, we could climb out through the skylight, four storeys up, crawl over the roof and get into our own flat through the balcony of a window that never shut properly.

So that's what the chopsticks are telling me about. That and the impossibility of using them to tackle roast leg of lamb. Now they've gone. And a small bit of me knows that quite soon, one of the children will turn up saying, 'You know those chopsticks you've got at the back of the drawer ...' They will be astounded and horrified to learn that part of the familiar backdrop to their lives has gone. And that they will have to fork out for their own sets of chopsticks. Sod's law is like that.

So there's half a reason perhaps for hanging on to this flotsam and jetsam. But why do we suddenly arrive at a point where we can jettison it? Why can I now face a chopstickless future? I don't know. There's just a point sometimes when clutter, instead of being a comfort, becomes a burden. Your dream centres on a space, free of jumble, with a log fire and walls of books.

Hardest to deal with, of course, is the stuff that has the most potent emotional baggage: the stuff that has to do with your parents or your children. My mother never threw anything away: old linen sheets were turned into pillowcases or handkerchiefs, old curtains became cushions, hand-knitted jerseys were unravelled and the good bits of wool handed out to be knitted into something smaller.

This wasn't meanness. She was the most generous woman imaginable. Partly it was a mindset brought on by the rationing and shortages of the Second World War. For her generation, recycling (not a word that anyone used) was a necessity, not the holier-than-thou thing it has become, with the Sunday trip to the bottle bank replacing attendance at church. But for her, I think, reusing things also implied respect for the time and care that had gone into creating them. And that's why I felt guilty when those rusty icing nozzles finally hit the waste bin.

MINIMALISM FOR THE MILLENNIUM

So how did it feel when you woke on the first morning of the new millennium with a hangover and a string of unfamiliar noughts at the top of the page? Different? Did the view outside the window have an unusual millennial glow about it? For me, sadly, no. Just the

same worn, muddy lawn, the same unruly jasmine, blackbirds toss-
ing mulch on to the paths like demented little road-menders.

Anyone who gardens knows that to plants, a date on the calendar means nothing. They aren't going to change just because some
notional boundary has been crossed in a man-made counting
system. The jasmine reacts to heat and cold, drought and starvation.
It works out its timetable to profit from or guard against whatever
is going on around it. It responds to its immediate environment.

My hope for the new millennium is that we, too, will return
to the same way of operating. Gardeners need to throw away the
rule books, and learn again to use their eyes, trust their instincts.
Instinct has a hard time of it in a culture which depends so heavily on facts. But why do we rely on facts, when facts themselves
are so unreliable? Take the pruning of roses. For as long as anyone
can remember, gardeners have been told to cut out twiggy and
'unproductive' growth on their rose bushes. But the most recent
research suggests that this growth has an important part to play. The
twiggy bits grow leaves rather than flowers and the leaves gather in
resources that the plant needs in order to produce good blooms on
its flowering stems.

Perhaps this will be arcane knowledge for the gardeners of the
coming millennium. If there is a trend at the moment, then it is
towards the minimalist garden. Much paving. Few plants. Much talk
about light and space. Little understanding that it is not kind to
plant a *Cedrus atlantica* 'Glauca' in a rather small aluminium tub.
However elegant the confluence may be between the dull polished
surface of the container and the silvery blue texture of the cedar's
needles, this is murder. And slow murder at that, so much worse
than a quick death.

Respect is what it comes down to. Although in the last ten years,
more words have been written about respect for the 'environment'
than you could read in a whole lifetime, the effect has been not to
draw us into this thing, but to separate us from it. If you really respect

other living things, you acknowledge their right to a life as full and as happy as you hope yours is going to be. If you stuff a cedar into a pot, to fulfil some transitory notion of style, then you deny the cedar the possibility of ever fulfilling what it set out to do. Its destiny is to grow into a fabulous monster at least 50 feet (15 metres) tall.

'Less is more' is the mantra of the minimalist moderns. The words are the architect, Mies van der Rohe's, which he used in the fifties to describe his spare, pared-down houses. Daringly, I used the phrase once in a talk. We were considering edging plants for a potager and I said that, for this particular job, the effect is generally better if you use one plant, rather than a mixture. 'What do you mean, less is more,' thundered a man in the audience. 'More is more.'

I've not used the words since. But Mies van der Rohe was preaching restraint. That can be good, as long as what you are left with after the restraining can stand scrutiny. When space is cleared out, every object or line left in it has to work very hard. The problem with the minimalist garden is that there are too few designers with the vision, expertise and perfectionism to bring the thing off.

Unfortunately, the archetypes for English designers working in the minimalist style seem often to be in Mexico. They croon over the stark shadows falling over half an acre of swept concrete patio, the only ornament an olive jar, artfully set against a wall (no windows – it's too hot in Mexico) of shocking pink. In Mexico, I'd be crooning as loud as anyone. These clean, clear lines are wonderfully restful, though I'd still argue we are talking architecture here, not gardening.

But does Mexico provide relevant role models for English gardeners? The ancient and indigenous adobe building style there needs only a tiny bit of tweaking and paring down to become an icon of modern minimalism. The landscape, from which the gardens flow, is harsh, often barren, and the light is bright, bright, bright. In terms of environment, a garden in Mexico could not be more different from one in England.

Minimalist designers cannot hide behind frills and embellish-
ments. That is to their credit. Too often, mediocre garden designers
rely on constant incident and glut to disguise the fact that, actually,
the bones of their design are very brittle indeed. So, if you take out
the possibility of decoration for its own sake, minimalist designers
are left with space, proportion and a few well-chosen materials to
do the job.

If the clean, uncluttered garden is to be the thing of the future,
I'd abandon Mexico and reach instead for a JCB. It's odd that with
these extraordinary, powerful, yet delicate machines to hand,
designers do not take more advantage of them. You no longer
need thirty men with pickaxes, shovels and wheelbarrows to turn
a sloping site into a series of horizontal terraces (instantly more
interesting).

No, they don't fit into every back garden. You need an access
point. But that still leaves plenty of places where they can be used.
You could use one to excavate the centre of a rectangular plot to
make a version of a sunken garden, but all green and grassy, with
perhaps a pleached walk of hornbeams set round the raised sides
of the rectangle. I see the minimalist garden of the future as one of
green, sculpted land forms, not of harsh concrete. We need green.
Every square yard of ground that is covered with tarmac, concrete
or paving slabs is another square yard unable to sop up rain when
it falls.

Sculpting the land isn't a new idea, of course. Eighteenth-century
gardeners did it beautifully. Go to the National Trust's garden,
Claremont, in Surrey, to see how stunning the effect can be. There,
a slope becomes a grassy amphitheatre, with parallel grass ledges
running round the curve of the slope like contour lines. There are
grass 'wings' too, sloping down either side, like the wings of a real
theatre.

The effect is like surreal soft sculpture. The form is clean and
geometric. Minimal, though they didn't use words like that in the

eighteenth century. But the grass covering suggests fluidity, the opposite of what the forms are saying. The American architect Charles Jencks has already shown how the twenty-first-century garden could look. At Portrack in the Scottish borders, he and his wife, the late Maggie Keswick, have laid out an extraordinary landscape of water, trees, swirling land forms and sculpted mounds. Maggie Keswick, an authority on Chinese gardens, was strongly influenced by Taoist theories of geomancy, a search for the best way to release the invisible energy locked up in natural land forms, not imposing design, but liberating it.

That's the difference between real geomancy and the type of gardening feng-shui we've recently heard too much about. One is about self-obsession (what will make ME feel better). The other is concerned with the land's own needs and potential. So, in this coming millennium, which is it to be? It, or us?

PEAR HEAVEN

I planted a pear tree as soon as we moved into our house. You can keep your apples: cold-fleshed, self-satisfied fruit. I'm for pears, melting pears, with skins speckled and freckled with russet spots and flesh that dissolves like butter in your mouth. Already I'm prowling up and down the pear trees – there are fourteen of them now in the garden – counting the crop, imagining the day, probably in October, when I can sink my teeth into the first 'Beurre Hardy' of the season.

'Beurre Hardy' has always kept a special place in my affections because it was the first pear I ever planted. It's a big, chunky pear, handsome, well conformed, with a shiny yellowish-green skin thickly overlaid with russet. The flesh is white with the faintest hint of pink, melting, juicy, completely without the graininess that ruins some good-looking pears. Hovering around it when you bite into it is a muted whiff of rose water. It is a Château Lafite of pears.

Planting that pear tree finally wiped out the envy I harboured all through my childhood against my brother. As children we both had gardens. Mine had a 'Beauty of Bath' apple tree in one corner. But my brother's garden had a pear tree. It grew tall and elegant and every summer my mother produced a clutch of muslin bags to tie over the fruit and keep it safe from wasps. No wasps ever bothered with my 'Beauty of Bath' apples.

The apples, being an early kind, could be picked and eaten straight from the tree. But there was a much greater ceremony attached to my brother's pears. To ripen properly, they had to be stored, not quite touching, in wooden boxes in a place that was grandly called the fruit room. It was in fact an old air-raid shelter, built half-underground.

It was a dark cool place. After the war (no bomb ever dropped near us, marooned in rural Wales) it was filled either side with slatted shelves to store fruit. It doubled up as a dungeon for our long, complicated and tensely exhilarating games of chasing, which ranged over miles of territory. If you were captured, you were shut in the fruit room, where you had to stay until a member of your side touched you through the jagged fly screen that half-covered the only window.

There was no thought of eating pears while you were a prisoner. Your heart was thumping too wildly, waiting for your release. I got the same frisson when I was sent to fetch in pears from that store to eat on autumn evenings. Choosing the right ones was a great responsibility. A pear comes to its climax very slowly, but, once there, collapses swiftly. If you are a pear fancier, there is no greater disappointment than to sink your teeth into what looks like a perfect fruit only to a find a grey, runny, slightly alcoholic mess just underneath the skin. Pears are like Russian statesmen. The outward appearance gives little indication of what is going on inside.

In October, I might bring in small 'Seckle' pears, yellowish brown, buffed up to red on the side that had caught the sun. In November, 'Louise Bonne of Jersey' would come into season: smooth yellow skin, covered in dots of russet and crimson – a rich, sugary pear with a whiff of muscat wine hidden in it. Towards December, if things had gone well in the store and the mice were not too greedy, 'Glou Morceau' would be at its best, greenish yellow freckled with grey, a big pear with a tender, sugary inside.

Finally, in the flat days after Christmas, my brother's pears would be ready, and though, to my jealous eyes, he seemed to have had very little to do with the crop, he would get the satisfaction of providing treats at the lowest ebb of the year. 'Josephine de Malines' was his pear, raised in 1830 by Major Esperen, a veteran of Napoleon's army, at Malines, a town in Belgium, said by one visitor to enjoy 'a repose bordering on stagnation', just right for pears. He – Esperen that is, not my brother – called the pear after his wife. It's a smallish fruit (but only the crudest judges measure performance in terms of size), with flesh that is not white like most pears but palest pink. The juice smells of hyacinths. I begrudged my brother his moment of glory, but nobody could deny that 'Josephine de Malines' is a fabulous pear.

My mother liked her pear brought in on an old china saucer left over from a tea set that had belonged to *her* mother: it had a swirly faded turquoise pattern edged with battered gold leaf. My father peeled his with the slim, black-handled pocket knife he always carried. He peeled fruit more thinly than anyone I ever knew – not out of meanness but because whatever he did, he did with care and attention.

Peeling an apple, he went round and round the fruit, so that the skin dropped off in a long, curly spiral. But a pear he tackled differently. He peeled from the stalk to the eye of the fruit in a series of smooth strokes, then cut the pear in quarters and ate them without ever dribbling juice down his chin.

I always ate a pear by pulling the stalk out first. I still do. You can then lunge into the fruit wholeheartedly, taking a great bite out of the stalk end, before slowing down and taking the rest of the fruit at a more leisurely pace. Edward Bunyard, the Edwardian fruit bat who wrote *The Anatomy of Dessert* in 1929, said that a pear should 'melt upon the palate with the facility of an ice'. The eighteenth-century Abbé Hardenpont of Mons is responsible for that meltingness, that butteriness. By careful breeding, he discovered that you could turn the grainy texture of wild pears into something far more ambrosial.

Only once have I been *seriously* unfaithful to the pear. It happened in Costa Rica, where we were wandering about in the rainforest that straddles the border between Costa Rica and Panama. We were looking for a waterfall, which we could hear but find no way down to. It was steaming hot, we were covered in mud and the need to plunge into cool water became so overwhelming, we swooped and slithered towards it straight down the mud slopes of the ravine, past ferns and vines, past orchids and the neat burrows of tarantula spiders, who sat placidly outside their front doors taking the evening air.

As we plunged downwards, the waterfall roared louder and louder, so that all other senses were overwhelmed by this one, engulfing noise, sucking us towards it. Like Tube trains suddenly emerging from a tunnel, we shot out from the dark, overhanging trees of the ravine into a clear patch of light by the edge of the river. The waterfall was above us, dashing its heart out into a deep pool below, surrounded by vast, smooth boulders. Pieces of rainbow splintered on the ferns that arched over the water.

Hot, sweaty, thickly plastered in mud, we jumped into the pool, splashing, shrieking. Hooligan behaviour, but it's the effect waterfalls have. Then we remembered the mangoes in the backpack. No mango has ever been endowed as magically as that Costa Rican one, stripped of its skin under the waterfall, its brilliant flesh fractured and reflected in a million drops of water, its juice running down my neck to mix with the waterfall's thunderous spray.

But the mango madness did not last. Under the greyer skies, the more sober landscapes of England, mangoes lost their magic. I realised it had been a typical holiday romance. The pear, which I had forgotten entirely during this wild, tropical Costa Rican fling, re-established itself as my number one love, and though I've been in tropical parts many times since, I've never gone all the way with a mango again.

CALIFORNIAN GOLD

To English eyes, the exraordinary garden at Lotusland, hidden away in the hills behind Santa Barbara, California, is like a giant film set for Walt Disney's *Fantasia*. Arriving at the house, a low Spanish-style hacienda washed over in shades of ochre, the first thing you see, framing the front door, is a vast and gangling cactus, with arms dangling down like a spiny octopus. This plant, *Euphorbia ingens*, sets the tone of what you will find in the rest of the garden: weird but wonderful cacti, superb succulents, rare cycads, flowering aloes and a forest of dragon trees (*Dracaena draco*).

The only thing more extraordinary than the garden itself, with its gorgeous tiles and fountains, its Moorish rills and lotus pools, is the woman who made it. Born in Poland in 1887, she soon abandoned her given name for the more glamorous-sounding title of Madame Ganna Walska. Given the speed at which she subsequently changed husbands, she was wise to stick to the label. Her friends could never have kept up.

Her first husband was a consumptive Russian count, quickly followed by an American neurologist twice her age. A few months after his death (there was never much of a breathing space between marriages) she hooked the man the newspapers called 'the richest bachelor in the world', Alexander Smith Cochran, but left him after two years for Harold McCormick, wallowing in the affluence provided by the International Harvester empire.

By her standards, this was a reasonably long liaison, lasting nine years. McCormick indulged her theatrical fantasies, bought her the Théâtre des Champs-Élysées in Paris, made sure theatres were full for her American operatic tours by supplying sackfuls of free tickets to all comers. There was a slight disaster in Chicago, though, when Edith McCormick, Harold's previous wife, bribed the theatre manager to cancel Madame Walska's debut. Edith won another round, too, when she bought all American rights in Puccini's operas, thwarting La Walska's ambition to star as Madame Butterfly.

Mostly though, she got her own way, though her final husband, Theos Bernard (the fifth, physicist Harry Grindell-Matthews, lasted only three years) was more than a match for her. Like her, he was an adventurer and must have thought he had struck gold when, in 1941, he first discovered Lotusland, then persuaded his patroness to buy it and install him there, to study yoga. Very west coast.

After four years of marriage, Madame Walska finally saw through Theos Bernard, who was twenty years younger than she was. After dispatching him, she settled into the longest relationship of her life – the love affair with the Lotusland garden, which lasted more than forty years. It was a reward she deserved after forty disastrous years failing to make the grade as an operatic diva.

Though the place is stuffed with extraordinary plants, she herself was not a plantsman. What she brought to the place was a sense of drama, a theatrical eye. The garden unfolds as a series of stage sets: a pool painted bright, sparkling white, with abalone shells lining the edge, and fountains made of giant clams from the South Pacific; a Japanese garden with evergreens clipped into floating cloud topiaries; a beautiful pebble mosaic made by her stonemason Oswald da Ros in 1969; a horticultural clock with signs of the zodiac cut from sheets of copper and bedded in among dwarf succulents. Many of the paths linking the different scenes are lined with blue-mauve chunks of glass, bought from the Arrowhead Water Company.

The cactus garden, heralded by the great drooping specimen by the front door, continues along the front of the house and round the side with formal sweeps of barrel cactus. It was one of the first projects that Madame Walska started at Lotusland, having hired Lockwood de Forest, Santa Barbara's best garden designer, to help her. But when, after a year, de Forest left California to serve in the Second World War, he wrote to her, saying, 'I never would have thought of using cactus at the front door, or many of the other plantings you have suggested. They are very handsome and I congratulate you.'

She had a good eye for placing plants and in the dry, canyon-filled landscape and the bright, unforgiving light of California, the cacti look as right and as pleasing as wisteria does with us, twisting its way round the front of an old manor house. She was mad on the golden barrel cactus *Echinocactus grusonii*, and planted them in great swathes between tall old man cacti *Cephalocereus senilis* and columns of the South American cactus *Cereus uruguayanus*. 'I want to have a monopoly for all barrels, grandfather, mother or babies,' she wrote to the plant collector Antonia Crowninshield, who dug up vast specimens from the Arizona desert and drove them west to the Lotusland garden.

She wasn't working on a blank canvas, though. The place had originally been a 37-acre nursery and some of the oldest trees there, like the Monterey cypress, date back to this period from 1882 onwards, when Kinton Stevens sold lemons and palms to the farmers and gardeners of Santa Barbara. The beautiful star-shaped

Moorish fountain appeared in the 1920s, designed by a Santa Barbara architect, George Washington Smith.

Madame Walska had the sense to leave the good bits of the garden alone, and enrich the areas in between. Working with Kinton Stevens's son, Ralph, she started in 1948 to make her blue garden, setting blue atlas cedars in place and underplanting them with great swathes of the blue fescue *Festuca glauca* and steely grey agaves. Mass planting was her forte and it gives the garden enormous strength and character.

It's not all hot and dry and spiky. One of the most successful areas is the fern garden, which Madame Walska started when she was already in her eighties. It is cool and green and lush, the huge fronds of tree ferns underplanted with masses of species begonias. Under the begonias is a cool green carpet of helxine (mind-your-own-business) which covers almost all the floor.

Equally luxuriant is the bromeliad garden, started originally in the shade of a coast live oak *Quercus agrifolia*. Bromeliads are stacked in the crooks of tree branches and swing in wooden baskets over more bromeliads planted in vast clumps in the earth below. It is a mesmerising place, and gazing out now at my own garden, with leaves drifting down from the trees on a damp November afternoon, I long to be there again. If you are in Santa Barbara this winter, don't miss it.

GRAND DESIGNS

On a stage one time with Sir Roy Strong and Natasha Spender, we were asked which designer of the past we would welcome to do a garden makeover on our own gardens. We were there discussing the garden as art, so it was an apposite question. As it turned out, none of us ever had or would commission others to do our garden thinking for us, but Natasha Spender thought that Lanning Roper wouldn't make too much of a mess of her Provençal garden.

The problem was, it would end up looking like all Lanning Roper's other gardens. He had a fixed way of doing things. He ordered many of his plants from Christopher Lloyd, whose nursery at Great Dixter in Sussex had just been set up when Roper was at his peak. 'Wherever he was working, the plant lists were always exactly the same,' remembered Mr Lloyd. 'It made things very easy for us, but I couldn't help thinking it must be a bit tedious for the garden owners.'

I plumped for the Edwardian architect-gardener Harold Peto. He was a one-look man, too. He did Italy: pencil-thin cypresses, pergolas dripping with vines, pools, topiary and vast quantities of urns, well-heads, statues and oil jars sent over from the Continent by the crateload. In fact, no look could be less appropriate for the kind of place we live in, but Peto intrigues me. Always has. I'd like the chance to talk to him and see what could be gauged from the face that in photographs is always in shadow under the brim of a wide-brimmed hat.

He was a loner and left no diaries or letters that might have given a clue to his make-up. No notebooks or drawings have been found describing the gardens he worked on. He published only one piece about his own garden, Iford Manor near Bradford-on-Avon, which is still one of my favourite gardens in England. He trained as an architect in the lush London practice run by Sir Ernest George, who at that stage was busy throwing up streets of fake Queen Anne houses in the squares round Sloane Street. Edwin Lutyens was a pupil there too, at exactly the same time.

Lutyens went on to have books written about him, exhibitions devoted to his work. His name is famous. Peto disappeared to the Riviera. Pictures of the gorgeous villas and gardens he made there, mostly for rich American clients, were regularly published in the pages of *Country Life* magazine, but though he was a much better garden maker than Lutyens, he never went into orbit in the same way. Why, I wonder? Partly, perhaps, because he never had a Gertrude Jekyll to boss him into prominence. Nor a wife with a good address book, which Lutyens's Lady Emily certainly had.

Garden designers say, of course, that they are there to interpret their clients' wishes. But if I ever did hire one (though I wouldn't) I would hope that he or she would do more than that. It would be good for me to be fed ideas that I might never have had myself. The garden would benefit from a totally fresh eye, and my own blind spots and prejudices could be challenged and contested. My own wishes, I can bring about myself.

But why wouldn't I ever want a real designer swanning round my patch? Let's leave aside the obvious problem of the bill. What I'd resent is the sense of being invaded. My garden is an extension of me, of the things that please me. Forced for most of our lives to operate in a world that is bizarre and irrational (as well as ugly), our gardens become bubbles, protective carapaces. In my garden, I can order the world in a way that fits my needs. The ordering, the making of this world, no matter how long it takes, gives one self-esteem (which is not the same thing as vanity or conceit). 'Remember, Anna,' a wise gardener said to me. 'A garden is a process, not a product.' In the hands of a garden designer, it has little option but to become a product.

Only Roy Strong was brave enough to voice publicly the thoughts that we all had privately. 'Anyone else in our garden?' he said vehemently. 'God forbid.'

Tasks for the Month

General

꙳ Save the turf from planting holes cut for trees and shrubs in established lawns and set it, grass side down, in the bottom of the hole. As it rots it will provide humus to improve soil structure.

꙳ Repair jobs on fences, trellises and boundary walls should be done through winter when climbers and wall shrubs are dormant and can easily be taken down from their supports.

꙳ It is often difficult to water trees and shrubs planted on a steep slope. Plant an old drainpipe or plastic soft-drink bottle with both ends cut off alongside the tree. Set it so the top just surfaces above the soil. Water delivered through the pipe will get straight to the roots of the tree.

꙳ Check newly planted evergreens for wind-rock: they offer far more wind resistance than deciduous trees and shrubs. Stamp down the soil around them so their roots can get a firm grip on it.

꙳ Terracotta pots that have been standing in saucers of water all summer should now have those saucers removed. Pots are less likely to crack open in icy weather if the compost is well drained. Raise pots on small, even blocks of wood to ease drainage problems. Where style is paramount, use terracotta lions' paws specially made for the job.

꙳ If possible, order seeds this side of Christmas.

꙳ Clean mowing machines after the last grass-cut of the year. Wash off all mud and grass and cover all the important shiny-looking bits of the engine with a thin layer of oil or grease.

꙳ Protect plants overwintering in cold frames by covering the glass with layers of sacking or hessian on frosty nights.

꙳ Plant new hedges of deciduous trees.

꙳ Overhaul water pumps used for fountains and waterfalls. Remove submersible pumps and store them safely.

Flowers

꙳ Plant tulips at the beginning of the month. They are excellent in tubs. You can also use them in windowboxes, but choose the shorter varieties and those of the Greigii and Kaufmanniana families with striped and mottled leaves. Miniature tulips such as *T. tarda* or *T. turkestanica* are charming in troughs and rockeries.

November

- Cut back summer sprawlers such as mallow, reducing branches to the base. New growth will start in spring.
- Do not cut back slightly tender plants, such as penstemon. They may put out fresh shoots which will get massacred by frosts.
- Check that the bulbs you are forcing inside for early flowering have not dried out. The compost should be just damp.
- Draw the leaves over the crowns of slightly tender plants such as red hot pokers and tie them up in a bundle to provide winter protection.
- Pile dry leaves on top of agapanthus and nerines for insulation.
- Continue to cut down stems of late summer perennials such as Michaelmas daisy, golden rod and perennial verbascum. Mulch thickly around the clumps.
- Plant new roses while growth is dormant. Climbing roses destined to grow against walls should be planted at least 15 inches (38 centimetres) away from the base of the wall. The soil closer to the wall will be too dry for the plant to thrive.
- Put cloches or panes of glass over Christmas roses (*Helleborus niger*) to keep the flowers clean and free from splashes of earth.
- Pick fallen leaves from rockeries where they may smother and rot alpine plants underneath. Top up the stone chippings around rock plants to improve drainage. Shelter lewisias with panes of glass.
- Protect plants which are prone to frost damage (hardy fuchsia, *Ceratostigma willmottianum*, California tree poppy (*Romneya coulteri*) and solanum). Mulch all around the plants with chipped bark, straw, leaves or bracken to insulate the roots.

Vegetables

- Plant garlic at the beginning of the month.
- In warmer parts of the country it may be worth trying an early row of broad beans.
- Sow a row of early peas, such as the versatile 'Douce Provence'.
- Protect the crowns of globe artichokes with loosely packed straw or bracken.
- Plant chicory roots in large pots containing sand, water them and put them somewhere dark.

- Harvest leeks and parsnips.
- Lift and store beetroot and celeriac.

Fruit

- Prune apple and pear trees after leaf fall. Cut out all dead, diseased or damaged branches and prune other growth selectively to eliminate crossing or rubbing branches.
- Plant new raspberry canes 18 inches (45 centimetres) apart in rows 6 feet (2 metres) apart. Prune hard after planting.
- Plant gooseberries, setting the bushes 5 feet (1.5 metres) apart.

Scethrog Tower (winter)

CHOOSING TREES

The Westonbirt Arboretum, near Tetbury in Gloucestershire, is a wonderful place to look at dogs. On the autumn colour trail this week was the most elegant Gordon setter I have seen for a long time, his black and tan coat gleaming against the brilliant yellow foliage of a shagbark hickory. From the understorey of box bushes burst wild braces of springer spaniels, flushing out the pheasant that existed only in their overheated minds. Staffordshire bulls with chests as impressive as Sly Stallone's rolled their way down the wide rides, between tall stands of bishop's pine.

Like a threnody woven through the birch and the beech, the oaks and the acers, was the wailing voice of a woman in a Barbour jacket and boots: 'Candy, Candy, here, here, HERE.' Candy, a staggeringly capricious cream-coloured labrador, dashed across Willesley Drive in the south part of the Silk Wood with the Barbour jacket in hot pursuit. She was there again at The Link, and, still screeching, in the Broad Drive. As the labrador lollopped past us for the seventh time, it turned its head and gave the closest thing to a wink I've ever seen on a dog. The two of them may be there still. Certainly the dog looked as though it could keep up the game for several days.

What I was supposed to be doing was looking for an answer to a perennial question. If there is room for only one tree in a garden, which tree should it be? For me, it would be a pear. Not the poncy, silver-leaved kind, but a proper pear, with snow-white blossom in spring and melting russetted fruit in autumn. I like the shape that a pear tree makes, rather narrow in proportion to its height. In a small garden, that is a useful attribute. So is the fact that a pear tree has more than one season of interest. That is easy to forget in the great lemming rush to the garden centre at Easter. But ask yourself always, 'What comes after the blossom?' In the case of many flowering cherries, the answer is a deafening silence.

Be clear in your mind what you want the tree to do. If it has to screen some hideous eyesore, then height will be an important consideration. Do you want to sit under it and eat supper in summer? If so, you will not want a tree that drops its branches too low to the ground. Above all, you need to be realistic about the tree's size and shape when mature. Weeping willows may look dreamily romantic in a nursery bed, but are totally unsuitable for all but the largest gardens. They grow fast, not only up but out. If you must have one, choose not the common weeping willow *Salix chrysocoma* but the more manageable *S. purpurea* 'Pendula', the purple osier which, trained as a standard, makes a charming small weeping tree that stops growing at 16 feet (5 metres).

The blue atlas cedar *Cedrus atlantica* 'Glauca' is another species that looks very fetching when it is small. Do not be taken in by this winsomeness. It will be a cuckoo in most suburban nests, growing to at least 80 feet (25 metres). If you want an evergreen, plant box or holly, both natives, but very slow-growing. This is what puts people off them. But if we plant only instant, short-lived trees, what will be left for future generations to enjoy?

There were some superb hollies at Westonbirt such as 'J. C. van Tol', with dark, shining, almost spineless leaves and huge crops of berries. I've also got a weakness for the silver hedgehog holly called 'Ferox Argentea'. It is well named, ferociously difficult to deal with as it has prickles not only on the edges but also on the surface of its leaves. The spines in this variety are creamy white and there is a band of the same colour round each leaf. But it is certainly not a tree for impatient gardeners. Even for a holly, this is slow.

Purple-leaved trees can be oppressive in small gardens. They are spectacular when the leaves first emerge in spring but as summer progresses, the colour becomes ever more heavy and dismal. If your garden is exposed, then avoid exotic species such as catalpa, the Indian bean tree, which has large leaves that are rather thin in texture. When the wind blows, they will tear rather than flutter. Robinia has small feathery leaves, offering no wind resistance at all, but the wood is brittle and liable to snap in a gale.

Nurseries sell trees as whips, feathers, half standards and standards. Some also offer extra heavy standards, or what they call advanced stock, which can mean a tree up to 20 feet (6 metres) high. This will be difficult to establish and keep on its feet without expert care. Whips have a single stem, feathers have small side branches. A half standard will have a stem clear of branches 4–5 feet (1½ metres) from the ground. A standard has a clear stem of 5–6 feet (1½–2 metres). Both kinds of standard should have been pruned to give a well-balanced canopy of branches. Whips and feathers are much cheaper, but you have to take on the responsibility of training them.

When you are choosing a tree at a garden centre, bear in mind that biggest is not always best. In its natural state, a tree has a root system as big as its top canopy of branches. Where trees are for sale, this is rarely feasible, but the bigger the disparity in the proportion of roots to shoots, the bigger the difficulty in getting the tree established.

Where trees are container-grown, a good nursery will repot them as they grow. As a rough rule of thumb, the tree should not be more than five times higher than the width of the container. Avoid top-heavy plants.

Trees kept in pots have a distinct tendency to make roots which whirl around in a restrictive spiral. It is difficult to straighten these out as you plant, so the tree never has a chance to anchor itself securely in the ground. Bare-rooted trees, carefully lifted any time after leaf fall, will often have better root systems than large container-grown trees. Some trees, however, such as davidia, liriodendron, eucalyptus and nothofagus (southern beech) resent disturbance at the roots and are better bought in containers.

SIX OF THE BEST

❧ SNOWY MESPILUS (*Amelanchier lamarckii*)
Twiggy low-domed tree with masses of small starry flowers in April. The leaves turn rose-red and yellow in autumn. Height 15 feet (4½ metres), spread 10 feet (3 metres). Thrives in any good garden soil.

❧ STRAWBERRY TREE (*Arbutus unedo*)
Small evergreen tree which eventually grows into a gnarled Arthur Rackam shape. Bell-shaped white flowers in autumn and red strawberry-shaped fruits. Bark shreds and peels. Not reliably hardy. Height 20 feet (6 metres), spread 10 feet (3 metres). Plant in a sheltered position. Protect young plants with mesh or bracken.

❧ THORN (*Crataegus prunifolia*)
A small, compact tree eventually developing a broad head. Showy round red fruit which stay on the tree well into winter. The polished oval leaves colour richly in autumn. Does well in light shade. Height 17 feet (5 metres), spread 14 feet (4 metres). *Crataegus* x *lavallei* is equally good.

❧ CRAB APPLE (*Malus hupehensis*)
A neat small tree, with stiff, markedly upright branches. Scented flowers in great abundance, pink in bud, open white in spring and are followed by yellow fruit flushed with red. Height 16 feet (5 metres), spread 12 feet (3½ metres). Does best in full sun.

֍ **KASHMIR MOUNTAIN ASH** (*Sorbus cashmiriana*)
Hanging heads of white flowers in late spring, and feathery, pinnate foliage, similar to our own native mountain ash.
Hanging clusters of fruit, pearl-white on red stems, persist
well into winter. Height 13 feet (4 metres), spread 12 feet (3½
metres). *Sorbus hupehensis* is as good, but rather more vigorous.

֍ **JUDAS TREE** (*Cercis siliquastrum*)
Clusters of purplish flowers without stems break directly
from the branches in spring. Very pretty rounded leaves, which
turn yellow in autumn. Light grey-green pods of seeds persist
through the winter. An elegant, slow-growing tree, best in light
shade. Height 20 feet (6 metres), spread 20 feet (6 metres)
(but not for fifty years or so).

GARDEN WORK: RIP

A kind reader recently sent me a little clutch of gardening magazines unearthed from the back of his shed. They date mostly from
the late forties, small format, densely printed, no colour, but lots of
how-to illustrations laid out in the style of strip cartoons. The same
man features in all of them. He has rolled-up sleeves, a waistcoat
and an assortment of hats. In summer magazines he wears a panama,
in winter ones a flat tweed cap. *Garden Work*, the mag is called, and
it is an uncompromising read. Fruit and veg, as you would expect
in the years of post-war rationing, take up much more space than
flowers. Rockeries, though, were treated seriously and dominated
the editorial page on 25 May 1946.

'Many of the rockery plants,' wrote the editor, 'which have been gladdening our hearts with colourful masses of bloom in recent weeks – Aubretia, Arabis, Gold Dust (*Alyssum saxatile*) – are unfortunately most rampant growers. Now that they are getting over, they begin to look very untidy and often they are found to be snatching *lebensraum* from less vigorous neighbours in the good old totalitarian way.' VE Day may have been celebrated only a year previously, but the war of the rockery thugs, stormtrooping aubretia and the like, raged on. Gardeners knew what they had to do. There could be no appeasement at Mon Repos.

War looms large in *Garden Work*'s blotting-paper pages. Full-page advertisements plug products such as 'Katakilla' derris insecticide to wipe out greenfly, blackfly, caterpillars, asparagus beetle, red spider, apple sucker and a suspiciously long list of other flying insects. DDT is among the favourite remedies recommended by Nutilis Famous Pest Controls. Accompanying the ad for Corry's Weed Death Weedkiller is a grinning human skull. The early use of Nopest guarantees perfect freedom from all garden and greenhouse pests, promise Goodalls Ltd of Birtley in Co. Durham. It's a big promise. They don't say what the active ingredient is, but in its way it must have been as awesome as the atom bomb.

Garden Work ran a consultation bureau for its readers, and here you read questions and answers that would fit just as easily into *BBC Gardeners' World* mag today. How do I renew an ageing lavender hedge? Why isn't my wisteria flowering? How do I treat clubroot on cabbages? Why are the leaves of my aloe turning brown? Even in 1946, when central heating had scarcely begun to penetrate private homes, the bureau chief suggested that the aloe was being kept in too warm a place indoors.

The only questions you wouldn't get today are the ones dealing with poultry and bee-keeping. The great wartime drive for self-sufficiency included honey and eggs as well fruit and veg. All were part of the gardener's remit. As *Garden Work* pointed out, with your own honey and home-bottled fruit, you could produce 'delicious points-free fruit dishes next winter'. But certain commodities were still in short supply, nets for fruit cages being one of them. The netmakers Edwards & Son of Bridport, who had spent the war years producing camouflage nets for tanks, said in May 1946 that they were now in a position to supply a limited quantity of pea and bean netting. The rest would have to wait.

The most recent of the *Garden Work* mags I have is dated 25 March 1950. Wartime imagery does not crop up with anything like the same frequency in this issue. On the cover is an ad for A Scientifically Designed Aluminium Lily Pool, transportable yet permanent. For just twelve guineas readers could order the rectangular pool together with two water lilies, eight choice corner plants, two oxygen plants, two floating plants, six ornamental fish, twelve water snails, shingle and a bag of fish food. Instant gardening is not a modern phenomenon.

In a curious way, though, war was critical to the success of a rigorously untitillating magazine such as *Garden Work*. Founded in 1913, it marched valiantly on until 1951, the year that gardeners began to ease off their leather boots and live a little. Who needed home-made, points-free fruit dishes when Clarence Birdseye could so simply provide a frozen equivalent? As the Festival of Britain flowered along the south bank of the Thames in London, *Garden Work* quietly wilted and died. RIP.

TAKING STOCK

'Taking stock' is a purposeful phrase. It implies order, objectives, plans, getting to grips with things. It's what shopkeepers do. And I told myself it was what I was doing as I mooched round outside one golden day in December. The sky was as blue as an Italian fresco, the light was brilliant and sparkling and the whole garden seemed to be holding its breath.

A lot of one's pleasure in a garden comes from just ambling around in it, without any special purpose. No, I hadn't a clipboard with me. No, I was not counting the number of pear trees, nor checking the level of the water in the rain butt. Nor was I particularly thinking of jobs that needed doing, though some sprang to mind as I wandered about, hands clasped round a fat mug of coffee. Stems of helianthus in the round border have not only died back but have splayed out awkwardly and are now leaning on the fresh green leaves of *Scilla peruviana*. The helianthus needs to be cut back.

Chiefly, I was thinking about the overall look of the garden. Is it still holding up, now that the hostas and rodgersias have melted away, the leaves dropped from the Judas trees and the annual flowers all gone from the pots? Is there sufficient structure to string it all together?

It's difficult to stand back sufficiently from your own garden, and see it with fresh eyes. Familiarity breeds acceptance. What is obvious at this season, though, is the way that the garden changes focus. It's like a hologram. Tilted one way you get the summer map, dominated by big humps of herbaceous stuff. Now the garden's tilted away from those and what I'm seeing (what I'd forgotten) is plain old *Cotoneaster horizontalis*, doing a stupendous job half-leaning on an old gatepost, hugging the contours of the bank below. The neat small leaves are ox-blood red, spectacular arching over the carpet of fox-coloured oak leaves that have dropped from the tree above.

In spring and summer, there's too much going on for me to notice the cotoneaster. If it is noticed, it's despised. From time to time I've thought, 'Lord, what a boring shrub. Let's have it out.' I hope I never say that again.

So much on the bank has died down that I can see right through to one of the paths that climbs up it in a long diagonal. Bordering the path on the far side is a carpet of ivy which stretches back to the trunks of the trees in the hedge, mostly holly and oak. Growing through a carpet of cyclamen leaves, big box balls, planted at regular intervals, highlight the line the path takes to the top of the bank. Scarcely noticed in summer, they are important now.

They are quiet combinations, box and ivy, holly and yew. But the tilt of the hologram tilts one's responses to the garden too. In this season, it doesn't have to provide surges of adrenalin. It just has to reassure me that what I'm looking at is not death, but retrenchment.

There's no better time than winter to assess whether the lines you've drawn to divide up spaces in the garden are the right lines and whether they are sufficiently bold. Wandering round Florence over Christmas made me doubly aware of this. The landscapes and gardens there are superb at this season because, in both, two of the most common elements are evergreen and contrast brilliantly the one with the other. First there are cypresses, taller and thinner than any we can successfully grow here. Then there are pine trees, low, mounded umbrella shapes of *Pinus pinea*, quite different from and much more numerous than our taller, craggier native pines.

Italian gardeners also have the olive tree to play with, and though these chug along happily as babies in town gardens in Britain, I can't see them settling as permanent grown-up features in our landscape. But in Italy they contribute a fine, silvery evergreenness to the overall picture and the trees themselves don't get too tall. At Hidcote, his Gloucestershire garden, the Edwardian gardener Lawrence Johnston tried to recapture the silveriness of the olive by planting holm oaks (*Quercus ilex*), but the tree is much bigger, and heavier in colour than the olive. It is good, but not as good.

So we can't copy everything we see and admire in Italian gardens, but they can remind us of some basic principles of planting. And one of the most important of those is a firm structure of evergreen.

Walk, for instance, in the Boboli Gardens, laid out for the Medici from 1550 onwards (closed the first and fourth Monday of each month, otherwise open daily in daylight hours). Or skirt round the back of the gardens, starting from the southern end of the Ponte Vecchio and take the Costa di San Giorgio, which leads past Galileo's house up to the thirteenth-century city gate, the Porta San Giorgio.

From this height, you get a delicious view out over the city, punctuated with the sudden exclamation marks of cypress. The pines make slower shapes, delaying the way your eye moves over the landscape. From the gate, turn sharp left and follow the city wall down to the next gate, the Porta San Miniato. The verge under the towering wall is packed with olive trees. Though only minutes from the centre of Florence, you could be in deep country here, *rus in urbe*.

From the Porta San Miniato with its studded doors, turn sharp right and start the long climb up the Via del Monte alle Croci to the stunning Romanesque church on top of the hill above. This approach will bring you to the great stairs that lead up to its marbled grey and white façade. The setting is immeasurably enhanced by the clipped evergreen hedges and shrubs planted on the steep banks either side.

Stay there a long time: Roman-pillared crypt, shimmering Byzantine mosaics, frescoes – there's much to see. Then slip out of the courtyard through the arch to the right of the shop and wander down to the Piazzale Michelangelo through the gardens laid out by a Florentine town planner, Guiseppe Poggi, at the beginning of the twentieth century. Though they are tired (grottoes and fountains clogged with litter), there is some good planting here: shiny camellias, viburnums clipped and classy, ferns dripping out of the roof of the grotto.

By the isolated Porta San Niccolo, turn left back towards the Ponte Vecchio, following the narrow Via San Niccolo. On both sides are the slightly forbidding façades of fourteenth- and fifteenth-century palazzos, privacy preserved inside. On a corner on the left at no. 55, you'll find a café/wine bar called Rifrullo. And here we sat for several hours, drinking the most wicked hot chocolate that's ever been put before me. Mind food only takes you so far. You need the real thing too.

PRINCIPLES OF PLANTING

Plants will mostly try to grow, whatever you do to them. Sometimes they will also die, even if you are the world's acknowledged expert on their care. But there is a lot that a gardener can do to help rather than hinder a plant's passage through life. Some plants, like some people, have quite specific requirements and it is crazy to ignore them. No iris is going to thank you for burying it, with a foot's depth of hefty clay on top of its sun-loving rhizomes.

The first principle is: do not plant the pot as well as the contents. New gardeners often do. There is a certain logic in doing so (plant easier to move if you have made the wrong decision about where to put it, roots not disturbed, job quicker and simpler to carry out) but this treatment does nothing for the long-term future of the plant in question. Roots must run.

The second principle is: dig a hole twice the size of the one you first thought of. The RSPCA would soon be on your doorstep if you crammed your dog into a kennel that only fitted it when it lay with its back legs crooked up to its belly and its head bent round to meet them. Plants, too, need space to spread.

A planting hole should be roughly twice the size of the rootball of the plant you are putting into it. When you have dug the hole, mix some compost or bonemeal into the pile of earth you have taken out. I often do this in a bucket. Fork over the base of the hole to loosen the earth. This is particularly necessary in stiff, clay soils. It may not be necessary at all in sandy ones.

Put one hand over the compost in the pot and tip it over to ease out the plant. If it has been sitting too long in a nursery or garden centre, you may need to bang the bottom of the pot sharply with your trowel to start it moving. Sometimes roots poke out through the drainage holes in the bottom of the pot. If the plant won't shift, either cut down the side of the plastic pot to release it, or trim some of the roots protruding from the bottom.

Gently tease out any roots that have been tightly coiled round the inside of the pot – a sign that nurserymen have been lazy about repotting. If you don't do this teasing, plants may never kick the roundabout habit. They will never become properly rooted and will be more at risk of being blown out of their holes in winter or dying of drought in summer.

Settle the plant in the prepared hole, spreading the roots around it like a skirt. If there are not enough roots to spread in all directions (roses are often very sparse in this respect), then make sure that you favour the side which will face the prevailing winds. In this country, this is often the south-west.

Use a cane to check that the soil on top of the rootball is just level with (or perhaps very slightly below) the level of the ground around it. You can adjust the level, of course, by adding soil to the bottom of the hole or digging it deeper if you didn't go far enough in the first place.

If you are planting a tree, drive your stake in now, while you can still see where it will go, clear of any major roots. Otherwise you risk doing a vampire act and battering the stake through the heart of the rootball. Fill in around the rootball with the soil and compost mixture. I find it easier to pour this in from a bucket, stopping every now and then to press the soil down with my bunched fist.

If you firm around the rootball in stages, like this, you can be reasonably sure that there will be no spaces where the roots are waving frantically, unable to make contact with sustaining soil. When you have filled the hole level with the surrounding ground, tread round the infill firmly, but not oppressively.

Water in the plant thoroughly. This means a whole watering can for each plant. No cheating. If you are planting trees, shrubs or moisture-loving perennials, follow up the watering with a thick mulch of muck, well-rotted compost or leaf mould, spreading it in a wide circle round the new plant. If you are lucky, your plant will not need any further titivation, in the way of shaping or pruning. The nursery should have done that for you.

But rose growers find that their customers complained if they sent out roses cut down as hard as they ought to be. They thought they weren't getting value for money. So, reluctantly, many rose growers send out plants which they haven't cut down much, together with strict instructions to the customer to do the cutting themselves, when the rose has been planted. How many people follow these directions?

On other shrubs – or trees – you may see diseased or damaged stems that will need to be cut back to fresh, healthy growth. Sometimes twigs get broken when a plant is in transit. Prune these back to a clean cut near an outward facing bud. Sometimes on a tree or shrub there is a branch that is awkwardly angled towards the centre of the head. Take this out, bearing in mind the kind of free, open outline you would like the shrub or tree to have when it is mature. For the same reason, take out any weak, straggling growths entirely, and shorten very long growths that you feel might eventually unbalance the shape of a tree or shrub.

I much prefer planting in the time leading up to Christmas than I do in spring. A plant has such a lot to do in spring. If you plant it in late autumn or early winter, it can concentrate on getting its understorey sorted out before it has to think about pushing out leaves and flowers. There are many exceptions of course. Snowdrops and aconites are best planted 'in the green', that is, in early spring after they have finished flowering, but before they lose their leaves. Bearded irises are also best planted when they have finished flowering. That is usually in late summer.

I mentioned irises at the beginning. They do best if they are planted with the rhizomes sitting on top of a little saddle of soil, which you can mould in the planting hole. Arrange the rhizome so that the roots drape down either side of the saddle, leaving the rhizome itself sitting mostly on top of the soil. And remember, when you are planting, think dog.

GO NUTS

The years of my childhood were punctuated by a regular series of marathon expeditions, which put down markers in each twelve-month that seemed far more immutable than Christmas, Easter or Harvest Festival. In spring there was the Globe Flower Trek, in summer the Climb to the Winberry Grounds, in autumn the Gathering of the Sweet Chestnuts and in winter the Great Watercress Hunt. My mother, who seemed perfectly normal to me when I was growing up, I now realise was rather extraordinary in her passionate identification with the landscape in which we lived. There was little point for her in being indoors if she could be out.

The sweet chestnut tree – there was only one in our patch of country – grew at the edge of parkland next to an old iron kissing-gate that let you through into the lane. It was an enormous tree, handsome in high summer with its long tassels of catkins, and good in autumn, too, when the toothed leaves turned butter-yellow. But we went to it for its nuts, not to write poems about its leaves.

The excitement of this expedition lay in the uncertainty of the outcome. Some years the ground under the tree would be littered with prickly cases, stretched fatly over the nuts inside. Other years there would be none. The tree's common name, Spanish chestnut, suggests the reason why. It is a native of southern Europe and northern Africa. It likes hot summers and fruits best when it gets them.

The laborious business of working your way through to the bit that you want is part of the pleasure of eating nuts. We ate a lot of sweet chestnuts in their raw and creamy state, breaking open the spiny covering, peeling off the shiny chestnut coat, then stripping away the hairy skin that is the last line of defence. The texture of raw chestnuts is not so floury as when they are roasted. Roasted is marginally better.

We used to push the chestnuts in the beds of hot wood ash that were rarely cleared out from the fireplaces during winter. Pricking them first was important, we were told, but nobody ever explained why. One year my brother, who had an admirably enquiring mind, pushed a batch in the hot ash without pricking them first. They exploded all over the hearth in a very satisfactory way, but shattered into so many bits that there was nothing left to eat. By a narrow margin, he decided that the explosion was not worth the loss of the nuts. Later, he managed to get the best of both worlds by devising a gunpowder mix that he buried in cocoa tins in the lawn and deto-nated with a longish fuse. Those blasts made the chestnuts' efforts pale by comparison.

You need space for a sweet chestnut, for in maturity, they are not only tall, but wide. The champion tree in Britain grows at Canford School in Dorset, a warty, burred beast 55 feet (17 metres) high and more than 13 feet (4 metres) round its massive trunk. Some of the biggest I know are in Burghley Park, Stamford, where they were planted in King Charles's time to provide winter fodder for the deer in the park. With age, their bark has become twisted like barley sugar and you could set up home inside their hollowed trunks.

It is one of the trees that the Romans are supposed to have intro-duced into Britain along with the sycamore. The tree that we made pilgrimages to was probably the wild species *Castanea sativa*, but there is a French selection, 'Marron de Lyon', which is available over here and has bigger, better fruit. Robert Hogg, the Victorian doyen of fruit fanciers, reckoned that 'Devonshire Prolific' was the only variety worth growing, but he was writing in 1875 and it doesn't seem to be offered now though it probably still exists somewhere, if only somebody could put a name to it.

Like sweet chestnuts, walnuts need space – and patience. You may have to wait twenty years before you get a crop. They grow slowly to make round-headed trees not usually (at least in this country) as tall as the sweet chestnut. The tallest walnut in Britain is at Boxted Hall, Suffolk (75 feet, 23 metres), the fattest at Gayhurst, Newport Pagnell, Buckinghamshire.

The ones we feasted on at home were brought into the weekly market by various farmers and were thin-shelled and creamy. Strands of black webbing still stuck to the outsides of the shell. They were called 'wet' walnuts and the taste was ambrosial, far removed from the aged, slightly rancid flavour of the nuts that pour into the shops every Christmas. Why do we wait for Christmas to bring us out in a nut rush, when we could be eating them long before? Nuts with port was the crowning glory of an epicurean Edwardian's meal. We seem now to have adopted the French habit of cheese with port instead. Nuts have acquired a faintly Fabian air: wholesome, of course, but not appealing to gourmands.

Old trees were mostly raised from seed and are of variable quality. Size, fertility, flavour and thickness of shell can all differ markedly. The shells were once almost as prized as the nuts. Jewellers put gold hinges on them, lined them with scraps of velvet and sold them as ring boxes.

Named varieties of walnut are now grafted. Look for *Juglans regia* 'Broadview' or 'Buccaneer', both of which are self-fertile. The most handsome cultivar is 'Laciniata', which has a slightly drooping habit and gorgeous leaves that are doubly pinnate. I have only seen it once, at Spetchley Park, near Worcester.

Choose only young walnut trees for planting as they resent being moved when they are older. Do not cut or prune them unless it is absolutely unavoidable. They bleed horribly when they are wounded. If it must be done, late summer is the best time.

Hazels are much easier to accommodate in small gardens, though the likelihood of getting any nuts will depend on the number of squirrels in the neighbourhood. Just as birds always have a keener eye on the strawberries than gardeners have, squirrels usually beat filbert fanciers to the crop. Hazels can either be filberts, which have a long husk that completely encloses the nut, or cobs, which have a husk shorter than the nut. The Kentish cob is just there to confuse. It is in fact a filbert.

Hazels set a crop with or without a sunny summer, unlike sweet chestnuts or walnuts. Left to themselves, they make multi-stemmed thickets, which you can plunder for pea sticks, bean poles and twiggy stems to weave into decorative supportive lattices for your French beans. You can use them as part of an informal boundary hedge or plant them as an understorey beneath oaks or beeches, the way they often grow in the wild.

Hazels do best in deep, damp limestone soils, but survive in a wide variety of situations, in sun or partial shade. You could use them to make an informal bit of woodland at the bottom of the garden, scattering snowdrops, anemones and bluebells under them for a spring display. They need not take up much room. The catkins, already showing now as rigid green caterpillars, are the male flowers which pollinate inconspicuous red female flowers on the same branches. Wind does the job well enough.

In the Kent orchards, where hazelnuts used to be grown in huge quantity (in 1900 there were 7,000 acres of hazel orchard in Britain – now there are just 250), the trees were kept on a single leg and very low. By repeated pruning, the nurserymen used to produce trees that were perhaps 16 feet (5 metres) wide but no more than 5–6 feet (1.5 metres) high. This made them much easier to pick. You don't have to prune, but you can shorten branches in March if you want and take out in late summer some of the wood that springs up from the centre of the bush.

Corylus avellana 'Cosford Cob' is one of the best of the cobs, with pale brown shells so thin you can crack them in your fingers, without nutcrackers. It produces an early crop of big, oblong nuts. *Corylus maxima* 'Kentish Cob' is an excellent filbert, shown at the Horticultural Society (not then Royal) in about 1812 by Mr Aylmer Lambert of Boynton in Wiltshire. It was then quite properly called 'Lambert's Filbert' but got taken up to such an extent by Kentish growers that poor old Lambert got forgotten. Remember him by planting his tree.

CHRISTMAS CHEER

Like an actor stuck in an over-long run of a play, I used to try and vary the lines of the Christmas script. This did not go down well with the rest of the cast. 'I thought we might put the angels in the sitting room this year,' I once said as we were unpacking the boxes of decorations from the cupboard (always the same boxes, always the same cupboard. Even the same wrapping paper – sheets of the *Radio Times c.* 1942).

There was a long frozen moment while a 'she *can't* be serious' look passed between the children. 'But the angels *always* go in the kitchen,' said the youngest finally. And that was the end of that. For the twenty-seventh time the angels took up their stations, blu-tacked to the panes of the kitchen window.

The first angel was made by the middle daughter at school when she was six. It is a silhouette cut out in black paper and filled in with different-coloured tissue papers. When the light shines through, it looks like stained glass. She was so pleased with it, she set up an angel factory and produced enough to make a chequerboard over the whole window. The time before the angels, none of them can remember.

I can. It belongs to that strange period when you first get married. Buried under the thin layer of shared experience lies a far thicker layer of the lives you led before you met. At Christmas these earlier lives burst through the new thin wrapping. Two cultures clash. Should the feast be at lunchtime or at night? The presents in the morning or the afternoon? Should there be a fairy or a star at the top of the Christmas tree? At stake is your own identity.

The dichotomy is only resolved when you begin to stage your own joint Christmas productions. This seems not to happen until you have your own children. Until then, you ricochet between other people's Christmases: your parents or his, usually both in rotating order, which means you spend most of your time celebrating on the M4 motorway.

The Queen's speech featured largely in my parents-in-law's Christmas, which was quite a shock to my system. In my own home in Wales, I had never heard it. We spent a good deal of Christmas Day outdoors, 'getting up an appetite' as my mother used to say. Quite often there was snow and I would wake to the curious bright light that reflected from it on to the walls of my bedroom, more thrilling even than the weight of the stocking at the end of the bed.

Christmas cards perpetuate the notion that snow is part of the Christmas package, but then they still plug Yule logs and stage-coaches too. It is weird that this Pickwickian image should prevail. No stagecoach driver worth his salt would ever have risked his horses in the sort of weather you see on cards.

There was snow the first Christmas we spent in our own home though there never has been since. It was the Christmas after the birth of our second daughter. Her arrival changed things. We were no longer two feckless adventurers racketing about with a baby in tow. We were a family. It was time to scramble the old rites, construct our own rituals. After that, we never went away at Christmas.

Despite (actually, because of) the children, the rituals *have* changed over the years. The changes are the natural ones that you expect as children grow up. When they were small, the feast was at lunchtime, the youngest in the high chair drawn up to the table, with the dog perched just below, ready, like an ever-open wastebin, to catch the droppings. Now the Christmas meal is at night.

We used to go to church on Christmas morning, where our children beadily compared Christmas presents with the other children in the valley. When they were teenagers, we started going to Salisbury Cathedral, where there is a thunderously magnificent service finishing after midnight on Christmas Eve.

This created a difficulty with the stockings. By the time we got back from Salisbury (more than an hour's drive away) I was swallowing myself with yawns. The children, conversely, were souped up and wanting to party. Protocol dictated that stockings should arrive on door knobs unseen, but I couldn't stay awake that long, so the children just pretended they couldn't see them. It was a ludicrous but carefully observed charade.

Stockings are an unchanging part of the ritual. The advantage of having older children is that they start to give you stockings in return and you also get a later start on Christmas morning. 'It's got to be light before you open them,' we used to insist when the children were small, but of course it rarely was.

That is when it is good to have grandparents in the house. 'Lovely, darling,' you can say at five o'clock in the morning as a three-year-old blows a hooter in your face. 'Go and show Grandpa.'

There has to be an orange, an apple and some nuts in the stocking, not because anyone is panting for them, but because there always was in my stocking at home. I used to crack the nuts by putting them under the leg of the bed and bouncing on the corner.

There was a perfectly good pair of nutcrackers in the dining room. But to get there you had to jump from the bottom stair to the mat in the hall. If your foot touched the wood in between you would be pulled for ever into its whorls and seams. That was a nasty prospect to face at half past four in the morning.

The stockings are as important now to the children as they have ever been. 'Why?' I asked, when we were talking about it recently. 'It's the beginning of the whole thing,' said the eldest. 'And you wouldn't buy us those presents if we didn't have stockings,' said the youngest, whose mystical side is rather less developed than the pragmatic.

All of them once believed in Father Christmas. None were traumatised when the Truth About Stockings finally emerged. They all said it added to the specialness of Christmas but somebody, somewhere, must have already written a thesis on the psychological damage inflicted by the Father Christmas figure. The Politics of Christmas: Towards a Gender Shift. St Nicholas: the New Terrorist.

Polemic is actually a less dangerous threat than the increasing number of houses without chimneys. We have always lived in places well endowed in that line, but I am not sure how you would field Father Christmas questions in a chimneyless flat. Perhaps new myths are being forged to fit: reindeers on roller blades, emailing Father Christmas rather than sending him a letter up the chimney.

The Christmas ritual that we have settled into still has elements in it from both our families. From mine comes the ritual morning walk, these days usually ending at a pub before coming home for soup.

From my husband's family comes the tradition of opening presents (apart from stockings) after lunch rather than before. And at his huge family Christmases, everyone did a turn of some kind. They sang or recited, danced or played the trumpet.

I would rather be subsumed into the wooden planks of the floor than do a turn, so this ritual was adapted to a slightly different purpose. Each Christmas he wrote a play, which, after the opening of the presents, he and the three children performed for the four grandparents. I was usually narrator and prompt.

The plots often involved mutinous reindeer. Once it was about three Christmas clowns and their encounter with a grolf – a starring role for my husband, dressed in a goatskin rug. He gave it his all and his all proved too much for Tilly, the youngest child.

As he lunged out from behind the sofa for his big scene, the script required that the Christmas clowns stand fast and see him off. But Tilly's nerve cracked and, howling, she charged across the room and buried her head in my lap. Like the well-trained troupers they were, the grandparents applauded wildly. There were prizes all round and rave reviews for the writer, but nevertheless, we haven't done a Christmas play since.

Tasks for the Month

General

ℰ Check that frost has not lifted the ground around newly planted shrubs and trees.

ℰ Dig over heavy soil, leaving it in large clods to be broken down by frost.

ℰ If necessary, shake snow from the branches of upright conifers to prevent them splaying out. A corset of large mesh netting wrapped round the tree will prevent this happening in future.

Flowers

ℰ Bring pots of bulbs into the warm when flower buds are showing through.

ℰ Bring roses grown in containers into the greenhouse. Prune them hard while still under cover. This will encourage them to flower earlier than usual next season.

ℰ Prune outdoor roses any time between now and early spring. The later time is safer in cold areas.

ℰ Continue to plant roses, ensuring that the roots are well spread out in the planting hole. Firm the soil around the roots and mulch around the base of the plant.

ℰ Continue to tidy beds and borders if the weather is kind.

ℰ Pinch out the tips of sweet pea plants after the second or third pair of leaves appears.

ℰ Indoor cyclamen are in full flood now. Unfortunately the conditions which they need to flourish are precisely those that are most difficult to provide in the average home. They like a cool temperature, somewhere around $55\,^{\circ}$F ($13\,^{\circ}$C), and bright light, but not direct sunlight. A north-facing windowsill usually suits them well. If the leaf stalks start stretching out in an ungainly way, the plant needs more light than it is getting. The compost should be moist but never wet. Keep water off the cyclamen tuber. Water it by standing the pot in a bowl of slightly tepid water.

ℰ Amaryllis, because they grow so fast and have flowers as subtle as a heavyweight's punch, make excellent presents for children. Choose bulbs with thick firm roots. Before planting, soak the base of the bulb and roots in lukewarm water for a few hours. Plant in a pot that is only just big enough, leaving the top third of the bulb exposed. Keep the pot in the warm and water sparingly until the flower stem starts to grow. Amaryllis should flower ten weeks after planting.

ﾟﾙ Hardware stores and garden centres often have half-price bulbs for sale at this time of the year. Tulips are a particularly good buy and will be least affected by late planting. Choose bulbs that are still plump and firm and avoid any that have begun to sprout. Look out for some of the early singles such as 'Apricot Beauty', darker inside than out, and 'Princess Margaret', a pink tulip fading to white at the base. Both are excellent in pots.

Vegetables

ﾟﾙ Continue to spread manure on the vegetable garden, leaving one area unmanured. This is where you should grow root crops. If grown in freshly manured ground, carrots and parsnips fork into multiple roots.

ﾟﾙ Harvest kohlrabi when the roots are about the size of a tennis ball.

Fruit

ﾟﾙ Prune autumn-fruiting raspberries down to ground level.

ﾟﾙ Prune vines when all leaves have fallen, reducing side shoots on mature plants to within one or two buds of the main stem.

Acknowledgements

The *Independent* invited me to be its gardening correspondent when the paper was first set up in 1986 and I have been writing a weekly column for them ever since. I am grateful to the editor for allowing me to reprint some of these columns in *The Curious Gardener*. I am also delighted that Howard Phipps, whose work I have admired for years, has allowed us to use a selection of his fine wood engravings to introduce each section. The book crystallised over lunch with Caradoc King, my agent at A. P. Watt. He paid. Thank you, Caradoc. At Bloomsbury, Bill Swainson has been an exemplary editor. I am indebted to him and also to Emily Sweet, the managing editor, and Sarah Greeno, who designed the jacket. My final thank you is to Penny Edwards, who once again has produced a very elegant book.

Index

A NOTE ON THE AUTHOR

Anna Pavord has been gardening correspondent for the *Independent* since the paper was founded in 1986. She is the author of eight previous books, including her bestseller *The Tulip* and *Searching for Order*. For many years she was associate editor of the magazine *Gardens Illustrated*, and she regularly fronts programmes for Radio 3 and 4. For ten year she was a member of the National Trust's Gardens Panel, the last five as chairman. She is also a member of English Heritage's Parks and Gardens Panel. In 2001 she was awarded the Gold Veitch Medal from the Royal Horticultural Society. For nearly forty years she has lived and gardened in Dorset. She is married and has three daughters.

A NOTE ON THE TYPE

The text of this book is set in Perpetua. This typeface is an adaptation of a style of letter that had been popularized for monumental work in stone by Eric Gill. Large scale drawings by Gill were given to Charles Malin, a Parisian punch-cutter, and his hand cut punches were the basis for the font issued by Monotype. First used in a private translation called *The Passion of Perpetua and Felicity*, the italic was originally called Felicity.